AF522232

MANAGEMENT OF HOSPITALITY ORGANIZATION

MANAGEMENT OF HOSPITALITY ORGANIZATION

By

Nancy Brown

DISCOVERY PUBLISHING HOUSE PVT. LTD.

NEW DELHI-110 002

Published by:
Tilak Wasan
DISCOVERY PUBLISHING HOUSE PVT. LTD.
4831/24, Prahlad Street, Ansari Road
Darya Ganj, New Delhi-110002 (India)
Phone : +91-11-23279245, 43764432
Fax : +91-11-23253475
E-mail : parul.wasan@gmail.com
discoverypublishinghouse@gmail.com
info@discoverypublishinggroup.com
web : www.discoverypublishinggroup.com

First Edition: **2011**
Reprint: 2019

ISBN: 978-81-8356-927-9

Management of Hospitality Organization

Printed at Mehra Offset Press, Delhi.

Preface

The hospitality industry consists of broad category of fields within the service industry that includes lodging, restaurants, event planning, theme parks, transportation, cruise line, and additional fields within the tourism industry. The hospitality industry is a several billion dollar industry that mostly depends on the availability of leisure time and disposable income. The importance of human resources management for hotels is very great. There are thousands of ways that a human resources manager can make a hotel run more smoothly and more efficiently. There are many different areas that can benefit from the experience and guidance of a human resources manager.

Therefore, it is very important to not undermine the manager's importance. Without the human resources manager a hotel is not the same or as pleasing to customers and employees. There are many other important roles in the housekeeping team at most hotels. In large hotels, there is usually a houseperson for each floor or section. This person is responsible for emptying the dirty linens and trash in housekeepers' carts and refilling their towels and amenities when needed. In some locations it is not possible for each housekeeper to empty and his cart throughout the day, so the houseperson is essential and makes his rounds continually, at least once an hour.

The job of a hotel housekeeper is to keep an assigned number of rooms clean. This includes a variety of services depending on the room's occupants. For a standard occupied room, this will involve basic cleaning duties. For a room where the occupants have just checked out, the job is more difficult and involves turning over nearly everything in the room. There are few companies in the world who manufacture of highest quality safes to be used in hotels. The strong boxes designed to protect the valuables of hotel guests against theft, are called 'hotel in room safes'. The world's leading hotels buy hotel safes for each room they have. The safes are installed in each hotel rooms for the best privacy of guests. The guests use hotel safes to store their travel documents and valuables while they are in the room or not.

—Author

CONTENTS

INTRODUCTION

Hospitality management is the academic study of the hospitality industry. Hospitality management studies provides a focus on management of hospitality operations including hotels, restaurants, cruise ships, amusement parks, destination marketing organizations, convention centers, country clubs, and related industries.

One of the most important departments of any hotel staff is human resources management. Proper human resources management can be the difference between a really well run hotel and a poorly one hotel. The human resources manager can control almost the whole feeling and presence of the entire hotel. This makes the importance of human resources management for hotels very evident.

There are several different areas in which human resources management is very important. One of these areas is for newly hired employees. The employees that are hired in a hotel can really alter the quality of service and the whole atmosphere of the hotel. This means that it is very important to pick upbeat, dedicated workers for each position. It is the job of the human resources manager to make sure that good people are chosen to work in the hotel.

A degree in hospitality management is often conferred from either a university college dedicated to the studies of hospitality management or a business school with a department in hospitality management studies. Degrees in hospitality management may also be referred to as hotel management, hotel and tourism management, or hotel administration. Degrees conferred in this academic field include Bachelors of Arts, Bachelors of Business Administration, Bachelors of Science, Masters of Science, MBA, and Doctorate of Philosophy.

In many cases, many hotel workers are only participating in hotel work because they can find nothing else to do. Not very many people have a dream of running or serving in a hotel environment. However, there are some people who do want to work in that capacity, and it is the job of the human resources manager to find those people.

Retention of employees is another large problem in the hotel service business. Since so many of the employees do not have hotel work as their ending career goals, many of them only work in a hotel for a short amount of time. Other employees may have to be let go because of poor work ethics or other issues.

However, there are ways that a hotel human resources manager can curb some of the desire and likelihood that employees will move to other jobs quickly. The importance of human resources management for hotels is very large in this area. Managers can provide good training and incentive programs that will cause employees to stay longer at the hotel. Having a clear progression plan to advance to higher levels of service will also cause employees to stick around much longer.

The issue of employee progression and promotion is also another large issue for the hotel industry. The importance of human resources management for hotels is proven in this area. Hotels which provide ways for employees to advance in position, or that provide training for employees so that they can gain skills necessary for an advanced position are very important to the retention rate of employees.

It is easy to implement services of this nature and the expense is negligible compared to the expense and time necessary to constantly find new employees to replace the ones that always leave shortly after being hired. One of the easiest things to implement is English lessons. Many hotel employees do not speak English very well, and so it is a great incentive for them to stay working at a hotel if they are offered English lessons.

The importance of human resources management for hotels is also important in the area of employee services. If the employees know they can come to the human resources manager whenever they have a problem or issue then it is easier for them to work in good conscience.

Many human resources departments implement different games and activities to make the work environment more interesting and fun for employees. There are many different services that a human resources manager can think of to help employee morale. Maybe the hotel could implement a babysitting service, or have a park day every year. These little services go a long way towards making happy employees. Happy employees make happy companies and happy customers.

As we can see, the importance of human resources management for hotels is very great. There are thousands of ways that a human resources manager can make a hotel run more smoothly and more efficiently. There are many different areas that can benefit from the experience and guidance of a human resources manager. Therefore, it is very important to not undermine the manager's importance. Without the human resources manager a hotel is not the same or as pleasing to customers and employees.

Bar management entails a wide range of responsibilities. Typically, bar managers handle daily details their employers prefer not to. Duties range from the general, like opening and closing the doors, to the intricate, as accounting and payroll. The more a bar manager can do for their employer the better. Here is bar management 101: the basics, employee issues, and working with distributors.

BAR MANAGEMENT BASICS

Managing a bar comes with responsibility. The biggest is the money. Due to the volume of cash dealt with on a daily basis, a bar manager must be trustworthy. A trusted bar manager can handle setting up tills along with calculating cash ins, outs, spills, comps, and inventory.

Cash in is the amount of money in the till at the end of the night. This amount includes cash, checks, and credit/debit receipts and is minus the original till and any cash outs or payouts. The original till is the amount of money in the register at opening.

Depending on an employer's preference, and the size of the establishment, cash outs or payouts are normally money drawn for tips and can be accounted for from credit/debit slips, checks, or tabs. Payouts may also come from any unexpected expenses incurred during a shift that require the bartender to draw money from the register. These are usually indicated by a receipt or bill of sale in the drawer.

Payouts for miscellaneous items are better handled by keeping a petty cash fund. This fund should be kept separate from the till. The fund should be enough to cover miscellaneous costs such as fruits, basic mixers, or even money for the jukebox to liven up the bar.

Spills and comps are often considered the same, as they are both not paid for. Spills are drinks that were either literally spilled or not made to customer satisfaction. Comps are free or complimentary drinks. Mainly clubs comp a drink to birthday, anniversary, or regular guests as a gesture of good will. It is good practice and generates repeat business.

Calculating inventory is dependent upon knowing output volume. Determining how much stock should be maintained is something every bar manager should know. Maintaining a record of sales, counting boxes of beer stocked, and recording liquor levels should give a manager accurate knowledge of how much supply you need.

Remember that your inventory is not limited to liquor and beer. Keep in mind mixers, garnishes, napkins, glassware and any other items your bar uses are a part of the inventory. A smooth operating bar relies on well-maintained stock and supplies.

EMPLOYEE ISSUES

THEFT

Theft is huge in the bar business. Honestly, dealing with a high volume of cash is tempting. Bartenders that steal from the bar, or your customers, should be watched for and terminated.

Bartenders should be trained to count their till and petty cash upon taking over the bar. This should be done in the presence of management. Any shortages or overages of the original till should be addressed immediately.

Stuffing the till with extra money can test a bartender's honesty. A good rule of thumb, an honest bartender will note excess and rectify it. The cash drawer becomes the responsibility of the bartender once it has been verified. To avoid any conflict, the bartender should be the sole person allowed access to the drawer once they take possession of it. The bartender is responsible for petty cash and till shortages.

Determining theft can be tricky. Bar managers should be observant, listen to, and possibly enlist, customers' help, and calculate shortages efficiently. Some bartenders use methods from the obvious as marking a tab or napkin to the obscure as stashing matches, making pencil marks on counters, or scuffing the floor to record their take of the till.

Registers have a no sale (n/s) option to open the drawer for change. When bartenders open the drawer for change, they may be taking money for their pocket. Hence a high number of n/s rings on the register, along with a shortage or a number of spills or comps should be looked into.

Bartenders abusing spills and comps tick off drinks, charge the customer, and pocket the money. Bartenders with a high number of spills should be watched to determine if there is theft involved.

Customers that run tabs make good targets for thieves. Some bartenders will "pad" tabs with an extra drink or two that was never served. Padding a tab is simple. Bartenders maintain two records of a tab. They charge for the padded tab and turn in the real tab.

After they complete the transaction, they re-ring the bill and mark for an over-ring if necessary. The overage is pocketed. This method does not work with credit/debit tabs if the customer pays the exact amount. However, a customer that rounds up totals for a cash back instances can be marked.

Padding Tabs and Drinking

Bartenders use padding a tab as a method to get drinks for themselves or their friends. Some customers like to buy drinks for the bartender. This makes money for the bar. However the drink should be saved for after the shift is up. A drinking policy for bartenders should be established and enforced.

Bartenders' drinking behind the bar is a liability. Service falters and bartenders lose track of what they are doing. Bar managers should watch for bartenders that drink while on shift. The problem should be addressed. If it persists, the bartender should be terminated.

When bartenders pad tabs to "buy" drinks for their friends, the customer buys the drinks unknowingly. Frankly, in a bar environment it is easy to lose track of how much you are buying. Especially if a customer is buying rounds or is a part of a large party. A bartender can easily mark up a few extras for a comrade and it goes completely unnoticed.

Moonlighters

Another issue to be aware of is moonlighting, where more than one job is held, it can be good or bad. Bartenders that moonlight can bring customers in or take them away. Take note of moonlighters pulling in traffic. This could be a means to increase business. Offer these bartenders more money, shifts, or incentives.

The flip side of a moonlighter is when they take business away. Newer employees could be working to bring business to their other bar. These are moles. The bar manager from the other establishment may have encouraged the bartender to take your business away or spy on your methods.

Lovers

Unfortunately, bartenders have personal relationships outside of the bar. It should be encouraged and enforced that your bartender's significant other remains away from the bar during their shift. Customers like to think their bartenders are available and are often romanticized about. You do not want a jealous lover causing problems with your customers. With everything else a bar manager has to deal with, adding a bar fight to the mix only leads to disaster.

Tasks and Miscellaneous

Bar managers should delegate chores to their bartenders. Depending on the type of bar, the amount of traffic it gets, and the amount of free time a bartender has, certain responsibilities should be given to the bartenders. A clean bar makes customers happy.

Cleaning tasks vary from washing glasses to wiping the bar top to basic dusting of fixtures. Stocking duties, cleaning and filtering the ice bin, and maintaining the refrigerator may need to be done by the bartender. Do not exclude preparing garnishes and mixers for shift changes.

Other issues a bar manager deals with includes excessive call-ins, tardiness, poor service, and bartenders bad mouthing customers or each other. These can be dealt with in a variety of ways, but the best method is communication. Usually, a bartender will make an effort to change if they are alerted.

DEALING WITH DISTRIBUTORS AND VENDORS

Distributors are your suppliers. A bar manager that can squeeze perks and specials out of the suppliers will make money for the bar. The more specials you can run, the better the sales.

Many times distributors have unadvertised specials. For instance, beer companies often give discounts for purchasing a certain number of cases. Inquire about specials often. Discounts can be filtered into lowering prices and running specials or happy hours.

Beer distributors also have promotional paraphernalia like bottle openers, cardboard and neon signs, coasters, napkins, and sometimes glassware. Developing a close relation with a beer distributor to get advertisement devices for your bar not only gives the bar atmosphere it increases sales.

Liquor distributors are an asset also. Often liquor companies like to run promotions for a new mixes. They have promotional tools for you too. The perks can range from T-shirts and hats to glassware. Do not forget to ask for signs. A good distributor will arm you with all the tools you need to sell their wares.

Restaurant and bar suppliers also run specials on glassware, barware, and napkins. Inquiring for specials lowers costs. Purchasing in bulk lowers costs. Lowering costs leads to increased profits. Profits make owners happy.

Vendors run the gamut from cigarette machines to gaming machines and pool tables. Cigarette machines are quickly being eliminated, but they are run and owned by a vender. Usually venders share a portion of the profits with the bar.

Vendors come on a scheduled day to count the incoming cash. The manager or owner should be present during the count for verification. It is good practice to change out quarters and small bills with vendors for use in the bar, as it keeps theses machines profitable and your bar stocked with plenty of change.

Vendors operate jukeboxes too. These are special and maintain ambiance for your bar when there is not a DJ or a band. The music should vary to accommodate many tastes. Consult with your bartenders and customers for requests. Your vendor should make any changes to the lineup you may require.

An organized, knowledgeable, and aware bar manager can take on any task. Knowing your basics, staying abreast with your bartenders, and maintaining a good rapport with your distributors and vendors is key. Keeping your thumb on the pulse of the bar, listening to customer feedback, and investing extra effort will keep your bar running smoothly.

PROFESSIONAL MANAGEMENT VS. ENTREPRENEURIAL MANAGEMENT

An entrepreneur has a dream. Skill, hard work, and luck turn that dream into a business success. At some point, as the company grows and matures, the founder faces a decision - should he/she continue to manage the company or stay with the dream.

Should the founder continue with entrepreneurial management or is it time to engage professional managers so the founder can devote more time to the company's core idea? It is a question that must continue to be faced as the company continues to grow.

When is the right time for the founder to relinquish control of his dream to a professional? Some would have you believe it has to happen as soon as the founder begins to look for outside capital. Others would have you believe it is never the right time.

The Merriam-Webster dictionary defines entrepreneur as "one who organizes, manages, and assumes the risks of a business or enterprise" and manager as "one that manages: as a : a person who conducts business or household affairs or b : a person whose work or profession is management".

As you can see from those definitions, there is a lot of overlap between the two. That's what makes the decision so hard. Many entrepreneurs are excellent managers. Often the founder's decision to manage the company or "manage the dream" is a win in either case for the company. In many cases, the decision hinges on the founder's definition of success. Does the founder want to grow the company into the biggest enterprise in its industry? Or would the founder rather limit growth to something that provides simply a good income and allows him/her to retain full control of the company and its goals and direction?

SELECT BIG COMPANIES

A gentleman we know started a small software company based on his skill as a programmer. He has a real talent for programming languages, a good feel for what the market wants, and the resultant ability to produce specialty applications for select large companies.

He also has keen business sense, an excellent ability to market his company's capabilities, and has earned an enviable reputation for quality and innovation. He has built a network of contacts among the top levels of his biggest customers. He has been able to see new trends coming and has been agile enough to adjust to take advantage of them.

As his company started to grow beyond the "three guys in a garage" stage, he found himself spending more time running the business than writing programs. So he hired a friend to manage the company so he could continue programming. He quickly learned that managing a growing company requires more skill than just friendship with the founder. He took the unpleasant, but necessary, step of eliminating the manager and resuming those duties.

He was continuing to struggle with his dilemma of running the company or continuing to program. He was doing both, but was concerned that he just didn't have the time or energy to do both of them well. It was a move that provided new possibilities at the same time as a watershed change in the industry provided new opportunities. He chose to retake full control of the business himself.

A couple of years later, after turning the company to a dramatically new course, he again stepped aside and again brought in professional management. The company has been very successful in their new market. And the founder again may find himself facing the decision of how much control he is willing to sacrifice to continue to grow. Will this be the time he surrenders majority control of the voting stock in exchange for a top-caliber management team? Or, will he decide that his current reward from the company is adequate for his needs?

A Tough Choice

It is tough for any entrepreneur to decide when, or whether, to relinquish control of their dream for the growth and freedom a professional management team can bring to their company. If you have made the choice, let us know how you decided, and when. If you are facing the decision, post your situation on our Management Forum, and see what guidance your peers can give you.

HOSPITALITY AND TOURISM MANAGEMENT

In America, Hospitality and Tourism Management curriculum follow similar core subject applications to that of a business degree but with a focus on hospitality management. Core subject areas include accounting, administration, finance, information systems, marketing, human resource management, public relations, strategy, quantitative methods, and sectoral studies in the various areas of hospitality business. Cornell University, University of Nevada, Las Vegas (UNLV), and University of Central Florida (UCF) are considered the top Hospitality Management undergraduate colleges in America. One of the newest graduate degree programs in hospitality management is offered by The George Washington University School of Business in Washington, D.C..

In addition to the core coursework above, degree-specific coursework normally includes:

- Restaurant Management (Examples: Management of Food and Beverage Operations, Food Science, Food Selection and Preparation, Food and Beverage Cost Control)
- Lodging Operations (Examples: Lodging Management, Hotel Operations, Resort Timeshare Management, Reservation Sales and Marketing, Hospitality Physical Plant)

- Global Tourism (Examples: Tourism Management, Airline Industry, Sustainable Tourism, Hospitality and Research Methods)
- Attractions Management (Examples: Theme Park Management, Entertainment Arts)
- Event Management (Examples: Event Industry, Catering Management, Hospitality Marketing Management)
- Food Preparation (Examples: Basic Food Preparation, Food Sanitation, Beer and Wine Labs)

Many hospitality programs require concurrent field experience within the industry in the form of internships or co-operative placements.

Several large hospitality corporations such as Marriott, Hilton Worldwide, IHG, Hyatt, Sasi park, Wyndham, beeran international Parks and Resorts, and various management companies offer internship programs as well as management training programs and direct placements for students majoring in Hospitality and Tourism Management. Similar to other business fields, management training programs and direct placement opportunities are highly competitive.

Hospitality Service

The concept of hospitality exchange, also known as "accommodation sharing", "hospitality services" and "home stay networks", refers to centrally organized social networks of individuals, generally travelers, who offer or seek accommodation without monetary exchange. These services generally connect users via the internet.

In 1949, Bob Luitweiler founded the first hospitality service called Servas Open Doors as a cross national, non-profit, volunteer run organization advocating interracial and international peace. In 1965, John Wilcock set up the Traveler's Directory as a listing of his friends willing to host each other when traveling.

In 1988, Joy Lily rescued the organization from imminent shutdown, forming Hospitality Exchange. In 1970, Jimmy Carter (then US President) announced the formation of Friendship Force International which has chapters in 57 countries today. In 2000, Veit Kuhne founded Hospitality Club, the first Internet-based service. In 2004, Casey Fenton started CouchSurfing, now the largest hospitality exchange organization.

Generally, after registering, members have the option of providing very detailed information and pictures of themselves and of the sleeping accommodation being offered, if any. The more information provided by a member improves the chances that someone will find the member trustworthy enough to be their host or guest. Names and addresses may be verified by volunteers. Members looking for accommodation can search for hosts using several parameters such as age, location, sex, and activity level.

Home stays are entirely consensual between the host and guest, and the duration, nature, and terms of the guest's stay are generally worked out in advance to the convenience of both parties. No monetary exchange takes place except under certain circumstances (e.g. the guest may compensate the host for food). After using the service, members can leave a noticeable reference about their host or guest.

Instead of or in addition to accommodation, members also offer to provide guide services or travel-related advice. The websites of the networks also provide editable travel guides and forums where members may seek travel partners or advice. Many such organizations are also focused on "social networking" and members organize activities such as camping trips, bar crawls, meetings, and sporting events.

Some networks cater to specific niche markets such as students, activists, religious pilgrims, and even occupational groups like police officers.

BENEFITS

Monetary Savings

As these networks provide accommodation at no charge, monetary savings can be significant.

Local Contact

Hospitality exchange gives travelers the chance to experience what life is like for people living in other places. In addition, making interpersonal connections and fostering understanding of different cultures may in the long run also be important to international relations. During hospitality exchanges, hosts may show off their local knowledge and exciting places 'off the tourist map'. Not only may travelers get a distinct experience, but they will also get a feel for the everyday lives of local residents.

Reciprocity

The concept behind Hospitality services is based on the pay it forward philosophy, gift economy, and reciprocal altruism.

Major Constraints

Lack of Guarantee

There is no contractual agreement between users in these systems. Reservations are made, but if they are for some reason broken, there is no higher authority to which one could plead for a refund or other compensation. The only repercussion will be the poor rating you give that user and your only consolation will be that your warning will deter others from visiting or hosting them. For those who feel insecure unless their travel arrangements are written in stone before departure, this system will not be comforting.

Potential Interpersonal Conflict or Awkwardness

There is a chance that guest and host will not get along. Perhaps there will be scheduling or ideological conflicts. Maybe you will find that hosts or visitors have misrepresented themselves. Perhaps the experience will not live up to your expectations.

Intense interpersonal communications in advance and a flexibility once you have arrived is your best bet. These experiences require additional planning and courtesy towards the demands of your host. Thus, your living conditions, length of stay, and overall experience will be circumscribed by the living conditions you enter into.

Digital Divide and Demographic Segregation

As use of these services generally requires access to the internet and knowledge of the English language, the sample population found in searches of these databases is really much less diverse than a geographical representation of worldwide users might suggest.

Security

Staying in someone's house, or inviting people into your house leaves open the possibility of being taken advantage of.

Important Websites

There are countless websites that serve the idea of hospitality service, with new ones appearing as this phenomenon becomes more popular. While this page is not intended to be a directory listing, here is a small sample of the well-established and long-standing networks:

- CouchSurfing - A very active network with over 2 million members in more than 200 countries
- Friendship Force International A network of chapters worldwide which concentrates on building under standing across cultures.
- Hospitality Club - A very active network with over 550,000 members in more than 200 countries
- Servas International - human rights and global peace oriented since 1949. A relatively small network now with over 15,000 members(?) with a very long history.
- Tripping - A global network of travelers with the motto "For Travelers, Not Tourists"
- BeWelcome

Specialized Networks

Some networks offer specialized hospitality services as given below:

- Lesbian and Gay Hospitality Exchange International
- Warm Showers - Hospitality network for touring cyclists
- Dachgeber - Hospitality network for touring cyclists in Germany with about 3000 members
- Pasporta Servo - for Esperanto speakers
- WWOOF - "Worldwide Opportunities on Organic Farms", help on the property is exchanged for food, accommodation, education and cultural interaction
- Freagle - "Free Camping, worldwide!" - Uniting Outdoor Lovers Through Hospitality and Mutual Help.
- HelpX - "Help Exchange", help is exchanged for food, accommodation, experience and cultural interaction
- Homeshare International - charitable organization providing exchange of housing for help in the home
- Ridester - ride sharing for travelers in USA

Hospitality Industry

The hospitality industry consists of broad category of fields within the service industry that includes lodging, restaurants, event planning, theme parks, transportation, cruise line, and additional fields within the tourism industry. The hospitality industry is a several billion dollar industry that mostly depends on the availability of leisure time and disposable income.

A hospitality unit such as a restaurant, hotel, or even an amusement park consists of multiple groups such as facility maintenance, direct operations (servers, housekeepers, porters, kitchen workers, bartenders, etc.), management, marketing, and human resources.

The hospitality industry covers a wide range of organizations offering food service and accommodation. The hospitality industry is divided into sectors according to the skill-sets required for the work involved. Sectors include accommodation, food and beverage, meeting and events, gaming, entertainment and recreation, tourism services, and visitor information.

Usage rate is an important variable for the hospitality industry. Just as a factory owner would wish to have his or her productive asset in use as much as possible (as opposed to having to pay fixed costs while the factory isn't producing), so do restaurants, hotels, and theme parks seek to maximize the number of customers they "process" in all sectors. This led to formation of services with the aim to increase usage rate provided by hotel consolidators. Information about required or offered products are brokered on business networks used by vendors as well as purchasers.

In viewing various industries, "barriers to entry" by newcomers and competitive advantages between current players are very important. Among other things, hospitality industry players find advantage in old classics (location), initial and ongoing investment support (reflected in the material upkeep of facilities and the luxuries located therein), and particular themes adopted by the marketing arm of the organization in question.

Very important is also the characteristics of the personnel working in direct contact with the customers. The authenticity, professionalism, and actual concern for the happiness and well-being of the customers that is communicated by successful organizations is a clear competitive advantage.

CONVENTION AND VISITOR BUREAU (CVB)

A convention and visitor bureau is the dominant form of destination marketing organization in the United States, but is found in other countries as well. Destination marketing organizations have many names - convention and visitors bureaus, visitors' bureaus, welcome centers, tourism bureaus, travel and tourism bureaus, information centers and more. Regardless of the name, these organizations offer many services to the traveling public. While each U.S. state has a department of travel and tourism, most counties and/or cities also have their own CVB, to promote a narrower geographical area.

Although there are many government and chamber of commerce bodies that have responsibility for marketing a destination to visitors and selling to conventions and meeting planners, most convention and visitors bureaus (CVBs) are non-profit organizations, working independently under the direction of a board of elected directors. The fundamental mission of a convention and visitor bureau is the promotion of the economic development of a destination through increasing visits from tourists and business travelers, which generates overnight lodging for a destination, visits to restaurants, and shopping revenues. Convention and visitor bureaus are the most important tourism marketing organizations in their respective tourist destinations, as they are directly responsible for marketing the destination brand through travel and tourism "product awareness" to visitors. While they primarily are funded through the collection of "bed taxes" on visitors, convention and visitors bureuas produce billions of dollars in direct and indirect revenue and taxes for their state and local economies with their marketing and sales expertise.

Services

Typically, a convention and visitors bureau provides information about a destination's lodging, dining, attractions, events, museums, arts and culture, history and recreation. Some even provide bus services, insider tips, top ten attraction and activity lists, blogs, photos, forums, free things to do, season-specific activity suggestions and more. The organization works with tourists and meeting planners to provide valuable information on their local area.

Their goal is to help make a visitor's trip or a conference attendees' meeting a much more enjoyable and rewarding experience. In many locations, they work closely with a convention center that will offer large spaces for larger meetings, trade shows, and conventions than can be accommodated in a single hotel. Usually, these organizations also have a local office where one can find maps, brochures, travel professionals, local insight, visitors guides, souvenirs and more.

Marketing Initiatives

A convention and visitor bureau's marketing initiatives are typically achieved through the following: trade association marketplaces, web pages, advertising, distribution of promotional and collateral material, direct sales, hosting familiarization tours for journalists and travel industry personnel, and sponsoring other hospitality functions. The target decision maker of these marketing initiatives is not typically a resident in the community.

Most often, if visitors are going to spend the night in a hotel, they reside at least 100 miles away. Thus, the marketing activity usually takes place or is directed outside the convention and visitors' bureau's community. Convention and visitors bureaus in larger destinations often will market nationally and globally, while smaller cities may focus just on their state or region.

DESTINATION MARKETING ASSOCIATION INTERNATIONAL

DMAI's mission statement is to enhance the professionalism, effectiveness, and image of destination marketing organizations worldwide. Destination Marketing Association International (DMAI) is a professional organization representing destination marketing organizations and convention and visitor bureaus worldwide.

As the world's largest resource for official destination marketing organizations (DMOs), Destination Marketing Association International represents over 1,500 professionals from 658 plus destination marketing organizations in more than 25 countries.

They provide members - professionals, industry partners, students and educators - with educational resources, networking opportunities and marketing benefits available worldwide.

They maintain an online bookstore and resource center, an e-mail discussion lists for members, professional certificates and designations (PDM, CDME), an accreditation program and an official online travel portal: OfficialTravelGuide.com. DMAI also owns the Meeting Information Network (MINT), the meetings and convention database.

Destination Marketing Association International (DMAI) is a professional organization representing destination marketing organizations and convention and visitor bureaus worldwide.

As the world's largest resource for official destination marketing organizations (DMOs), Destination Marketing Association International represents over 2,500 professionals from 650 plus destination marketing organizations in more than 30 countries.

They provide members - professionals, industry partners, students and educators - with educational resources, networking opportunities and marketing benefits available worldwide.

They maintain an online bookstore and resource center, an e-mail discussion lists for members, professional certificates and designations (PDM, CDME), an accreditation program and an official online travel portal: OfficialTravelGuide.com. DMAI also owns the empowerMINT.com, formerly called Meeting Information Network (MINT), the meetings and convention database.

DMAI was founded in 1914 as the International Association of Convention Bureaus (IACB) to promote sound professional practices in the solicitation and servicing of meetings, conventions and tourism. In 1975, the association changed its name for the first time to become the International Association of Convention and Visitors Bureau (IACVB), to reflect the growing importance of consumer travel. In August of 2005, the association changed its name for the second time to become Destination Marketing Association International.

Hotel Manager

A hotel manager is a person who holds a management occupation within a hotel, motel, or resort establishment. Management titles and duties vary by company. In some hotels the title hotel manager or hotelier may solely be referred to the General Manager of the hotel. Small hotels may have a small management team consisting of only two or three managers while larger hotels may often have a large management team consisting of various departments and divisions.

Hotel managers are generally exposed to long shifts that include late hours, weekends, and holidays due to the 24 hour operation of a hotel. The common workplace in hotels is a fast-paced environment, with high levels of interaction with guests, employees, investors, and other managers.

Upper management consisting of senior managers, department heads, and General Managers may sometimes enjoy a more desirable work schedule consisting of a more traditional business day including weekdays and days off on holidays.

A typical organizational chart for a mid-scale to large hotel:

- General Manager

Director of Room Operations

- Front Office Manager
- Front Desk Manager (s)
- PBX Supervisor
- Reservations Manager (may report to Sales in some hotels)
- Guest Services Manager
- Bell Captain
- Concierge Supervisor
- Executive Housekeeper
- Housekeeping Manager(s)
- Laundry Supervisor
- Custodial Supervisor

Director of Sales & Marketing

- Senior Sales Manager
- Sales Manager(s)
- Sales Coordinator (s)
- Catering Manager
- Marketing Manager
- Revenue Manager
- Convention Services Manager(s)
- Event Manager (s)

Director of Food & Beverage

- Restaurant Manager(s)
- Room Service Manager
- Bar Manager
- Director of Catering

Chief Engineer

Director of Human Resources

Director of Security

Spa & Recreation Manager

Director of Finances / Controller

Director of Information Technology

Background and training required varies by management title and duties involved. Industry experience has proven to be an essential qualification for nearly any management occupation within the lodging industry.

Basic qualifications for a management occupation within a hotel usually consist of the following:

- Industry Experience is the main factor
- Education

  A high school diploma is a required qualification for any management occupation.

A degree in Hospitality management studies or equivalent Business degree is often required or strongly preffered

A graduate degree may be desired for a General Manager position but is often not required with sufficient management experience and tenure.

GENERAL MANAGER

General Manager is a descriptive term for certain executives in a business operation. It is also a formal title held by some business executives, most commonly in the hospitality industry.

A manager may be responsible for one functional area, but the general manager is responsible for all areas. Sometimes, most commonly, the term general manager refers to any executive who has overall responsibility for managing both the revenue and cost elements of a company's income statement. This is often referred to as profit & loss (P&L) responsibility. This means that a general manager usually oversees most or all of the firm's marketing and sales functions as well as the day-to-day operations of the business. Frequently, the general manager is also responsible for leading or coordinating the strategic planning functions of the company.

In many cases, the general manager of a business is given a different formal title or titles. Most corporate managers holding the titles of chief executive officer (CEO) or president, for example, are the general managers of their respective businesses. More rarely, the chief financial officer (CFO), chief operating officer (COO), or chief marketing officer (CMO) will act as the general manager of the business. Depending on the company, individuals with the title managing director, regional vice president, country manager, product manager, branch manager, or segment manager may also have general management responsibilities.

In consumer products companies, general managers are often given the title brand manager or category manager. In professional services firms, the general manager may hold titles such as managing partner, senior partner, or managing director.In non-profit enterprises, the general manager is often given the title executive director.

ROLE IN HOTEL

In hotels, the General Manager is the executive manager responsible for the overall operation of a hotel establishment. The General Manager holds ultimate authority over the hotel operation and usually reports directly to a corporate office or hotel owner.

Common duties of a General Manager include hiring and management of a management team, overall management of hotel staff, budgeting and financial management, creating and enforcing business objectives and goals, managing projects and renovations, management of emergencies and other major issues involving guests, employees, or the facility, public relations with the media, local governments, and other businesses, and many additional duties.

The extent of duties of a hotel General Manager vary significantly depending on the size of the hotel and company; for example, General Managers of smaller hotels may have additional duties such as accounting, human resources, payroll, purchasing, and other duties that would usually be handled by other managers or departments in a larger hotel.

Business Telephone System

A business telephone system is any of a range of a multiline telephone systems typically used in business environments, encompassing systems ranging from small key systems to large scale private branch A business telephone system differs from simply using a telephone with multiple lines in that the lines used are accessible from multiple telephones, or "stations" in the system, and that such a system will often provide additional features related to call handling. Business telephone systems are often broadly classified into "key systems", "hybrid systems", and "private branch exchanges".

Into the 21st century, the distinction between key systems and PBX has become increasingly confusing. Early electronic key systems used dedicated handsets which displayed and allowed access to all connected PSTN lines and stations.

The modern key system now supports SIP, ISDN, analog handsets (in addition to its own proprietary handsets - usually digital) as well as a raft of features more traditionally found on larger PBX systems. Their support for both analog and digital signalling, and of some PBX functionality gives rise to the "Hybrid" designation.

A hybrid system will typically have some call appearance buttons that directly correspond to individual lines and/or stations, but may also support directly dialing to extensions or outside lines without selecting a line appearance.

The modern key system is usually fully digital (although analog variants persist) and some systems embrace VOIP. Indeed, key systems now can be considered to have left their humble roots and become small PBXes. Effectively, the aspects that distinguish a PBX from hybrid a key system are the amount, scope and complexity of the features and facilities offered.

Hybrid systems are a common tool in the financial services industry used on trading floors. These advanced hybrid key systems generally only require attached PBXs for interaction with backroom staff and voicemail. These systems commonly have their front end units referred to as Turrets and are notable for their presentation of hoot-n-holler circuits. Multiple Hoots are presented to multiple users over multiplexed speakers to multiple locations.

A key system was originally distinguished from a private branch exchange (PBX) in that it allowed the station user to see and control the calls directly, manually, using lighted line buttons, while a private branch exchange operated in a manner similar to the public telephone system, in the calls were routed to the correct destination by being dialed directly. Technologically, private branch exchanges share lineage with central office telephone systems, and in larger or more complex systems, may rival a central office in capacity and features.

Key systems are primarily defined by their individual line selection buttons for each connected phone line, a feature shared with hybrid systems. New installations of true 'key' systems have become less common, as hybrid systems and private branch exchanges of comparable size now have similar costs and greater functionality.

Key systems can be built using three principal architectures: electromechanical shared-control, electronic shared-control, or independent keysets.

Electromechanical Shared-control Key Systems

Before the advent of large-scale integrated circuits, key systems were typically composed of electromechanical components (relays) as were larger telephone switching systems. In the 1960s, 1A1 key systems simplified wiring with a single KTU for both line and station termination, and increased the features available.

As the 1A1 systems became commonplace, requirements for intercom features increased. The original intercom KTUs, WECo Model 207, were wired for a single talk link, that is, a single conversation on the intercom at a time. The WECo 6A dial intercom system provided two talk links and was often installed as the dial intercom in a 1A1 or 1A2 key system.

Unfortunately, the 6A systems were complex, troublesome and expensive, and never became popular. The advent of 1A2 technology in the 1970s simplified key system set up and maintenance. These continued to be used throughout the 1980s, when the arrival of electronic key systems with their easier installation and greater features signaled the end of electromechanical key systems.

Two obscure key systems were used at airports for air traffic control communications, the 102 and 302 key systems. These were uniquely designed for communications between the air traffic control tower and radar approach control (RAPCON) or ground control approach (GCA), and included radio line connections.

Automatic Electric Company also sold a family of key telephone equipment, but it never gained the widespread use enjoyed by Western Electric equipment.

Electronic Shared-control Systems

With the advent of LSI ICs, the same architecture could be implemented much less expensively than was possible using relays. In addition, it was possible to eliminate the many-wire cabling and replace it with much simpler cable similar to (or even identical to) that used by non-key systems. Electronic shared-control systems lead quickly to the modern hybrid telephone system, as the features of PBX and key system quickly merged. One of the most recognized such systems is the AT&T Merlin.

Additionally, these more modern systems allowed a vast set of features including:

- Answering machine functions
- Remote supervision of the entire system
- Automatic call accounting
- Speed dialing
- Caller ID
- Station-specific limitations (such as no long distance access or no paging)
- Selection of signaling sounds

Features could be added or modified simply using software, allowing easy customization of these systems. The stations were easier to maintain than the previous electromechanical key systems, as they used efficient LEDs instead of incandescent light bulbs for line status indication.

Independent Keysets

LSI also allowed smaller systems to distribute the control (and features) into individual telephone sets that don't require any single shared control unit. Generally, these systems are used with a relatively few telephone sets and it is often more difficult to keep the feature set (such as speed-dialing numbers) in synchrony between the various sets.

Private Branch Exchange

A private branch exchange (PBX) is a telephone exchange that serves a particular business or office, as opposed to one that a common carrier or telephone company operates for many businesses or for the general public. PBXs are also referred to as:

- PABX - private automatic branch exchange
- EPABX - electronic private automatic branch exchange

PBXs make connections among the internal telephones of a private organization-usually a business-and also connects them to the public switched telephone network (PSTN) via trunk lines. Because they incorporate telephones, fax machines, modems, and more, the general term "extension" is used to refer to any end point on the branch.

PBXs are differentiated from "key systems" in that users of key systems manually select their own outgoing lines, while PBXs select the outgoing line automatically. Hybrid systems combine features of both.

Initially, the primary advantage of PBXs was cost savings on internal phone calls: handling the circuit switching locally reduced charges for local phone service. As PBXs gained popularity, they started offering services that were not available in the operator network, such as hunt groups, call forwarding, and extension dialing. In the 1960s a simulated PBX known as Centrex provided similar features from the central telephone exchange.

Two significant developments during the 1990s led to new types of PBX systems. One was the massive growth of data networks and increased public understanding of packet switching. Companies needed packet switched networks for data, so using them for telephone calls was tempting, and the availability of the Internet as a global delivery system made packet switched communications even more attractive. These factors led to the development of the VoIP PBX. (Technically, nothing was being "exchanged" any more, but the abbreviation PBX was so widely understood that it remained in use.)

The other trend was the idea of focusing on core competence. PBX services had always been hard to arrange for smaller companies, and many companies realized that handling their own telephony was not their core competence. These considerations gave rise to the concept of hosted PBX. In a hosted setup, the PBX is located at and managed by the telephone service provider, and features and calls are delivered via the Internet. The customer just signs up for a service, rather than buying and maintaining expensive hardware. This essentially removes the branch from the private premises, moving it to a central location.

History

The term PBX was first applied when switchboard operators ran company switchboards by hand. As automated electromechanical and then electronic switching systems gradually began to replace the manual systems, the terms PABX (private automatic branch exchange) and PMBX (private manual branch exchange) were used to differentiate them. Solid state digital systems were sometimes referred to as EPABXs (electronic private automatic branch exchange). Now, the term PBX is by far the most widely recognized? The acronym is now applied to all types of complex, in-house telephony switching systems, even if they are not private, branches, or exchanging anything.

PBXs are distinguished from smaller "key systems" by the fact that external lines are not normally indicated or selectable at an individual extension. From a user's point of view, calls on a key system are made by selecting a specific outgoing line and dialing the external number. A PBX, in contrast, has a dial plan. Users dial an escape code (usually a single digit; often the same as the first digit of the local emergency telephone number) that connects them to an outside line (DDCO or Direct Dial Central Office in Bell System jargon), followed by the external number. Some modern number analysis systems allow users to dial internal and external numbers without escape codes by use of a dialplan which specifies how calls to numbers beginning with certain prefixes should be routed.

System Components

A PBX will often include:

- The PBX's internal switching network.
- Microcontroller or microcomputer for arbitrary data processing, control and logic.
- Logic cards, switching and control cards, power cards and related devices that facilitate PBX operation.
- Stations or telephone sets, sometimes called lines.
- Outside telco trunks that deliver signals to (and carry them from) the PBX.
- Console or switchboard allows the operator to control incoming calls.
- Uninterruptible power supply (UPS) consisting of sensors, power switches and batteries.
- Interconnecting wiring.
- Cabinets, closets, vaults and other housings.

CURRENT TRENDS

One of the latest trends in PBX development is the VoIP PBX, also known as an IP-PBX or IPBX, which uses the Internet Protocol to carry calls. Most modern PBXs support VoIP. ISDN PBX systems also replaced some traditional PBXs in the 1990s, as ISDN offers features such as conference calling, call forwarding, and programmable caller ID. However, recent open source projects combined with cheap modern hardware are sharply reducing the cost of PBX ownership.

For some users, the private branch exchange has gone full circle as a term. Originally having started as an organization's manual switchboard or attendant console operated by a telephone operator or just simply the operator, they have evolved into VoIP centres that are hosted by the operators or even hardware manufacturers. These modern IP Centrex systems offer essentially the same service, but they have moved so far from the original concept of the PBX that the term hardly applies at all.

Even though VoIP gets a great deal of press, the old circuit switched network is alive and well, and the already bought PBX's are very competitive in services with modern IP Centrexes. Currently, there are four distinct scenarios in use:

- PBX (Private and Circuit Switched)
- Hosted/Virtual PBX (Hosted and Circuit Switched) or traditional Centrex
- IP PBX (Private and Packet Switched)
- IP Centrex or Hosted/Virtual IP (Hosted and Packet Switched)

Since in reality people want to call from the IP side to the circuit switched PSTN (SS7/ISUP), the hosted solutions usually have to maneuver in both realms in one way or another. The distinctions are seldom visible to the end user.

FOOD MANAGEMENT

Food Management is a general term for a number of career paths in food preparation and food service management. It encompasses restaurant operation and institutional food services. Food managers plan meals, control budgets and costs and are responsible for new product development and quality assurance.

A food manager is responsible for all aspects of food safety, ranging from storage to serving customers. The details vary, but most states have specific legal requirements for companies that work with food. A trained food manager is responsible for supervising the food handling practices. Food safety legislation is focused on reducing the occurrences of food-borne illness and disease from commercially prepared food.

Food-borne illness are often referred to as food poisoning. There are several different types of bacteria, naturally present in food, that can cause food poisoning. Proper food handling techniques can significantly reduce the frequency of food related illnesses. There are four areas of responsibility for food managers: food transportation, temperature, preparation and service.

Food transportation rules are typically centered on the length of travel time and the packaging of the food. A manager working in a food production facility is responsible for ensuring that the food is packed in appropriate containers for shipment. Depending on the industry, there may be sterilization, temperature limits or packaging requirements that must be met. For example, there are strict rules surrounding the packaging and transportation of hot cooked meals for home delivery. These requirements include sterile food containers, limited transportation time and temperature maintenance within a specific range.

The rules surrounding safe food transportation cover both large and small organizations. For example, Meals on Wheels is a charitable organization that arranges the delivery of hot meals for seniors and shut-ins. A food manager working for this organization is responsible for ensuring that all the food is packed in sterile containers and transported safely.

The temperature requirements are critical to avoiding food-borne illnesses. The food temperature must be maintained within the appropriate range at all times. The food manager is responsible for ensuring that the food safety protocols are followed at all times. Hot foods must be kept hot and cold foods kept cold.

It is the primary responsibility of the food manager to ensure that the specific requirements surrounding food handling and production are enforced. Staff training, supervision and reinforcement are all part of the job. These rules apply in all settings where food is prepared.

Food service is closely related to food production and storage. The same cleanliness, temperature and food exposure time lines apply in both cases. The food manager in a restaurant or institution must ensure that staff is following the safe food handling techniques at all times.

WHAT IS A FOOD MANAGER?

A food manager usually works for a restaurant, catering business, food service commissary or institutional food service. The food manager is responsible for setting up and following systems to ensure food quality from a taste, nutrition and food safety viewpoint. He may be responsible for any aspect of the food delivery including budgeting and cost controls, menu planning and food preparation.

Skills Needed

The food manager should be skilled in food preparation techniques. A basic background in accounting and marketing are helpful, as well as communication and management skills. Stamina is required because food managers often work long hours on their feet, under the pressure of deadlines. The ability to communicate and work well with a team are essential.

Employment Opportunities

Job opportunities for skilled food managers are excellent, especially for those possessing degrees in an area of food management. Food managers work in entry-level management positions at restaurants, hotels, bed and breakfast inns, catering businesses, nursing homes and hospitals, as well as commercial and institutional food service.

Educational Requirements

There are no educational requirements for food preparation positions. States can require licenses in food safety which usually involves taking a short course and passing an exam. Many food managers do not have degrees, but possession of a certificate or degree smooths entry into the profession and enhances promotional opportunities. Certificates are available in one year, associate degrees take two years and bachelor degrees are available in an average of four years.

Students in food management programs study food preparation, food safety, nutrition, menu planning, storing and handling food. Courses are usually required in basic accounting and marketing. Many programs will include an internship where students gain practical experience while still in school.

Salary Potential

Entry-level food managers often start in the $20,000 to $28,000-a-year range. Managers with degrees often start higher, in the range of $30,000 to $35,000. With advancement and experience, salaries rise to about $45,000. Food managers are often paid a base salary with bonuses based on performance and profitability. Food Managers can move into corporate food management where salaries often climb to $100.000 or more. These figures are current as of June 2009.

CHAPTER–2

HOUSEKEEPING OPERATIONS

Housekeeping is the act of cleaning the rooms and furnishings of a home. It is one of the many chores included in the term housework. Housecleaning includes activities such as disposing of rubbish, cleaning dirty surfaces, dusting and vacuuming. As the saying goes, "the difference is in the details." Those details are the charge of the Housekeeping Department. As one of the most integral departments within the hotel, the Housekeeping Department is responsible for the immaculate care and upkeep of all guest rooms and public spaces.

The housekeeping department is responsible for the cleanliness, appearance, and condition of the entire hotel. This includes public areas such as the lobby, public rest rooms, and meeting rooms as well as individual guest rooms.

A hotel's income depends on the number of rooms occupied at any given moment. It is the housekeeping department's responsibility to efficiently keep as many rooms as possible in a ready condition. Information regarding ready rooms, those ready for a new guest, must be conveyed to the front office immediately, or a sale might be lost. With computerized communications systems, the housekeeping department can convey room availability to the front desk almost instantaneously.

The housekeeping department can also be responsible for more glamorous jobs such as interior decorating and arranging fresh flowers for VIPs. Don't think only of running a vacuum cleaner when you hear the word "housekeeping." An efficiently managed housekeeping department is vital to the smooth operation of a hotel.

BASIC DUTIES OF THE HOUSEKEEPING DEPARTMENT

Guest Rooms. Cleaning guest rooms involves the following: Bed linen is changed daily, the furniture is dusted, ashtrays emptied, and the carpet vacuumed. The bathroom sink, toilet, tub, and floor are scrubbed. Clean towels are put in place. Supplies such as matches, soap, shampoo, tissue, and hotel literature are left.

The rooms must be kept in good repair. The executive housekeeper makes periodic checks for maintenance needs. For example, certain rooms might need to be closed for a day or so in order that they can be painted. The housekeeper keeps track of those rooms that need redecorating; for example, frayed bedspreads may need to be replaced. In some hotels, a maintenance request form is left on the night stand for the guests' convenience. This form is filled out and brought to the front desk for any nonurgent repairs.

Public Rooms. Cleaning public rooms is almost a 24-hour job in a large hotel. Of course, the lobby must be kept spotless for that all-important first ...

Eye for Detail

Individuals who excel in our Housekeeping Departments have an eye for detail and a commitment to the training, development and motivation of a diverse group of talented employees. In a competitive hotel market, it is service and cleanliness that really make an impact on our guests and determine whether they will return.

It may also involve some outdoor chores, such as removing leaves from rain gutters, washing windows and sweeping doormats. The term is often used also figuratively in politics and business, for the removal of unwanted personnel, methods or policies in an effort at reform or improvement.

When selecting the best hotel for a vacation, most people will assess the size of the rooms, hotel amenities, location and reviews. An important factor that is usually overlooked unless it is unsatisfactory is the work of the housekeeping staff. These hardworking individuals ensure that messy rooms are miraculously spotless at the end of the day. Hotel housekeeping is a difficult and demanding job that requires much more than might be expected.

The job of a hotel housekeeper is to keep an assigned number of rooms clean. This includes a variety of services depending on the room's occupants. For a standard occupied room, this will involve basic cleaning duties. For a room where the occupants have just checked out, the job is more difficult and involves turning over nearly everything in the room.

A check-out room must be so neat and clean that the new occupants cannot tell that another family may have vacated the room only a few hours earlier. Some occupants who are in the hotel room when the housekeeper arrives or are perhaps ill and spending the day in bed may prefer service known as trash and towels. This is exactly how it sounds.

The housekeeper will provide fresh clean towels and toiletries and remove the trash, but otherwise leave the room alone. If a guest leaves a later service sign on the door, the room must be revisited, perhaps several times throughout the day until the sign is removed. However, some guests forget to remove this sign entirely. Depending on the hotel this may mean that they will not receive any service, or it may mean they receive a phone call offering later service.

Some locations will even leave a set of clean towels and toiletries outside the door. One last consideration is rooms that have been vacant for several days. Though they have already been cleaned and turned over, these rooms must be revisited so the housekeeper can sweep and dust, ensuring that the room doesn't look dusty and abandoned when new guests arrive.

Specific Duties of a Housekeeper

The specific duties of a housekeeper may vary from one hotel to the next, but usually include several standard jobs. The first is making the beds. A good housekeeper should be able to make each bed in about a minute. Unless there are very obvious stains, the sheets and pillowcases are rarely changed daily. The average amount of time for sheets to be left unchanged is three days. However, this also varies from one hotel to the next. In very expensive locations the sheets are changed daily. The number of sheets and pillows on the bed can also vary. While a standard hotel bed has a bottom sheet, top sheet, blanket and comforter, nicer hotels will have a sheet both beneath and on top of the blanket. Some less-expensive hotels may not have a blanket at all.

Hotel beds are typically made with the comforter covering the entire bed and are almost always made this way when guests first check in. However, during a guest's stay, the comforter may only be folded neatly at the bottom of the bed. Next, the housekeeper must refresh any amenities in the room, such as coffee. End tables and desks may be straightened, but the guest's items are generally left as they are.

Small touches such as closing the doors of a television cabinet can give a room a finished look very quickly. If there is a porch or balcony, this should be swept and any ashtrays need to be emptied. Lastly, the trashcans in the rooms will be emptied, and the carpets swept. Moving on to the bathroom, the housekeeper will wipe down the tub, toilet, sink and counter. Towels will be changed and amenities will be refreshed.

In a check-out room, the bathroom is cleaned more thoroughly with a variety of cleaning agents, usually including bleach. Small touches are important here, such as carefully folding the towels. Each hotel has its own preferred method for folding and placing the towels. The toilet paper must be folded to a neat point as well. In some hotels, the tip of the toilet paper is even pressed with a stamp featuring the hotel's logo or name.

Time Frame

Most housekeepers work a typical eight-hour day. However, this day is usually filled with nonstop activity. Most hotels give each housekeeper between 15 and 20 rooms each day. An occupied room should take no more than 15 minutes to complete and a check out should take no more than half an hour. This is often a difficult schedule to keep considering the state of some rooms. In hotels with large suites, a housekeeper may be given around ten suites to complete each day. Suites often take much longer because of the additional amenities. Stoves, counters and refrigerators need to be cleaned.

If a dishwasher is present, the housekeeper will often be required to load and unload any dishes. In a suite there are also usually several bedrooms and bathrooms, all requiring attention. Housekeepers must always stay conscious of the time of day. The typical hotel check-out time is 11 a.m. Vacated rooms need to be cleaned as soon as possible to be ready for the usual 3 p.m. check-in time.

Most housekeepers have a set area in the hotel for which they are responsible. This means that they are not assigned an equal number of occupied rooms and check-outs each day. Some days can be very easy, with all rooms occupied. However, some days--especially weekends--can be extremely difficult when nearly every room is a check-out.

Responsibility of a Housekeeper

Though the typical housekeeper is responsible for a number of hotel rooms, there are many other important roles in the housekeeping team at most hotels. In large hotels, there is usually a houseperson for each floor or section. This person is responsible for emptying the dirty linens and trash in housekeepers' carts and refilling their towels and amenities when needed. In some locations it is not possible for each housekeeper to empty and his cart throughout the day, so the houseperson is essential and makes his rounds continually, at least once an hour.

The houseperson is also responsible for vacuuming hallways, dusting banisters and woodwork and cleaning any common areas on the floor. Another member of the housekeeping staff is usually assigned to the lobby area. In large hotels this can include the check-in area, pool, fitness center, childcare center, laundry facility and a variety of other areas. Lobby housekeepers usually make their rounds through these areas several times throughout the day.

If a guest calls for special amenities such as a microwave or crib, or other items that are not typically left in the room such a toothbrush, sewing kit or matches, these are often provided by another hardworking member of the housekeeping staff, sometimes called a runner. Hotels with minibars and turn-down service usually leave these specific tasks to separate members of the staff as well.

Considerations

When staying in any hotel, it is considered polite to tip the housekeeper. If you decline service for most or all of your stay your tip can be significantly less, but you should still keep in mind that the housekeeper prepared the room before you arrived, and will need to turn it over after you leave.

For guests who receive service every day, a typical tip is two or three dollars per day. You can leave this tip daily or in a lump sum when you check out. The tip should be in bills, not change. For the housekeeper to be sure that the tip is intended for them, it should be left in a conspicuous place such as on the pillow.

You may also want to leave a note with it. If you are only leaving a tip when you check out it can be left most anywhere and the housekeeper will assume that it is intended for them. Either method will work, but leaving a small tip daily will often let the housekeeper know that you are a considerate guest and may earn a few special touches.

Housecleaning is done to make the home look better and be safer and easier to live in. Without housecleaning limescale builds up on taps, mold grows in wet areas, bacterial action make the garbage disposal and toilet smell and cobwebs accumulate. Tools used in housecleaning include vacuum cleaners, brooms, mops and sponges, together with cleaning products such as detergents, disinfectants and bleach.

Removal of Litter

Disposal of rubbish is an important aspect of house cleaning, the reasons for this are psychological, social and practical. Plastic bags are designed and manufactured specifically for the collection of litter. Many are sized to fit common waste baskets and trash cans. Paper bags are made to carry aluminum cans, glass jars and other things. Recycling is possible with some kinds of litter.

Dusting

Over time dust accumulates on household surfaces. As well as making the surfaces dirty, when dust is disturbed it can become suspended in the air, causing sneezing and breathing trouble. It can also transfer from furniture to clothing, making it unclean. Various tools have been invented for dust removal; Feather and lamb's wool dusters, cotton and polyester dust cloths, furniture spray , disposable paper "dust cloths", dust mops for smooth floors and vacuum cleaners. Vacuum cleaners often have a variety of tools to enable them to remove not just from carpets and rugs, but from hard surfaces and upholstery.

Removal of Dirt

Examples of dirt or "soil" can be dry coffee spills and jelly drips or muddy footprints on carpet. Equipment used with a cleaner might be a bucket and sponge. A modern tool is the spray bottle, but the scientific principle is the same.

Household Chemicals

Various household cleaning products have been developed to facilitate the removal of dust and dirt, for surface maintenance, and for disinfection. Products are available in powder, liquid or spray form. The basic ingredients determine the type of cleaning tasks for which they are suitable. Some are packaged as general purpose cleaning materials whilst others are targeted at specific cleaning tasks such as drain clearing, oven cleaning, lime scale removal and polishing furniture.

Household cleaning products provide aesthetic and hygiene benefits but are also associated with health risks for the users, and building occupants. The US Department of Health and Human Services offers the public access to the Household Products Database. This database provides consumer information for over 4,000 products based on information provided by the manufacturer through the Material Safety Data Sheet.

Surfactants lower the surface tension of water, making it able to flow into smaller tiny cracks and crevices in soils making removal easier. Alkaline chemicals break down known soils such as grease and mud. Acids break down soils such as lime scale, soap scum, and stains of mustard, coffee, tea, and alcoholic beverages. Some solvent-based products are flammable and some can dissolve paint and varnish. Disinfectants stop smell and stains caused by bacteria.

When multiple chemicals are applied to the same surface without full removal of the earlier substance, the chemicals may interact. This interaction may result in a reduction of the efficiency of the chemicals applied (such as a change in pH value caused by mixing alkalis and acids) and in cases may even emit toxic fumes. An example of this is the mixing of ammonia-based cleaners (or acid-based cleaners) and bleach. This causes the production of chloramines that volatilize (become gaseous) causing acute inflammation of the lungs (toxic pneumonitis), long-term respiratory damage, and potential death.

Residue from cleaning products and cleaning activity (dusting, vacuuming, sweeping) have been shown to impact indoor air quality (IAQ) by redistributing particulate matter (dust, dirt, human skin cells, organic matter, animal dander, particles from combustion, fibers from insulation, pollen, and polycyclic aromatic hydrocarbons) that gaseous or liquid particles become adsorbed to. The particulate matter and chemical residual will of be highest concentrations right after cleaning but will decrease over time depending upon levels of contaminants, air exchange rate, and other sources of chemical residual. Of most concern are the family of chemicals called VOCs such as formaldehyde, toluene, and limonene.

Volatile organic compounds (VOCs) are released from many household cleaning products such as disinfectants, polishes, floor waxes, air-freshening sprays, all purpose cleaning sprays, and glass cleaner. These products have been shown to emit irritating vapors. VOCs are of most concern due to their tendency to evaporate and be inhaled into the lungs or adsorbed to existing dust, which can also be inhaled. It has been found that aèrosolized (spray) cleaning products are important risk factors and may aggravate symptoms of adult asthma, respiratory irritation, childhood asthma, wheeze, bronchitis, and allergy.

Other modes of exposure to potentially harmful household cleaning chemicals include absorption through the skin (dermis), accidental ingestion, and accidental splashing into the eyes. Products for the application and safe use of the chemicals are also available, such as nylon scrub sponge and rubber gloves. It is up to the consumer to keep themselves safe while using these chemicals. Reading and comprehending the labels is important.

There is a growing consumer and governmental interest in natural cleaning products and green cleaning methods. The use of nontoxic household chemicals is growing as consumers become more informed of the health effects of many household chemicals, and municipalities are having to deal with the expensive disposal of household hazardous waste (HHW).

Tools

'Modern housecleaning tools' is almost an oxymoron. There are few areas where someone from 50 years ago could step into the same job today, but housecleaning is an area where there has been very little change. Brooms remove debris from floors and dustpans carry dust and debris swept into them, buckets hold cleaning and rinsing solutions, vacuum cleanerss and carpet sweepers remove surface dust and debris, chamois leather and squeegees are used for window-cleaning, and mops are used for washing floors.

Yard

A home's yard and exterior are sometimes subject to cleaning. Exterior cleaning also occurs for safety, upkeep and usefulness. It includes removal of paper litter and grass growing in sidewalk cracks. Rain gutters, doormats, pools and the screens and glass of windows are also cleanable. Yard junk-removal might occur and porch clutter removal. The paint of door frames might be washed or an old piñata thrown away.

Floor Cleaning

Floor cleaning is a major occupation throughout the world. The main job of most cleaners is to clean floors.

The principal reasons for floor cleaning are:

- To prevent injuries due to tripping or slipping. Injuries due to slips and trips on level floors are a major cause of accidental injury or death. Bad practice in floor cleaning is itself a major cause of accidents.
- To beautify the floor.
- To remove stains, dirt, litter and obstructions.
- To remove grit and sand which scratch and wear down the surface.
- To remove allergens, in particular dust.
- To prevent wear to the surface e.g. by using a floor wax or protective sealant.
- To make the environment sanitary e.g. in kitchens.
- To maintain an optimum traction e.g. for dance floors.

Methods of Floor Cleaning

The treatment needed for different types of floors is very different. For safety it is most important to ensure the floor is not left even slightly wet after cleaning or mopping up.

Sawdust is used on some floors to absorb any liquids that fall rather than trying to prevent them being spilt. The sawdust is swept up and replaced each day. This was common in the past in pubs and is still used in some butchers and fishmongers.

It used to be common to use tea leaves to collect dirt from carpets and remove odours. Nowadays it is sill quite common to use diatomaceous earth, or in fact any cat litter type material, to remove infestations from floors.

Wood Flooring

Wood flooring should be treated completely differently depending on whether it waxed or oiled, or whether it has a polyurethane coating. It is important to determine the type of finish of a wood floor and always treat it the appropriate way, for instance it is difficult to clear wood floor wax from a polyurethane floor.

Reducing the Need for Cleaning

Good well-maintained entrance matting can dramatically reduce the need for cleaning. For public and office buildings about 80 to 90% of the dirt is tracked in from outside. Installing a total of 15 feet of matting consisting of both indoor and outdoor sections will remove about 80% of this. Thus about two-thirds of the dirt can be removed at the entrance. BS 7953 'Entrance flooring systems. Selection, installation and maintenance' has standards relating to barrier matting.

Carpet Cleaning

Carpet cleaning, for beautification, and the removal of stains, dirt, grit, sand, and allergens can be achieved by several methods, both traditional and modern. Clean carpets are recognized by manufacturers as being more visually pleasing, potentially longer-lasting, and probably healthier than poorly maintained carpets.

Sanitary Maintenance magazine reports that carpet cleaning is widely misunderstood, and chemical developers have only within recent decades created new carpet-care technologies. Particularly, encapsulation and other green technologies work better, are easier to use, require less training, save more time and money, and lead to less resoiling than prior methods.

The professional carpet-cleaning industry is primarily educated and unofficially governed by the Institute of Inspection, Cleaning, and Restoration Certification (IICRC). It is a nonprofit certifying body for the specialized fabric-cleaning industry that sets modern carpet-cleaning standards. It accepts five basic dry and wet professional cleaning methodologies.

Dry-cleaning

Many dry carpet-cleaning systems rely on specialized machines; dry carpet-cleaning machines include those manufactured by Brush and Clean, Host Dry, and Whittaker System. These systems are mostly technically "very low moisture" (VLM) systems, relying on dry compounds complemented by application cleaning solutions, and are growing significantly in market share due in part to their very rapid drying time, a significant factor for 24-hour commercial installations. Dry-cleaning and "very low moisture" systems are also often faster and less labor-intensive than wet-extraction systems.

Heavily soiled areas require the application of manual spotting, or of pretreatments, preconditioners, or "traffic-lane cleaners", which are detergents or emulsifiers that break the binding of different soils to carpet fibers over a short period of time, commonly sprayed onto carpet prior to the primary use of the dry-cleaning system. One chemical dissolves the greasy films that bind soils and prevent effective soil removal by vacuuming. The solution may add a solvent like d-limonene, petroleum byproducts, glycol ethers, or butyl agents. The amount of time the pretreatment "dwells" in the carpet should be less than 15 minutes, due to the thorough carpet brushing common to these "very low moisture" systems, which provides added agitation to ensure the pretreatment works fully through the carpet.

Dry Compound

A biodegradable absorbent powder and cleaning compound may be spread evenly over carpet and brushed or scrubbed in. For small areas, a household hand brush can work such a compound into carpet pile; dirt and grime is attracted to the compound, which is then vacuumed off, leaving carpet immediately clean and dry. For commercial applications, a specially designed cylindrical counter-rotating brushing system is used, without a vacuum cleaner. Machine scrubbing is more typical, in that hand scrubbing generally cleans only the top third of carpet.

Encapsulation

In the 1990s, new polymers began literally encapsulating (crystallizing) soil particles into dry residues on contact, in a process now regarded by the industry as a growing, up-and-coming technology; working like "tiny sponges", the deep-cleaning compound crystals dissolve and absorb dirt prior to its removal from the carpet. Cleaning solution is applied by rotary machine, brush applicator, or compression sprayer.

Dry residue is vacuumable immediately, either separately or from a built-in unit of the cleaning-system machine. According to ICS Cleaning Specialist, evidence suggests encapsulation improves carpet appearance, compared to other systems; and it is favorable in terms of high-traffic needs, operator training, equipment expense, and lack of wet residue. Encapsulation also avoids the drying time of carpet shampoos, making the carpet immediately available for use.

The use of encapsulation to create a crystalline residue that can be immediately vacuumed (as opposed to the dry powder residue of wet cleaning systems, which generally requires an additional day before vacuuming) has recently become an accepted method for commercial and residential carpet maintenance.

Bonnet

After club soda mixed with cleaning product is deposited onto the surface as mist, a round buffer or "bonnet" scrubs the mixture with rotating motion. This industry machine resembles a floor buffer, with an absorbent spin pad that attracts soil and is rinsed or replaced repeatedly. The bonnet method is not strictly dry-cleaning and involves significant drying time, and usually only addresses the top third of carpet, making it a quick solution rather than a deep cleaning of dirt or odor as considered suitable for valuable carpet. To reduce pile distortion, the absorbent pad should be kept well-lubricated with cleaning solution.

When there is a large amount of foreign material below the carpet backing, extraction with a wet process may be needed. The spin-bonnet method may not be as capable of sanitizing carpet fibers due to the lack of hot water, but a post-cleaning application of an antimicrobial agent is used to make up for this. Compared to steam cleaning, the small amounts of water required with spin-bonnet carpet cleaning favor water-conservation considerations.

Wet-cleaning

Wet-cleaning systems naturally require drying time, which has led to customer fears and concerns about very slow drying, the risk of discoloration returning during drying, and odors, bacteria, fungi, molds, and mildews. Balancing the need for rapid drying (attributable to lower flow rate through the cleaning jets of a spray system) and the need to remove the most soil (attributable to higher flow rate) is a key technique that must be mastered by carpet-cleaning technicians.

Pretreatments similar to those in dry-cleaning and 'very low moisture' systems are employed, but require a longer dwell time of 15 to 20 minutes, because of lower amounts of carpet agitation. Ideal pretreatments should rinse easily and leave dry, powdery, or crystalline residue that can be flushed without contributing to resoiling.

Steam Cleaning

In high-pressure hot water extraction ('steam cleaning'), after preconditioning with an alkaline agent, agitation with a grooming brush, and appropriate dwell time, a pressurized manual or automatic cleaning tool (such as a wand) passes over the surface several times to thoroughly rinse out all preconditioner, residue, and particulates, and, using an acetic acid solution, to restore neutral fiber pH. The acid rinse thus neutralizes the alkaline residues, and can contribute to softening cleaned fabrics.

Richard Smith from Modern Carpet Cleaning in Chico California recomends using a post applied alkalie neautralizer after cleaning. Neatralizing the carpet after cleaning will leave it softer and help it stay clean longer.

Rather than soaps, the steam-cleaning system uses detergent-based solutions that dry to a powder or crystal. The surface is dried to avoid saturation, typically taking 3-4 hours if done correctly; inexperienced carpet-cleaning companies sometimes overwet carpeting, leading to mold and recurring stains (arising from the "wicking" effect, whereby deeper soils are water-driven upward along carpet fibers, thus reconstituting visible stains). Some carpet-cleaning solutions are carbonated to dissolve organic material more effectively. Beyond these treatments, antistaining and antisoiling products can be applied by the carpet owner, and have for this reason become recognized in the carpet-cleaning industry as some of its biggest profit centers.

Extraction is by far the most important step in this process. Since the hot-water extraction method uses much more water than other methods like bonnet or shampoo cleaning, proper extraction is critical to avoid oversaturation. When carpet is saturated, there is a risk that soils and residue from deep in the carpet fiber and backing will "wick" up to the surface, resulting in browning, or the carpet layers may delaminate.

Hot-water extraction generally involves slower drying times, lower production rates, and more labor-intensive processes than dry carpet cleaning. Drying time may also be decreased by extra use of fans, air conditioning, and/or outdoor ventilation.

Older surfaces, such as double jute-backed carpets and loose rugs with natural foundation yarns, could shrink after a wet treatment, leading to suppositions that wet-cleaning could also remove wrinkles. However, this notion is antiquated and this method could also occasionally tear seams or uproot strips. Newer carpets, such as with synthetic backing and foundation yarns, do not shrink, and they smooth easily; in such carpets, wrinkles indicate an underlying problem, such as adhesive, that may need a certified carpet inspector to determine.

Shampoo

Wet shampoo cleaning with rotary machines, followed by thorough wet vacuuming, was widespread until about the 1970s, but industry perception of shampoo cleaning changed with the advent of encapsulation. Hot-water extraction, also regarded as preferable, had not been introduced either. Wet shampoos were once formulated from coconut oil soaps; wet shampoo residues can be foamy or sticky, and steam cleaning often reveals dirt unextracted by shampoos.

Since no rinse is performed, the powerful residue can continue to collect dirt after cleaning, leading to the misconception that carpet cleaning can lead to the carpet getting "dirtier faster" after the cleaning.

When wet-shampoo chemistry standards converted from coconut oil soaps to synthetic detergents as a base, the shampoos dried to a powder, and loosened dirt would attach to the powder components, requiring vacuuming by the consumer the day after cleaning.

Household Processes

Other household carpet-cleaning processes are much older than industry standardization, and have varying degrees of effectiveness as supplements to the more thorough cleaning methods accepted in the industry.

Vacuum

Vacuum cleaners use air pumps to create partial vacuums to suck up dust and dirt, usually from floors and carpets. Filtering systems or cyclones collect dirt for later disposal. Models include upright (dirty-air and clean-air), canister and backpack, wet-dry and pneumatic, and other varieties. Robotic vacuum cleaners have recently become viable as well.

Vacuum-cleaner manufacturers are widespread and include Aerus LLC, Bissell Carpet Sweepers, Black & Decker DustBuster, Dirt Devil, Dyson, Electrolux, Eureka, Goblin Vacuum Cleaners, the Hoover Company, the Kirby Company, Nilfisk-Advance, Numatic International Limited, the Oreck Corporation, Regina Vacuum Cleaners, Rexair LLC, Samsung Electronics

Stain Removal

Tea leaves and cut grass were formerly common for floor cleaning, to collect dust from carpets, albeit with risks of stains. Ink was removed with lemon or with oxalic acid and hartshorn; oil with white bread or with pipe clay; grease fats with turpentine; ox gall and naphtha were also general cleaners.

Ammonia and chloroform were recommended for acid discoloration. Benzine and alum were suggested for removing insects; diatomaceous earth and material similar to cat litter are still common for removing infestations. Some traditional methods of stain removal remain successful and ecological. Caution should be addressed when treating natural fibers such as wool.

The longer the stain material remains in the carpet, the higher the chance of permanent color change, even if all the original stain material is removed. Immediately blotting (not rubbing) the stain material as soon as possible will help reduce the chances of permanent color change. Artificial food coloring stains are generally considered permanent stains (Kool-Aid, Gatorade, Listerine, soda, etc.). These may be removed by professionals with heat-transfer stain-reducing chemicals, but carry risks of burning the carpet. Stain removal products can be combined with anti-allergen treatments to kill house dust mites.

Other

Carpet rods, rattan rugbeaters, and carpet-beating machines for beating out dust, and also brooms, brushes, dustpans, and shaking and hanging were all carpet-cleaning methods of the 19th century; brooms particularly carry risks of wear.

Misconceptions

Robert Wittkamp (1942-2007), IICRC-certified master cleaning technician with 30 years' expertise in carpet cleaning, commented that old wives' tales persist and thrive within the industry. For instance, the concept that walking barefoot on a carpet may lead to damage from body oils has not been supported or disproven by standardized reports or testing or by industry evidence.

Vacuum Cleaner

A vacuum cleaner, commonly referred to as a vacuum in the U.S. and generally as a hoover in the UK, is a device that uses an air pump to create a partial vacuum to suck up dust and dirt, usually from floors. The dirt is collected by either a dustbag or a cyclone for later disposal. Vacuum cleaners, which are used in homes as well as in industry, exist in a variety of sizes and models: from small battery-operated hand-held devices to huge stationary industrial appliances that can handle several hundred litres of dust before being emptied.

The vacuum cleaner evolved from the carpet sweeper via manual vacuum cleaners. The first manual models, using bellows, came in the 1860s, and the first motorised models came in the beginning of the 20th century.

Daniel Hess

Daniel Hess of West Union, Iowa, USA invented a vacuum cleaner in 1860. Calling it a carpet sweeper instead of a vacuum cleaner, his machine did, in fact, have a rotating brush like a traditional vacuum cleaner, which also possessed an elaborate bellows mechanism on top of the body to generate suction of dust and dirt. Hess received a patent (U.S. No. 29.077) for his invention of the vacuum cleaner on July 10, 1860.

Ives W. McGaffey

The first manually-powered cleaner using vacuum principles was the 'Whirlwind,' invented in Chicago, USA in 1868 by Ives

W. McGaffey. The machine was lightweight and compact, but was difficult to operate because of the need to turn a hand crank at the same time as pushing it across the floor. McGaffey enlisted the help of The American Carpet Cleaning Co. of Boston to market it to the public. It was sold for $25.

It is hard to determine how successful the Whirlwind was, as most of them were sold in Chicago and Boston, and it is likely that many were lost in the Great Chicago Fire of 1871. Only two are known to have survived, one of which can be found in the Hoover Historical Center.

McGaffey was but one of many 19th-century inventors in the United States and Europe who devised manual vacuum cleaners. He obtained a patent (U.S. No. 91,145) on June 8, 1869.

Melville Bissell

In 1876, Melville Bissell of Grand Rapids, Michigan, USA created a vacuum cleaner for his wife, Anna, to clean up sawdust in carpeting. Shortly after, Bissell Carpet Sweepers were born. After Melville died unexpectedly in 1889, Anna took control of the company and was one of the most powerful businesswomen of the day.

John S. Thurman

On November 14, 1898, John S. Thurman of St. Louis, Missouri, USA. submitted for patent (U.S. No. 634,042) a "pneumatic carpet renovator". It was issued on October 3, 1899. Thurman created a gasoline powered carpet cleaner for the General Compressed Air Company. In a newspaper advertisement from the St. Louis Dispatch, Thurman offered his invention of the horse drawn (which went door to door) motorized cleaning system in St. Louis.

He offered cleaning services at $4 per visit. By 1906, Thurman was offering built-in central cleaning systems that used compressed air, yet featured no dust collection. Thurman's machine is sometimes considered the first vacuum cleaner. However, the dust was blown into a receptacle rather than being sucked in, as in the machine now used. In later patent litigation, Judge Augustus Hand ruled that Thurman "does not appear to have attempted to design a vacuum cleaner, or to have understood the process of vacuum cleaning."

H. Cecil Booth

Hubert Cecil Booth has the strongest claim to inventing the motorized vacuum cleaner in 1901. As Booth recalled decades later, in 1901 he attended "a demonstration of an American machine by its inventor" at the Empire Music Hall in London. The inventor is not named, but Booth's description of the machine conforms fairly closely to Thurman's design, as modified in later patents. Booth watched a demonstration of the device which blew dust off the chairs, and thought it would be much more useful to have one that sucked dust. He tested the idea by laying a handkerchief on the seat of a restaurant chair, putting his mouth to the handkerchief, and then trying to suck up as much dust as he could onto the handkerchief. Upon seeing the dust and dirt collected on the underside of the handkerchief he realized the idea could work.

Booth created a large device, driven first by an oil engine, and later by an electric motor. Nicknamed the "Puffing Billy", Booth's petrol-powered, horse-drawn vacuum cleaner relied upon air drawn through a cloth filter. Gaining the royal seal of approval, Booth's motorized vacuum cleaner was used to clean the carpets of Westminster Abbey prior to Edward VII's coronation in 1901. Booth received his first patents on February 18 and August 30, 1901.

Booth started the British Vacuum Cleaner Company and refined his invention over the next several decades. Though his "Goblin" model lost out to competition from Hoover in the household vacuum market, his company successfully turned its focus to the industrial market, building ever-larger models for factories and warehouses. Booth's company lives on today as a unit of pneumatic tube system maker Quirepace Ltd.

Booth gave the vacuum cleaner its start. His first vacuum cleaner, called "puffin Billy," was made of a piston pump. It did not contain any brushes; all the cleaning was done by suction through long tubes with nozzles on the ends. It was a large machine, mounted in a horse-drawn van that was pulled through the streets. The vans of the British Vacuum Cleaning Company (BVCC) were bright red; uniformed operators would haul hose off the van and route it through the windows of a building to reach all the rooms inside.

Booth was harassed by complaints about the noise of his vacuum machines and was even fined for frightening horses. The BVCC's most prestigious engagement was cleaning the carpets in Westminster Abbey in London before the 1901 coronation of King Edward VII and Queen Alexandra.

David T. Kenney

Nine patents granted to the New Jersey, USA inventor David T. Kenney between 1903 and 1913 established the foundation for the American vacuum cleaner industry. Membership in the Vacuum Cleaner Manufacturers' Association, formed in 1919, was limited to licensees under his patents.

Walter Griffiths

In 1905 "Griffith's Improved Vacuum Apparatus for Removing Dust from Carpets" was another manually operated cleaner, patented by Walter Griffiths Manufacturer, Birmingham, England. It was portable, easy to store, and powered by "any one person (such as the ordinary domestic servant)," who would have the task of compressing a bellows-like contraption to suck up dust through a removable, flexible pipe, to which a variety of shaped nozzles could be attached. This was arguably the first domestic vacuum-cleaning device to resemble the modern vacuum cleaner.

Hermann Bogenschild

German immigrant engineer Hermann Bogenschild filed a patent in 1906 for a mechanical 'dust removing apparatus.' Emigrating from Berlin to Milwaukee in 1892, Bogenschild's device was mounted on wheels for portability and its motor was connected to a hose and filter system.

James Murray Spangler

In 1907, James Murray Spangler, a janitor from Canton, Ohio, USA invented the first practical, portable vacuum cleaner. Crucially, in addition to suction that used an electric fan, a box, and one of his wife's pillowcases, Spangler's design incorporated a rotating brush to loosen debris. Unable to produce the design himself due to lack of funding, he sold the patent in 1908 to William Henry Hoover who had Spangler's machine redesigned with a steel casing, casters, and attachments. Subsequent innovations included the first disposal filter bags in the 1920s and the first upright vacuum cleaner in 1926.

Hoover

Spangler patented his rotating-brush design June 2, 1908, and eventually sold the idea to his cousin's husband, Hoover. He was looking for a new product to sell, as the leather goods produced by his 'Hoover Harness and Leather Goods' company were becoming obsolete, because of the invention of the automobile.

In the United States, Hoover remains one of the leading manufacturers of household goods, including vacuum cleaners; and Hoover became very wealthy from the invention. Indeed, in Britain the name Hoover became synonymous with the vacuum cleaner so much so that one "hoovers one's carpets". Initially called 'The Electric Suction Sweeper Company', their first vacuum was the 1908 Model O, which sold for $60.

Constellation

Hoover is also notable for an unusual vacuum cleaner, the Hoover Constellation, which is a cylinder type but lacks wheels. Instead, the vacuum cleaner floats on its exhaust, operating as a hovercraft, although this is not true of the earliest models. They had a swivel top hose with the intention being that the user would place the unit in the center of the room, and work around the cleaner.

Introduced in 1952, they are collectible, and are easily identified by the spherical shape of the housing. They tended to be loud, had poor cleaning power, and could not float over carpets. But they remain an interesting machine; restored, they work well in homes with lots of hardwood floors.

The Constellations were changed and updated over the years until discontinued in 1975. These Constellations route all of the exhaust under the vacuum using a different airfoil. The updated design is quiet even by modern standards, particularly on carpet as it muffles the sound. These models float on carpet or bare floor-although on hard flooring, the exhaust air tends to scatter any fluff or debris around.

Hoover has now re-released an updated version of this later model Constellation in the US (model # S3341 in Pearl White and # S3345 in stainless steel). Changes include a HEPA filtration bag, a 12 amp motor, a suction turbine powered rotating brush floor head, and a redesigned version of the handle, which tended to break. This same model was marketed in the UK under the Maytag brand as the Satellite because of licensing restrictions.

The 5.2 amp motor on older US units provides respectable suction but they all lack a motorized brush head. Therefore they generally work better on hard floors or short pile rugs. Old units take Hoover type J paper bags but the slightly smaller type S allergen filtration bags can be easily trimmed to fit the retaining notches on the old vacuums. Replacement motors are still available from Hoover US for some models.

Hoover made another hovering vacuum cleaner model called the Celebrity in 1973. It has a flattened "flying saucer" shape. Hoover added wheels to it make it a conventional cylinder model after a brief run as a hovering vacuum. It uses type H bags.

Nilfisk

In 1910, P.A. Fisker patented a vacuum cleaner using a name based on the company's telegram address-Nilfisk. It was the first electric vacuum cleaner in Europe. His design weighed just 17.5 kg and could be operated by a single person. The company Fisker and Nielsen was formed just a few years before. Today the Nilfisk vacuums are delivered by Nilfisk-Advance.

Electrolux Model V

The first vacuum cleaners were bulky stand-up units and not easily portable. But in 1921 Electrolux launched the Model V, that was designed to lie on the floor on two thin metal runners. This innovation, conceived by Electrolux founder Axel Wenner-Gren, became a standard feature on generations of future vacuum cleaners.

There is a recorded example of a 1930s Electrolux vacuum cleaner surviving in use for over 70 years, finally breaking in 2008.

Post-World War II

For many years after their introduction, vacuum cleaners remained a luxury item; but after World War II they became common among the middle classes. They tend to be more common in Western countries because, in most parts of the world, wall-to-wall carpeting is uncommon and homes have tile or hardwood floors, which are easily swept, wiped, or mopped.

Vacuum cleaners working on the cyclone principle became popular in the 1990s, although some companies (notably Filter Queen and Regina) have been making vacuum cleaners with cyclonic action since 1928. Modern cyclonic cleaners were adapted from industrial cyclonic separators by British designer James Dyson in 1985. He launched his cyclone cleaner first in Japan in the 1980s at a cost of about US$1,800 and later the Dyson DC01 upright in the UK in 1993 for £200. It was expected that people would not buy a vacuum cleaner at twice the price of a normal cleaner, but it later became the most popular cleaner in the UK.

Cyclonic cleaners do not use bags instead, the dust collects in a detachable, cylindrical collection vessel. Air and dust are blown at high speed into the collection vessel at a direction tangential to the vessel wall, creating a vortex. The dust particles and other debris move to the outside of the vessel by centrifugal force, where they fall due to gravity, and clean air from the center of the vortex is expelled from the machine after passing through a number of successively finer filters at the top of the container. The first filter is intended to trap particles which could damage the subsequent filters that remove fine dust particles. The filters must regularly be cleaned or replaced to ensure that the machine continues to perform efficiently. Since Dyson, several other companies have introduced cyclone models, including Hoover, Bisell, Eureka, Electrolux, etc and the cheapest models are no more expensive than a conventional cleaner.

In early 2000 several companies developed robotic vacuum cleaners. Some examples are Roomba, Robomaxx, Intellibot, Trilobite and FloorBot. These machines propel themselves in patterns across a floor, cleaning surface dust and debris into their dustbin. They usually can navigate around furniture and find their recharging stations. Most robotic vacuum cleaners are designed for home use, although there are more capable models for operation in offices, hotels, hospitals, etc. Some such as the Roomba are equipped with an impeller motor to create an actual vacuum. By the end of 2003 about 570,000 units were sold worldwide.

In 2004 a British company released Airider, a hovering vacuum cleaner that floats on a cushion of air. It has claimed to be light weight and easier to maneuver (compared to using wheels), although it is not the first vacuum cleaner to do this-the Hoover Constellation predated it by at least 35 years.

Technology

A vacuum's suction is caused by a difference in air pressure. An electric fan reduces the pressure inside the machine. Atmospheric pressure then pushes the air through the carpet and into the nozzle, and so the dust is literally pushed into the bag.

Tests have shown that vacuuming can kill 100% of young fleas and 96% of adult fleas.

A British inventor has developed a new cleaning technology known as Air Recycling Technology which instead of using a vacuum uses an air stream to collect dust from the carpet. This technology was tested by the Market Transformation Programme (MTP) and shown to be more energy efficient than the vacuum method. Although working prototypes exist Air Recycling Technology is not currently used in any production cleaner.

Configurations

Upright vacuum cleaners are common in the U.S., Britain and several Commonwealth countries, but very unusual in Continental Europe. They take the form of a cleaning head, onto which a handle and bag are attached. Upright designs usually employ a rotating brushroll or beater bar, which removes dirt through a combination of sweeping and vibration.

There are two types of upright vacuums; dirty-fan/direct air (found mostly on commercial vacuums), or clean-air/fan-bypass (found on most of today's vacuums).The older of the two designs, direct-fan cleaners have a large impeller (fan) mounted close to the suction opening, through which the dirt passes directly, before being blown into a bag. The motor is often cooled by a separate cooling fan. Because of their large-bladed fans, and comparatively short airpaths, direct-fan cleaners create a very efficient airflow from a low amount of power, and make great carpet cleaners.

Their 'above-floor' cleaning power is less efficient, since the airflow is lost when it passes through a long hose.Fan-bypass uprights have their motor mounted after the bag. Dust is removed from the airstream by the bag, and usually a filter, before it passes through the fan. The fans are smaller, and are usually a combination of several moving and stationary turbines working in sequence to boost power. The motor is cooled by the airstream passing through it.

Fan-bypass vacuums are good for both carpet and above-floor cleaning, since their suction does not significantly diminish over the distance of a hose, as it does in direct-fan cleaners. However, their air-paths are much less efficient, and can require more than twice as much power than direct-fan cleaners to achieve the same results.

The least common upright vacuum cleaners use a drive-belt powered by the suction motor to rotate the brush-roll. However, a more common design of dual motor upright is available. In these cleaners, the suction is provided via a large motor, while the brushroll is powered by a separate, smaller motor, which does not create any suction. The brush-roll motor can sometimes be switched off, so hard floors can be cleaned without the brush-roll scattering the dirt. It may also have an automatic cut-off feature, which shuts the motor off if the brush-roll becomes jammed, protecting it from damage.

Cylinder models (in the U.S. also often called canister models) dominate the European market. They have the motor and dust collector (using a bag or bagless) in a separate unit, usually mounted on wheels, which is connected to the vacuum head by a flexible hose. Their main advantage is flexibility, as you can attach different heads for different tasks, and maneuverability (the head can reach under furniture and makes it very easy to vacuum stairs and vertical surfaces.

Many cylinder models have power heads, as standard or add-on equipment, which contain the same sort of mechanical beaters as in upright units, making them as efficient on carpets as upright models. Such beaters are driven by a separate electric motor or a turbine which uses the suction power to spin the brushroll via a drive belt.

Robotic vacuum cleaners are a form of carpet sweeper with limited suction power, which move autonomously, usually in a mostly chaotic pattern ("random bounce"). Some come back to a docking station to charge their batteries, and a few are able to empty their dust containers into the dock as well.

Hand-held vacuum cleaners, either battery-operated or mains powered, are also popular for cleaning up smaller spills, such as the Black & Decker DustBuster, introduced in 1979, and the various hand-held models from Dirt Devil, first introduced in 1984.

Drum models are essentially heavy-duty industrial versions of cylinder vacuum cleaners, where the cylinder consists of a large vertically positioned drum, which can be stationary or on wheels. These models, which can store over 200 litres (53 US gallons), are often hooked up to compressed air and utilize the venturi effect.

Wet or wet/dry or shop vacuum cleaners are a specialized form of the cylinder/drum models that can be used to clean up wet or liquid spills. They commonly can accommodate both wet and dry soilage; some are also equipped with a switch or exhaust port for reversing the airflow, a useful function for everything from clearing a clogged hose to blowing dust into a corner for easy collection.

Pneumatic or pneumatic wet/dry vacuum cleaners are a specialized form of wet/dry models that hook up to compressed air. They commonly can accommodate both wet and dry soilage, a useful feature in industrial plants and manufacturing facilities.

Back-pack vacuum cleaners are commonly used for commercial cleaning: they allow the user to move rapidly about a large area. They are essentially cylinder vacuum cleaners strapped on the user's back.

Central vacuum cleaners, also known as built-in or ducted, are a type of cylinder models which have the motor and bag unit located in a central location in the building and provide vacuum inlets throughout the building: only the hose and head need be carried from room to room, and the hose is commonly 8 m (25 ft) long, allowing a large range of movement without changing vacuum inlets. Plastic piping connects the inlets to the central unit. The vacuum head may be unpowered or have beaters operated by an electric motor or an air-driven turbo.

The dirt bag in a central vacuum system is usually so large that emptying or changing needs to be done less often, perhaps once per year.

Chapter–3

Security Operations

Today, more than ever, hotel security has grown to encompass more than just emergency and evacuation plans, a stern visit to a rowdy room, or a security guard at the hotel's entrance. Like all other large facilities in a post 9/11 world, hotels must protect themselves and their guests against terrorists looking for a high-throughput environment that would draw media and public attention in the case that an event transpires there.

In the case that a hotel is not mandated to undergo a hotel security risk assessment by local or national authorities, it must take this responsibility upon itself. That is, a professional risk assessment will help a hotel identify its assets, the potential threats to those assets, and the magnitude of losses in the event that the threat manifests. Finally, and perhaps most importantly, a risk assessment will draw conclusions and provide workable recommendations and countermeasures to be implemented by the hotel management. Although a professional risk assessment prevents a formidable investment for the hotel itself, it is the most imperative investment that the entity can make.

Most hotels have a security manager or chief of hotel security operations who is responsible for a crew of security guards. Today's managers and their teams must be professionally trained and educated regarding modern threats that face the hotel security industry. In addition to knowing how to properly monitor security technologies such as CCTV, access-control and other integrated hotel security systems, today's hotel security [http://www.thepsos.com/hotels] managers and officers must be trained in identifying suspicious behaviors, interpreting body language and cris-response intervention.

Thirdly, many countries or states have collective hotel associations that provide a supportive community network for local hotels. Some examples include the IH&RA (International Hotel & Restaurant Association), the AH&LA (American Hotel and Lodging Association), the EHMA (European Hotel Managers Association) and the IHA (Israeli Hotel Association). These fraternal organizations are the ideal platform for hotels to gain support in regards to how their counterparts are providing services to their clients.

Finally, hotels must have an orderly system in place whereby they are periodically updated about the local and/or national security warning level by law-enforcement bodies. Many national and/or local law enforcement bodies make this aspect of hotel security a requirement. That is, the hotels in a given area must be willing to have a consistent flow of dialogue between police or state security forces, and themselves. Through updates, and even set standards, these hotels will be better equipped to provide the best to their guests.

SECURITY OPERATIONS CENTER

A Security Operations Center (SOC) is a centralized unit in an organization that deals with security issues, on an organizational and technical level. An SOC within a building or facility is a central location from where staff supervises the site, using data-processing technology. Typically, it is equipped for controlling CCTV monitoring, lighting, alarms, and vehicle barriers.

In IT Organizations

SOC of IT or as recently called SIEM "Security Information and Event Management" or just SEM with no "Information" has different type of work that is pure technical.

For more Information take a look at Security Operations Centers in IT world and Security Event Manager.

SOCs of the United States Government

The Transportation Security Administration in the United States has implemented Security Operations Centers for most airports that have federalized security. The primary function of TSA Security Operations Centers are to act as a communication hub for security personnel, law enforcement, airport personnel and various other agencies involved in the daily operations of airports.

SOCs are manned 24-hours a day by SOC Watch Officers. Security Operations Center Watch Officers are trained in all aspects of airport and aviation security and are often required to work abnormal shifts. SOC Watch Officers also ensure that TSA personnel follow proper protocol in dealing with airport security operations.

The SOC is usually the first to be notified of incidents at airports such as the discovery of prohibited items/contraband, weapons, explosives, hazardous materials as well as incidents regarding flight delays, unruly passengers, injuries, damaged equipment and various other types of potential security threats. The SOC in turn relays all information pertaining to these incidents to TSA federal security directors, law enforcement and TSA headquarters.

Bouncer of Bar

A bouncer is an informal term for a security guard employed at venues such as bars, nightclubs or concerts to provide security, check legal age, and refuse entry to a venue based on criteria such as intoxication, aggressive behavior, or attractiveness. Bouncers are often required where crowd size, clientele or alcohol consumption may make arguments or fights commonplace.

In the United States, civil liability and court costs related to the use of force by bouncers are "the highest preventable loss found within the [bar] industry..." and other countries have found similar issues related to the excessive use of force. Studies suggest that one of the reasons that some bouncers emphasise physical force is their self image as a strongly masculine group, which requires them to respond to aggression in violent ways. In many countries, federal or state governments have taken steps to professionalise the industry by requiring bouncers to have training, licensing, and/or a criminal records background check.

In the 1990s and 2000s, increased awareness of the risks of lawsuits and criminal charges (particularly in the United States and industrialised world) have led many bars and venues to train their bouncers to use communication and conflict resolution skills rather than brute force against troublemakers.

However, the earlier history of the occupation suggests that the stereotype of bouncers as rough, tough, physical enforcers has indeed been the case in many countries and cultures throughout history. Historical references also suggest that the 'doorman' function of guarding a place and selecting who can have entry to it (the stereotypical task of the modern bouncer) could at times be a honorific and evolve into a relatively important position.

Ancient Times

The significance of the doorman as the person allowing (or barring) entry is found in a number of Mesopotamian myths (and later in Greek myths descended from them), including that of Nergal overcoming the seven doormen guarding the gates to the Underworld.

In 1 Chronicles 26 of the Old Testament, the Levitical Temple is described as having a number of 'gatekeepers' - amongst their duties are "protect[ing] the temple from theft", from "illegal entry into sacred areas" and "maintain[ing] order", all functions they share with the modern concept of the bouncer, though the described temple servants also serve as holy persons and administrators themselves (it is noted that some administrative function is still present in today's bouncing in the higher position of the supervisor).

The Romans had a position known as the 'Ostiarius' (doorkeeper), initially a slave or other such inferior personage, who guarded the door, and sometimes ejected unwanted people from the house whose gate he guarded. The term later become a low-ranking clergy title.

Plautus, in his play Bacchides (written approximately 194-184 BC), mentions a "large and powerful" doorman / bouncer as a threat to get an unwelcome visitor to leave.

Tertullian, an early Christian author living mainly in the 1st century AD, while reporting on the casual oppression of Christians in Carthage, noted that bouncers were counted as part of a semi-legal underworld, amongst other 'shady' characters such as gamblers and pimps.

Modern Times

During the late 19th and early 20th centuries, US saloon-keepers and brothel madams hired bouncers to remove troublesome, violent, or dead-drunk patrons, and protect the saloon girls and prostitutes. The word "bouncer" was first popularized in a novel by Horatio Alger, Jr., called The Young Outlaw, which was first published in 1875. Alger was an immensely popular author in the 19th century, especially with young people and his books were widely quoted. In Chapter XIV, entitled "Bounced", a boy is thrown out of a restaurant because he has no money to pay for his dinner:

- "Here, Peter, you waited on this young man, didn't you?" "Yes, sir." "He hasn't paid for his breakfast, and pretends he hasn't got any money. Bounce him!" If Sam was ignorant of the meaning of the word 'bounce,' he was soon enlightened. The waiter seized him by the collar, before he knew what was going to happen, pushed him to the door, and then, lifting his foot by a well-directed kick, landed him across the sidewalk into the street. This proceeding was followed by derisive laughter from the other waiters who had gathered near the door, and it was echoed by two street urchins outside, who witnessed Sam's ignominious exit from the restaurant. Sam staggered from the force of the bouncing, and felt disgraced and humiliated to think that the waiter who had been so respectful and attentive should have inflicted upon him such an indignity, which he had no power to resent."

An 1883 newspaper article stated that "'The Bouncer' is merely the English 'chucker out'. When liberty verges on license and gaiety on wanton delirium, the Bouncer selects the gayest of the gay, and - bounces him!"

In US Western towns in the 1870s, high-class brothels known as "good houses" or "parlour houses" hired bouncers for security and to prevent patrons from evading payment. "Good house"-style brothels "...considered themselves the cream of the crop, and [the prostitutes working there] scorned those who worked in (or out of) saloons, dance halls, and theatres." The best bordellos looked like respectable mansions, with attractively-decorated parlours, a game room and a dance hall.

For security, "somewhere in every parlor house there was always a bouncer, a giant of a man who stayed sober to handle any customer who got too rough with one of the girls or didn't want to pay his bill." The "protective presence" of bouncers in high-class brothels was "...one of the reasons the girls considered themselves superior to [lower-class] free-lancers, who lacked any such shepherds."

In Wisconsin's lumberjack days, bouncers would physically remove drinkers who were too drunk to keep buying drinks, and thus free up space in the bar for new patrons. The slang term 'snake-room' was used to describe a "...room off a saloon, usually two or three steps down, into which a bar-keeper or the bouncer could slide drunk lumber-jacks head first through swinging doors from the bar-room." In the late 19th century, until Prohibition, bouncers also had the unusual role of protecting the saloon's buffet. To attract business, "...many saloons lured customers with offers of a "free lunch"-usually well salted to inspire drinking, and the saloon "bouncer" was generally on hand to discourage [those with too] hearty appetites".

In the late 19th century, bouncers at small town dances and bars physically resolved disputes and removed troublemakers, without worrying about lawsuits. In the main bar in one Iowa town, "...there were many quarrels, many fights, but all were settled on the spot. There were no court costs [for the bouncers or the bar]; only some aches and pains [for the troublemakers]."

In the 1880s and 1890s, bouncers were used to maintain order in the "The Gut", the roughest part of New York's Coney Island, which was filled with "ramshackle groups of wooden shanties", bars, cabarets, fleabag hotels and brothels. Huge bouncers patrolled these venues of vice and "roughly ejected anyone who violated the loose rules of decorum" by engaging in pick-pocketing, jewellry thieving, or bloody fights.

During the 1890s, San Diego had a similarly rough waterfront area and redlight district called the 'Stingaree', where bouncers worked the door at brothels. Prostitutes worked at the area's 120 bawdy houses in small rooms, paying a fee to the procurer who usually was the bouncer or 'protector' of the brothel. The more expensive, higher-class brothels were called "parlour houses", and they were "run most decorously", and the "best of food and drink was served." To maintain the high-class atmosphere at these establishments, male patrons were expected to act like gentlemen; "...if any customer did or said anything out of line, he was asked to leave. A bouncer made sure he did".

20TH CENTURY

Bouncers in pre-World War I United States were also sometimes used as the guardians of morality. As ballroom dancing was often considered as an activity which could lead to immoral conduct if the dancers got too close, some of the more reputable venues had bouncers to remind patrons not to dance closer than nine inches to their partners. The bouncers' warnings tended to consist of light taps on the shoulder at first, and then progressed to sterner remonstrations.

In the 1930s, bars in the bawdiest parts of Baltimore, Maryland docks hired bouncers to maintain order and eject aggressive patrons. The Oasis club, operated by Max Cohen, hired "...a lady bouncer by the name of Mickey Steele, a six-foot acrobat from the

Pennsylvania coal fields. Mickey was always considerate of the people she bounced; first asking them where they lived and then throwing them in that general direction. She was succeeded by a character known as 'Machine-Gun Butch' who was a long-time bouncer at the club".

In the Weimar Republic in the Germany of the 1920s and early 1930s, doormen protected venues from the fights caused by Nazis and other potentially violent groups (such as Communists). Such scenes were fictionalised in the movie Cabaret. Hitler surrounded himself with a number of former bouncers such as Christian Weber; the SS originated as a group designated to protect party meetings.

In early Nazi Germany, some bouncers in underground jazz clubs were also hired to screen for Nazi spies, because jazz was considered a "degenerate" form of music by the Nazi party. Later during the Nazi regime, bouncers also increasingly barred non-German people (such as foreign workers) from public functions, such as 'German' dances at dance halls.

Bouncers also often come into conflict with football hooligans, due to the tendency of groups of hooligans to congregate at pubs and bars before and after games. In the United Kingdom for example, long-running series of feuds between fan groups like The Blades and groups of bouncers in the 1990s were described by researchers.

Bouncers have also been known to be associated with criminal gangs, especially in places like Russia, Hong Kong or Japan, where bouncers may often belong to these groups or have to pay the crime syndicates to be able to operate. In Hong Kong, triad-connected reprisal or intimidation attacks against bouncers have been known to occur.

Hong Kong also features a somewhat unusual situation where some bouncers are known to work for prostitutes, instead of being their pimps. Hong Kong police have noted that due to the letter of the law, they sometimes had to charge the bouncer for illegally extorting the women when the usually expected dominance situation between the sex worker and her 'protector' was in fact reversed.

In the 1990s and 2000s, a number of bouncers have written "tell-all" books about their experiences on the door. They indicate that male bouncers are respected by some club-goers as the ultimate 'hard men', while at the same time, these bouncers can also be lightning rods for aggression and macho posturing on the part of obnoxious male customers wanting to prove themselves. Bouncing has also started to attract some academic interest as part of ethnographic studies into violent subcultures. Bouncers were selected as one of the groups studied by several English researchers in the 1990s because their culture was seen as 'grounded in violence', as well as because the group had increasingly been 'demonised', especially in common liberal discourse (see Research section of this article).

RESEARCH AND SOCIOLOGY

Outside Studies

In the early 1990s, an Australian government study on violence stated that violent incidents in public drinking locations are caused by the interaction of five factors: aggressive and unreasonable bouncers, groups of male strangers, low comfort (e.g., unventilated, hot clubs), high boredom, and high drunkenness. The research indicated that bouncers did not play as large a role "... as expected in the creation of an aggressive or violence prone atmosphere [in bars]." However, the study did show that "...edgy and aggressive bouncers, especially when they are arbitrary or petty in their manner, do have an adverse effect." The study stated that bouncers:

"...have been observed to initiate fights or further encourage them on several occasions. Many seem poorly trained, obsessed with their own machismo, and relate badly to groups of male strangers. Some of them appear to regard their employment as giving them a licence to assault people. This may be encouraged by management adherence to a repressive model of supervision of patrons ("if they play up, thump 'em"), which in fact does not reduce trouble, and exacerbates an already hostile and aggressive situation. In practice many bouncers are not well managed in their work, and appear to be given a job autonomy and discretion that they cannot handle well."

A 1998 article "Responses by Security Staff to Aggressive Incidents in Public Settings" in the Journal of Drug Issues examined 182 violent incidents involving crowd controllers (bouncers) that occurred in bars in Toronto, Canada. The study indicated that in 12% of the incidents the bouncers had good responses, in 20% of the incidents, the bouncers had a neutral response; and in 36% of the incidents, the bouncers "... responses were rated as bad-that is, the crowd controllers enhanced the likelihood of violence but were themselves not violent." Finally, "... in almost one-third of incidents, 31 per cent, the crowd controllers' responses were rated as ugly. The controllers' actions involved gratuitous aggression, harassment of patrons and provocative behaviour."

Inside Studies

At least one major ethnographic study also observed bouncing from within, as part of a British project to study violent subcultures. Beyond studying the bouncer culture from the outside, the group selected a suitable candidate for covert, long-term research. The man had previously worked as a bouncer before becoming an academic, and while conversant with the milieu, it required some time for him to re-enter bouncing work in a new locality.

The study has, however, attracted some criticism due to the fact that the researcher, while fulfilling his duties as a bouncer and being required to set aside his academic distance, would have been at risk of losing objectivity - though it was accepted that this quandary might be difficult to resolve.

One of the main ethical issues of the research was the participation of the researcher in violence, and to what degree he would be allowed to participate. The group could not fully resolve this issue, as the undercover researcher would not have been able to gain the trust of his peers while shying away from the use of force.

As part of the study it eventually became clear that bouncers themselves were similarly and constantly weighing up the limits and uses of their participation in violence. The research however found that instead of being a part of the occupation, violence itself was the defining characteristic, a "culture created around violence and violent expectation".

The bouncing culture's insular attitudes also extended to the recruitment process, which was mainly by word of mouth as opposed to typical job recruitment, and also depended heavily on previous familiarity with violence. This does not extend to the prospective bouncer himself having to have a reputation for violence - rather a perception was needed that he could deal with it if required. Various other elements, such as body language or physical looks (muscles, shaved heads) were also described as often expected for entry into bouncing - being part of the symbolic 'narratives of intimidation' that set bouncers apart in their work environment.

Training on the job was described as very limited, with the new bouncers being 'thrown into the deep end' - the fact that they had been accepted for the job in the first place including the assessment that they should know what they are doing (though informal observation of a beginner's behaviour was commonplace). In the case of the British research project, the legally required licensing as a bouncer was also found to be expected by employers before applicants started the job (and as licensing generally excluded people with criminal convictions, this kept out some of the more unstable violent personalities).

Personality and Behaviour

Although a common stereotype of bouncers is that of the thuggish brute, a good club security staff member requires more than just physical qualities such as strength and size: "The best bouncers don't "bounce" anyone... they talk to people" (and remind them of the venue rules).

An ability to judge and communicate well with people will reduce the need for physical intervention, while a steady personality will prevent the bouncer from being easily provoked by customers. Bouncers also profit from good written communication skills, because they are often required to document assaults in an incident log or using an incident form. Well-kept incident logs can "cover the employee's back" if criminal charges or a lawsuit later arise from an incident.

However, British research from the 1990s also indicates that a major part of both the group identity and the job satisfaction of bouncers is related to their self image as a strongly masculine person who is capable of dealing with - and dealing out - violence; their employment income plays a lesser role in their job satisfaction. Bouncer subculture is strongly influenced by perceptions of honour and shame, a typical characteristic of groups that are constantly in the public eye.

Factors in enjoying work as a bouncer were also found in the general prestige and respect that was accorded to bouncers, sometimes bordering on hero worship. The camaraderie between bouncers (even of different clubs), as well as the ability to work "in the moment" and outside of the drudgery of typical jobs were also often cited.

The same research has also indicated that the decisions made by bouncers, while seeming haphazard to an outsider, often have a basis in rational logic. The decision to turn certain customers away at the door because of too casual clothing is for example often based on the perception that the person will be more willing to fight (compared to someone dressed in expensive attire). Many similar decisions taken by a bouncer during the course of a night are also being described as based on experience rather than just personality.

Use of Force

Excessive Force

Movies often depict bouncers physically throwing patrons out of clubs and restraining drunk customers with headlocks, which has led to a popular misconception that bouncers have (or reserve) the right to use physical force freely. However, in many countries bouncers have no legal authority to use physical force more freely than any other civilian-meaning they are restricted to reasonable levels of force used in self defense, to eject drunk or aggressive patrons refusing to leave a venue, or when restraining a patron who has committed an offence until police arrive. Lawsuits are possible if injuries occur, even if the patron was drunk or using aggressive language.

With civil liability and court costs related to the use of force as "the highest preventable loss found within the industry..." (US) and bars being "sued more often for using unnecessary or excessive force than for any other reason" (Canada), substantial costs may be incurred by indiscriminate violence against patrons-though this depends heavily on the laws and customs of the country. In Australia, the number of complaints and lawsuits against venues due to the behaviour of their bouncers has been credited with turning many establishments to using former police officers to head their in-house security, instead of hiring private firms.

According to statistical research in Canada, bouncers are as likely to face physical violence in their work as urban-area police officers. The research also found that the likelihood of such encounters increased (with statistical significance) with the number of years the bouncer had worked in his occupation. Despite popular misconceptions, bouncers in Western countries are normally unarmed. Some bouncers may carry weapons such as expandable batons for personal protection, but they may not have a legal right to carry a weapon even if they would prefer to do so.

Alternatives

Use of force training programs teach bouncers ways to avoid using force and explain what types of force are considered allowable by the courts. Some bars have gone so far as to institute policies barring physical contact, where bouncers are instructed to ask a drunk or disorderly patron to leave - if the patron refuses, the bouncers call police. However, if the police are called too frequently, it can reflect badly on the venue upon renewal of its liquor licence.

Another strategy used in some bars is to hire smaller, less threatening or female bouncers, because they may be better able to defuse conflicts than large, intimidating bouncers. The more 'impressive' bouncers, in the often tense environments they are supposed to supervise, are also often challenged by aggressive males wanting to prove their machismo. Large and intimidating bouncers, whilst providing an appearance of strong security, may also drive customers away in cases where a more relaxed environment is desired.

In addition, female security staff, apart from having fewer problems searching female patrons for drugs or weapons, and being able to enter women's wash rooms to check for illegal activities, are also considered as better able to deal with drunk or aggressive women.

In Australia, for example, women comprise almost 20% of the security industry and increasingly work the door as well, using "a smile, chat and a friendly but firm demeanor" to resolve tense situations. Nearly one in nine of Britain's nightclub bouncers are also women, with the UK's 2003 Licensing Act giving the authorities "discretionary power to withhold a venue's licence if it does not employ female door staff."

This is credited with having "opened the door for women to enter the profession.". However, female bouncers are still a rarity in many countries, such as in India, where two women who became media celebrities in 2008 for being "Punjabs first female bouncers" were soon sacked again after accusations of unbecoming behaviour.

Regulation and Training

In many countries, a bouncer must be licensed and lacking a criminal record to gain employment within the security/crowd control sector. In some countries or regions, bouncers may be required to have extra skills or special licenses and certification for first aid, alcohol distribution, crowd control, or fire safety.

Canada

In Canada, bouncers have the right to use reasonable force to expel intoxicated or aggressive patrons. First, the patron must be asked to leave the premises. If the patron refuses to leave, the bouncer can use reasonable force to expel the patron. This has been upheld in a number of court cases. Under the definition of 'reasonable force', "it is perfectly acceptable [for the bouncer] to grab a patron's arm to remove the patron from the premises." However, "Only in situations where employees reasonably believe that the conduct of the patron puts them in danger can they inflict harm on a patron and then only to the extent that such force is necessary for self defence."

In Alberta, bar and nightclub security staff will have to take a new, government-run training course on correct bouncer behaviour and skills before the end of 2008. The six-hour 'ProTect' course will, among other subjects, teach staff to identify conflicts before they become violent, and how to defuse situations without resorting to force.

In Ontario, courts have ruled that "a tavern owes a twofold duty of care to its patrons. It must ensure that it does not serve alcohol which would apparently intoxicate or increase the patron's intoxication. As well, it must take positive steps to protect patrons and others from the dangers of intoxication." Regarding the second requirement of protecting patrons, the law holds that "customers cannot be ejected from your premises if doing so would put them in danger [e.g., due to the patron's intoxication]. Bars can be held liable for ejecting a customer who they know, or should know, is at risk of injury by being ejected."

In Ontario, bartenders and servers have to have completed the Smart Serve Training Program, which teaches them to recognise the signs of intoxication. The Smart Serve program is also recommended for other staff in bars who have contact with potentially intoxicated patrons, such as bouncers, coat check staff, and valets. The Smart Serve certification program encourages bars to keep Incident Reporting Logs, to use as evidence if an incident gets to court. With the August 2007 Private Security and Investigative Services Act, Ontario law also requires security industry workers, including bouncers to be licensed.

New Zealand

In New Zealand, there is no national-level regulation of bouncers as of 2006. The New Zealand Security Association supports the Hospitality Association of New Zealand's efforts to introduce certification for bouncers, doormen and other people responsible for security at bars and sporting events. The association argues that security officers should be "...properly trained professionals, not just a 'big thug' to stand at the door.", decrying the practice of using "unlicensed, untrained security staff". The organisation has been lobbying the New Zealand government to introduce legislation on training requirements for bar security staff.

Singapore

Singapore requires all bouncers to undergo a background check and attend a 5-day 'National Skills Recognition System' course for security staff. However, many of the more professional security companies (and larger venues with their own dedicated security staff) have noted that the course is insufficient for the specific requirements of a bouncer and provide their own additional training.SIA

United Kingdom

In the UK, bouncers (called 'door supervisors') must hold a license from the Security Industry Authority. The training for a door supervisor licence takes 30 hours, and includes issues such as behaviour, conflict management, civil and criminal law, searching and arrest procedures, drug awareness, recording of incidents and crime scene preservation, licensing law, equal opportunities and discrimination, health and safety at work,physical intervention, and emergency procedures. One current provider of training is the British Institute of Innkeeping Awarding Body.

According to the BBC, a leaked government communication (Oct 2010) favours the abolition of the SIA as a further example of the Conservative Party's widespread cuts, with the SIA being an example of one of the many Quangos the Conservatives intend to disband. Whilst this may alleviate to some extent the financial burden on employers and individuals alike, the vast majority of the industry sees this as a retrograde step, fearing a return of the organised criminal element to the now regulated industry.

Republic of Ireland

In the Republic of Ireland all potential doormen (Bouncers) must complete a FETAC level 4 course in Door Security Procedures. This allows them to apply for a PSA license (Private Security Authority) The PSA vet all applicants before issuing a license, Subsequently some past convictions will disqualify an applicant from working in the security industry.

The license issued by the PSA entitles the holder of the license to work on pubs,clubs and event security. It is to be noted that currently event security is an unlicensed sector in Ireland and one does not require a PSA license to provide a security service at an event. However the PSA in conjunction with some of the major security companies in Ireland are in the process of regulating the events sector, As a means for continuous development of standards.

United States

Requirements for bouncers vary from state to state, with some examples being:

California

In California, Senate Bill 194 requires any bouncer or security guard to be registered with the State of California Department of Consumer Affairs Bureau of Security and Investigative Services. These guards must also complete a criminal background check, including submitting their fingerprints to the California Department of Justice and the Federal Bureau of Investigation. Californians must undertake the "Skills Training Course for Security Guards" before receiving a security licence. Further courses allow for qualified security personnel to carry batons upon completion of training.

New York

In New York State, it is illegal for a bar owner to knowingly hire a felon for a bouncer position. Under Article 7 General Business Law, bars and nightclubs are not allowed to hire bouncers without a proper license. Under New York state law only a Private Investigator or Watch, Guard and Patrol Agency can supply security guards/bouncers to bars

Notable Names

- Al Capone, Chicago-based gangster, worked as a bartender/bouncer in his early life.
- Bas Rutten, retired Dutch-American mixed martial artist MMA and kickboxer, was a bouncer for many years.
- Christopher Meloni, American actor known for his near opposite roles as the protective and committed Detective Elliot Stabler on the NBC drama series Law & Order: Special Victims Unit, and as the bisexual serial killer Chris Keller on HBO's Oz.
- Dave Batista, better known by his ring name, Batista, American professional wrestler currently signed to World Wrestling Entertainment on its SmackDown brand.
- Geoff Thompson, British bouncer and author of the book Watch My Back.

- Glenn Ross, Northern Irish bouncer and strongman.
- Lenny McLean, British bare-knuckle boxing heavyweight champion who also worked as a head doorman at London nightclubs.
- Michael Clarke Duncan, American actor and former bouncer who also worked as a bodyguard for various celebrities.
- Mr. T (Laurence Tureaud, aka. "Clubber Lang"), American actor, former bouncer and twice winner of the "America's Toughest Bouncer" competition.
- Road Warrior Animal (Joseph Laurinaitis), a professional wrestling tag-team star who worked as a bouncer.
- Vincent D'Onofrio, American actor on Law & Order: Criminal Intent.
- Vin Diesel, American actor who created his 'Vin Diesel' pseudonym to protect his anonymity while working as a bouncer.
- Kimbo Slice, is a Bahamian-American mixed martial arts fighter. He became famous for street fights which were spread on the Internet.
- Ivan 'Doc' Holiday, Canadian bouncer and author of The Cooler's Grimiore.
- Jon Venables, one of the ten year olds who murdered James Bulger in 1993, is believed to have worked as a bouncer, but because of reporting restriction it can't be confirmed.

Other Meanings

In Animals

Some types of ant species have evolved a sub-specialisation that has been called a 'bouncer', and performs a similar function (throwing intruders outside) for its fellows. The majors of the Australian Dacetine Orectognathus versicolor ants have massive blunt mandible jaws which are of little use to the prey-capture techniques this trap jaw species normally engages in. Instead, they spend much of their time guarding the nest opening, their jaws cocked. When foreign ants venture close, the force of the mandibles is sufficient to throw back the intruder for a significant distance, a defense behaviour which is thought to also protect the guard against physical or chemical injury that it might sustain in more direct battle.

In Social Control

Some critics have noted that the European Union has assigned the job of being its border security 'bouncers' to various non-EU North African countries like Morocco, Algeria or Libya, who are to turn away refugees (often with severe ill-treatment) before they can reach Europe to request asylum, analogous to a club bouncer turning away undesirable customers.

In a similar analogy, some social theorists have expressed the state itself as a form of 'bouncer' which "pushes and punches drifters [people who do not conform with social norms] back to where they are supposed to be" - though, depending on society, some states may be much more heavy-handed and proactive in this.

Security Guard

A security guard (or security officer) is usually a privately and formally employed person who is paid to protect property, assets, or people. Often, security officers are uniformed and act to protect property by maintaining a high visibility presence to deter illegal and inappropriate actions, observing (either directly, through patrols, or by watching alarm systems or video cameras) for signs of crime, fire or disorder; then taking action and reporting any incidents to their client and emergency services as appropriate.

Since at least the Middle Ages in Europe, the term watchman was more commonly applied to this function. This term was carried over to North America where it was interchangeable with night-watchman until both terms were replaced with the modern security-based titles. Security guards are sometimes regarded as fulfilling a private policing function.

Functions and Duties

Many security firms and proprietary security departments practice the "detect, deter, observe and report" methodology. Security officers are not required to make arrests, but have the authority to make a citizen's arrest, or otherwise act as an agent of law enforcement at the request of a police officer, sheriff, and others.

In addition to the methodology mentioned above, a private security officer's primary duty is the prevention and deterrence of crime. Security personnel enforce company rules and can act to protect lives and property. In fact, they frequently have a contractual obligation to provide these actions. Security officers are often trained to perform arrest and control procedures (including handcuffing and restraints), operate emergency equipment, perform first aid, CPR, take accurate notes, write detailed reports, and perform other tasks as required by the contractee they are serving.

Many security officers are required to go through additional training mandated by the state for the carrying of weapons such as batons, firearms, and pepper spray (e.g. the Bureau of Security and Investigative Services in California has requirements that a license for each item listed must be carried while on duty). Some officers are required to complete police certification for special duties.

Positions are also set to grow in the U.S., with 175,000 new security jobs expected before 2016. In recent years, due to elevated threats of terrorism, most security officers are required to have bomb-threat training and/or emergency crisis training, especially those located in soft target areas such as shopping malls, schools, and any other area where the general public congregate.

One major economic justification for security personnel is that insurance companies (particularly fire insurance carriers) will give substantial rate discounts to sites which have a 24-hour presence; for a high risk or high value venue, the discount can often exceed the money being spent on its security program.

This is because having security on site increases the odds that any fire will be noticed and reported to the local fire department before a total loss occurs. Also, the presence of security personnel (particularly in combination with effective security procedures) tends to diminish "shrinkage," theft, employee misconduct and safety rule violations, property damage, or even sabotage. Many casinos hire security guards to protect money when transferring it from the casino to the casino's bank.

Security personnel may also perform access control at building entrances and vehicle gates; meaning, they ensure that employees and visitors display proper passes or identification before entering the facility. Security officers are often called upon to respond to minor emergencies (lost persons, lockouts, dead vehicle batteries, etc.) and to assist in serious emergencies by guiding emergency responders to the scene of the incident, helping to redirect foot traffic to safe locations, and by documenting what happened on an incident report.

Armed security officers are frequently contracted to respond as law enforcement until a given situation at a client location is under control and/or public authorities arrive on the scene.

Patrolling is usually a large part of a security officer's duties. Often these patrols are logged by use of a guard tour patrol system, which require regular patrols. The most commonly used form used to be mechanical clock systems that required a key for manual punching of a number to a strip of paper inside with the time pre-printed on it.

Recently, electronic systems have risen in popularity due to their light weight, ease of use, and downloadable logging capabilities. Regular patrols are, however, becoming less accepted as an industry standard, as it provides predictability for the would-be criminal, as well as monotony for the security officer on duty.

Random patrols are easily programmed into these systems, allowing greater freedom of movement and unpredictability. Global positioning systems are also easing their way into the market as a more effective means of tracking officer movement and patrol behavior.

Personnel

Although security officers differ greatly from police officers, military personnel, federal agents/officers, and the like, Australia and the United States have a growing proportion of security personnel that have former police or military experience, including senior management personnel. On the other hand, some security officers, young people in particular, use the job as practical experience to use in applying to law enforcement agencies.

Types of security personnel and companies

Security personnel are classified as either of the following

- "in-house" or "proprietary" (i.e. employed by the same company or organization they protect, such as a mall, theme park, or casino); formerly often called works police or security police in the United Kingdom
- "contract," working for a private security company which protects many locations.
- "Public Security," "Private Police Officers," or security police
- "Private Patrol Officers", vehicle patrol officers that protect multiple client premises.
- "Parapolice", aggressive firms that routinely engage in criminal investigation and arrests.

Industry terms for various security personnel include: security guard, security agent, security officer, safety patrol, private police, company police, security enforcement officer and public safety. Other job titles in the security industry include bouncer, bodyguards, executive protection agent loss prevention, alarm responder, hospital security officer, mall security officer, crime prevention officer, private patrol officer, and private patrol operator.

State and local governments sometimes regulate the use of these terms by law-for example, certain words and phrases that "give an impression that he or she is connected in any way with the federal government, a state government, or any political subdivision of a state government" are forbidden for use by California security licensees by Business and Professions Code Section 7582.26. So the terms "private homicide police" or "special agent" would be unlawful for a security licensee to use in California. Similarly, in Canada, various acts specifically prohibits private security personnel from using the terms Probation Officer, law enforcement, police, or police officer.

Alberta and Ontario probibit the use of the term 'Security Officer' which is in widespread use in the United States for many decades. Recent changes to the act have also introduced restrictions on uniform and vehicle colours and markings to make private security personnel clearly distinctive from police personnel. Some sources feel that some of these restrictions are put in place to satisfy the Canadian Police Association.

There is a marked difference between persons performing the duties historically associated with watchmen and persons who take a more active role in protecting persons and property. The former, often called "guards," are taught the mantra "observe and report," are minimally trained, and not expected to deal with the public or confront criminals.

The latter are often highly trained, sometimes armed depending on contracts agreed upon with clientele, and are more likely to interact with the general public and to confront the criminal element. These employees tend to take pride in the title "Security Officer" or "Protection Officer" and disdain the label of "guard."

Ironically enough, there may be no relationship between duties performed and compensation-many mall "security officers" who are exposed to serious risks make less per hour than "industrial security guards" with less training and responsibility. However, there are now more positions in the security role that separate not just the titles, but the job itself. The roles have progressed and so have the areas for which security people are needed. All security jobs vary in pay and duties at present.

The term "agent" is particularly problematic in the security industry because it can describe not only a civil legal relationship between an employee and their employer or contractor ("agent of the owner" in California PC 602), but also describes a person in government service ("Special Agent Jones of the Federal Bureau of Investigation.") However we should then also consider the fact that this title is also made available to banking agents, loan agents and real estate agents.

Security "agents" found in loss prevention and personal or executive protection (bodyguards) typically work in plainclothes, without a uniform, and are usually highly trained to act lawfully in direct defense of life and/or property. There is also confusion with bail enforcement agents, or as they are popularly known "bounty hunters," who are sometimes regulated by the same agencies which regulate private security.

Security personnel are essentially private citizens, and therefore are bound by the same laws and regulations as the citizenry they are contracted to serve, and therefore are not allowed to represent themselves as law enforcement under penalty of law.

Any person who conducts a business or is employed in a security related field within Australia is required to be licensed. Each of the six states and two territories of Australia have separate legislation that covers all security activities. Licensing management in each state/territory is varied and is carried out by either police, Attorney General's Department, Justice Department or the Department of Consumer Affairs.

All persons licensed to perform security activities are required to undertake a course of professional development in associated streams that are recognised nationally. This has not always been the case and the introduction of this aspect should regulate the educational standards/knowledge base expected so that the particular job can be competently undertaken.

Strict requirements are laid down as to the type of uniform and badging used by security companies. Uniforms or badging that may be confused with a police officer are not permitted similarly, the use of the title 'Security Police' or 'Private Detective' are unacceptable. Whilst the term security guard is used by companies, government bodies and individuals, the term security officer is deemed more suitable. 'Bouncers' are Crowd Controllers and Store Detectives are Loss Prevention or Asset Protection Officers.

Security Officers are not permitted to carry firearms, handcuffs or batons unless they have a legitimate requirement to do so and then only when working and have the appropriate sub-class accreditation to their license.

Canada

In Canada, private security falls under the jurisdiction of Canada's ten provinces and three territories. All ten of Canada's provinces and one of its territories (the Yukon) have legislation that regulates the contract security industry. These eleven jurisdictions require that companies that provide security guard services and their employees be licensed.

Most provinces in Canada regulate the use of handcuffs and weapons (such as firearms and batons) by contract security companies and their employees, either banning such use completely or permitting it only under certain circumstances.

Canada's federal laws also restrict the ability of security guards to be armed. For example, section 17 of Firearms Act makes it an offence for any person, including a security guard, to possess prohibited or restricted firearms (i.e. handguns) anywhere outside of his or her home.

There are two exceptions to this prohibition found in sections 18 and 19 of the Act. Section 18 deals with transportation of firearms while Section 19 deals with allowing persons to carry such firearms on their persons to protect their lives or the lives of other persons, or for the performance of their occupation (Armour Car Guards, Licensed Trappers), provided an Authorization to Carry (ATC) is first obtained.

British Columbia

Private security in the province of British Columbia is governed by two pieces of legislation: the Security Services Act and the

Security Services Regulation. These laws are administered and enforced by the Security Programs and Police Technology Division of the Ministry of Public Safety and Solicitor General.

The legislation requires that guards must be at least 19 years old, undergo a criminal background check, and successfully complete a training course. As far as weapons, British Columbia law severely restricts their use by security guards. Section 11(1)(c) of the Security Services Regulation prohibits security personnel from carrying or using any "item designed for debilitating or controlling a person or animal", which the government interprets to include all weapons. As well, section 11 forbids private security from using or carrying restraints, such as handcuffs, unless authorized by the government. However, as in other parts of Canada, armoured car guards are permitted to carry firearms.

In the past, only personnel that worked for contract security, that is, security companies, were regulated in British Columbia. However, as of September 1, 2009, in-house security guards and private investigators came under the jurisdiction of the Security Services Act and Security Services Regulation. The same occurred to bodyguards and bouncers, effective November 1, 2009.

Europe

Armed private security are much rarer in Europe, and nonexistent in many countries, such as the United Kingdom, The Netherlands and Switzerland. In developing countries (with host country permission), an armed security force composed mostly of ex-military personnel is often used to protect corporate assets, particularly in war-torn regions.

As a requirement of the Private Security Industry Act 2001, the UK now requires all contract security guards to have a valid Security Industry Authority license. The licence must be displayed when on duty, although a dispensation may be granted for store detectives, bodyguards and others who need to operate without being identified as a security guard.

This dispensation is not available to Vehicle Immobilisers. Licenses are valid for three years and require the holders to undergo formal training, and are also to pass mandatory Criminal Records Bureau checks. Licences for Vehicle Immobilisers are valid for one year. Armed guarding and guarding with a weapon are illegal.

In Finland, all contract security guards are required to have a valid license granted by police. Temporary license is valid for four months and normal license for five years. License requires a minimum 40-hour course for temporary license and 60 hours more for a normal license. Additionally a narrow security vetting is required. The 40-hour course allows the carrying of a fixed-length baton and handcuffs, separate training and license is required for the security guard to carry pepper spray, extendable baton or a firearm.

Rehearse of weapons usage is mandatory every year and is regulated by the Ministry of The Interior, to ensure the safe handling of pepper spray and such. In Finland, a security guard has the right to detain a person "red-handed", or seen committing a crime and the right to search the detained individual for harmful items and weapons. An individual who has been forcefully detained can only be released by the police. All companies providing security guarding services are also required to have a valid license from Ministry of the Interior.

In The Netherlands security guards Beveiligingsbeambte must undergo a criminal backgroundcheck by the local police department in the area where the private security company is located. To become a securtiy guard in The Netherlands a person must complete the basic training level 2 Beveiliger2, to complete the training a trainee must undergo a three month intership with a private security company that is licensed by the svpb, this is the board that controls security exams.

A trainee guard must pass for his diploma within one year, if the trainee does not pass he is not allowed to work anymore until the trainee completes his training with a positive result, after a positive result a new ID can be issued and is valid for three years, after that the guard must undergo a backgroundcheck by the local police again. Security guards in The Netherlands are not allowed to carry any kind of weapon or handcuffs. Every uniformed security guard in The Netherlands must have the V symbol on its uniform to ensure the public they are dealing with a private guard, this rule is mandatory by thé Ministry of justice.

Security uniforms may not look like similar to police uniforms, and may not contain any kind of rank designation, and the collor yellow or gold are not allowed to used because the Dutch police uses gold accents in their uniforms, also wearing a uniformcap is not longer allowed. Every new uniform design or addition must be approved by the ministry of justice before use. A patrol vehicle may not look like a police striped vehicle. The only private security guards that are allowed to carry firearms are those who work for the military or Dutch National bank (De Nederlandsche Bank) this is were the national gold reserve can be found.

Norway

In Norway security officers are called "Vektere", there are a couple of different types of vektere. You have the normal uniformed and/or civil-clothing officers who normally watch over private and semi-public properties. The government can also hire vektere in public places, like for instance the Parliament. The security officers at the Parliament has a little more power by the law than private security officers.

Security officers must undergo three weeks of coursing and internship. They are allowed to work for six months after one week of introduction course. It's also possible to take Security as a High School major, with 2 years of school and 2 years of trainee positions at private companies which will give the officer a certificate from the government. This certificate will make it easier to get a job, and slightly higher pay. It will also make it easier to get a job elsewhere in the security industry. The certificate can also be taken privately by security officers who have had a minimum of 5 years working experience.

In addition to normal "vektere" there also is a special branch for "Ordensvakter" which normally works as bouncers or security at concerts and similar types of events. Ordensvakter has to undergo an extra week of coursing and learn Technics on how to handle drunk people and people on different drugs. They also learn about the alcohol laws of Norway (who are rather strict). The local police in the police district has to approve each Ordensvakt.

In the 1990s, bouncers had a bad reputation, specially in Oslo for being to brutal and rough with people. And the police had no control over who worked as bouncers. After the government forced training and mandatory ID-cards for bouncers it has gotten much better. And the police of Oslo now even says that Ordensvakter are helping the police finding crime that otherwise would not be reported.

In 2007 several Securitas officers harshly arrested a thief on Karl Johans Gate (the main street of Oslo). This was filmed with a mobile camera by some pedestrians and created a media storm on Security Officers taking the law in their own hands. When it later came to a fact that the thief attacked the security guards when they approached him the charges where dropped on the security guards.

But the police said that they would be harsher in the criminal background checking of people working as Security Guards. Before 2007 security guards where checked when they applied for a job, but not while they where working. And the companies employing the guards got massive critic for not checking criminal records suffice, and some times not at all.

Now people in private security is being checked annually. And the police have the authority to withdraw the companies licence for operating if they do not send in lists of employees. The Police in Norway has later been widely criticized for not checking this properly, and when they do, Security Guards still work for months before anything is done. The big security company G4s stated after critic from the police about hiring criminals that they cannot do anything about the problem, because the police is the only instance who has the possibility to check the records.

Today it is around 15,000 people working within private security in Norway. For comparison the police have around 10,000 employees in total.

Notable companies operating in Norway:

- Securitas
- G4S
- Vaktservice
- Hafslund infratek
- ISS A/S (formerly Personellsikring)
- ProSec - Professional Security (mainly event security)

Hong Kong

In Hong Kong, the term Security Officer refers to a senior staff member who supervises a team of security personnel. The staff who work under security officers' supervision are called Security Guards.

Legislation

Before 1 October 1996, private security personnel were regulated by the Watchmen Ordinance. However, there were many problems with that system of regulation-for example, there were no restrictions as to whom may establish private security service companies to provide security services to a client. Also, there was no regulation of people whom may perform installation of security systems.

Some employers hired "caretakers" instead of security guards to avoid their responsibilities under the ordinance (in formal definition, "caretakers" are supposed to provide facilities management service, although security service, which provided to residential properties, takes some parts of facilities management service). As a result, the Hong Kong Government enacted a wholly new law, the Security and Guarding Services Ordinance (Chapter 460), to replace the Watchmen Ordinance.

According to the Security and Guarding Services Ordinance: No individual shall do, agree to do, or hold himself/herself out as doing, or as available to do, security work for another person unless he/she does so-

- under and in accordance with a permit; or
- otherwise than for reward.

Security work means any of the following activities-

- guarding any property;
- guarding any person or place for the purpose of preventing or detecting the occurrence of any offence; (Replaced 25 of 2000 s. 2)
- installing, maintaining or repairing a security device;
- designing for any particular premises or place a system incorporating a security device.

Security device means a device designed or adapted to be installed in any premises or place, except on or in a vehicle, for the purpose of detecting or recording- (Amended 25 of 2000 s. 2)

- the occurrence of any offence; or
- the presence of an intruder or of an object that persons are, for reasons of security, not permitted to bring onto the premises or place or any other premises or place.

Qualification

Any applicant who wishes to apply for a Security Personnel Permit (SPP) must:

- He/she have been living in Hong Kong for at least 5 years. (This requirement may have been changed)
- No criminal record.
- At least 18 years old when submitting his/her application.
- Have passed a mandatory 16 hour training course and have been granted a certificate of the course.
- If the applicant is over 65 years old, he/she must submit his/her health examination report.

Although the Security and Guarding Services Industry Authority (SGSIA) is the agency in charge of the security service industry, all applicants must submit their application and pay the fee by mail or in person to Hong Kong Police Force(License Section).

Permit

Security Personnel Permit was separated to four types: A, B, C, and D.

- Type A permit holder was permitted to work in a 'single-block' residential building; they are not allowed to carry firearms. No age limit.
- Type B permit holder was permitted to work in any type of properties, but they also are not allowed carry firearms. The maximum age limit of this permit is 65.
- Type C permit holder was permitted to work as an armed guard. (Usually, they are members of the cash transport car crew.) The maximum age limit of this permit is 55.
- Type D permit holder was permitted to design, install, and repair security devices. No maximum age limit.

The permit is valid for five years. All holders must renew their permit before it expires, or they will lose their qualification to work, as such, until their permit is renewed.

The type A and Type B security service are gradually combined with property management service, though the boundary between these two industries is unclear.

Power of Arrest

Security Guards in Hong Kong do not have special powers of arrest above that of the ordinary citizen, i.e. citizen's arrest, also known locally as the '101 arrest power.' The Section 101 in the Criminal Procedure Ordinance addresses that arrest of an offender by a private citizen is allowed in certain circumstances if the offender is attempting an arrestable offense. Once arrested, the suspect must be delivered to a police office as soon as possible.

An arrestable offence is defined as any crime carrying a sentence of more than 12 months imprisonment. No security personnel are allowed to search other person, nor are they allowed to get personal information from other people, with the exception of some specific circumstances.

Israel

In Israel, almost all security guards carry a firearm, primarily to prevent terror attacks. Security guards are common: they perform entrance checks at shopping malls, transportation terminals, government and other office buildings, and many stores. Many locations with a high number of visitors, such as the Jerusalem Bus Station, employ X-ray machines to check passenger's bags; in other places, they are opened and visually inspected. As of 2009, private security guards have also replaced official security forces at some checkpoints inside and on the border of the West Bank, as well as the crossings to Gaza.

Malaysia

In August 2007, Malaysia banned hiring of foreign security guards following a rape and murder of a student by a Pakistani security guard.

Security guard companies need to apply to the Ministry of Internal Security.

South Africa

Main article: Private security industry in South Africa

Security guards along with the rest of the private security industry are regulated under Act 56 of 2001, Private Security Industry Regulation Act.

United States

Private security guards have outnumbered police officers since the 1980s, predating the heightened concern about security brought on by the September 11, 2001, attacks. The more than 1 million contract security officers, and an equal number of guards estimated to work directly for U.S. corporations, dwarf the nearly 700,000 sworn law enforcement officers in the United States.

Most states require a license to work as a security officer. This license may include a criminal background check and/or mandated training requirements.

Most security officers do not carry weapons and have the same powers of arrest as a private citizen, called a "private person" arrest, "any person" arrest, or "citizen's arrest." If weapons are carried, additional permits and training are usually required. Armed security personnel are generally used to protect sensitive sites such as government and military installations, armored money transports, casinos, banks (or other financial institutions), nuclear power plants, etc. However, armed security is quickly becoming a standard for vehicle patrol officers and on many other non-government sites.

Security guard/officer continue to gain broader responsibilities. A growing trend is the increased use of private security to support services previously provided by police departments. James F. Pastor addresses substantive legal and public policy issues which directly or indirectly relate to the provision of security services. These can be demonstrated by the logic of alternative or supplemental service providers.

The use of private police has particular appeal because property or business owners can directly contract for public safety services, thereby providing welcome relief for municipal budgets. Finally, private police functions can be flexible, depending upon the financial, organizational, political, and situational circumstances of the client.

Arizona Licensed security companies are required to provide eight hours of pre-assignment training to all persons employed as security guards before the employee acts in the capacity of a security guard. There is a state-mandated curriculum that must be taught, and subjects covered must include criminal law and laws of arrest, uniforms and grooming, communications, use of force, general security procedures, crime scene preservation, ethics and first response.

California

Security Guards are required to obtain a license from the Bureau of Security and Investigative Services (BSIS), of the California Department of Consumer Affairs. Applicants must be at least 18 years old, undergo a criminal history background check through the California Department of Justice (DOJ) and the Federal Bureau of Investigation (FBI), and complete a 40-hour course of required training. This required training is broken down into smaller training sections and time-lines.

The first is 8-hours of BSIS-designed instruction on powers to arrest and weapons. Then, within 30 days of getting the individual officers license, they must receive 16-hours of training on various mandatory and elective courses. Finally, within 6-months of getting their license, they must receive an additional 16-hours of training on various mandatory and elective courses.

California security officers are also required to complete 8-hours of annual training on security-related topics, after the first, above mentioned 40-hours are complete.

The training and exam may be administered by any private patrol operator or by any of a large number of certified training facilities. This training can be classroom or online. ,

New Jersey As of 2006 all security personnel must undergo a state mandated certified training program. This law commonly referred to SORA is the state's effort to increase the quality of security personnel.

New Mexico As of 2008 all security guards must undergo FBI background checks and a certified training program. Guards who carry firearms must also undergo additional training with a firearm through an approved firearms instructor and pass a phycological exam. The security industry is regulated through New Mexico Regulation and Licensing Division.

Oklahoma Security officers in Oklahoma are licensed by CLEET (Council on Law Enforcement Education and Training). To be licensed as an unarmed officer an individual must be at least 18 years of age and undergo 40 hours of classroom training and pass criminal history checks. Armed guards must be 21 years of age, have another 40 hours of classroom training, qualify with their firearm and pass a psychological evaluation.

Pennsylvania No licensing requirements to be an unarmed security guard. However, armed security guards must undergo and successfully complete a 40 hour training course (including shooting range time) in order to be certified to carry weapons and on watch while on duty under the Lethal Weapons Training Act (commonly referred to as Act 235 certification). Certification involves qualifying on a pistol range, with firing of 50 rounds of ammo larger than a .380acp. You are also required to qualify on a shotgun. The certification is good for five years at which time an eight hour refresher course must be taken or the certification is revoked.

South Carolina All Security Officers have the same authority and power to make an arrest as Sheriff's Deputies, while on the property they are paid to protect. Most companies prohibit this authority by policy due to lack of confidence and liability fears. Private Officers may respond to calls for service, make arrests and use blue lights and traffic radar. They may also be specially authorized by the State Law Enforcment Division (SLED), to issue Uniform Traffic Tickets to violators.

Security Officers are licensed or registered (as appropriate) by SLED for one year at a time. Training for unarmed officers is 8 hours, an additional 8 hours is required for a security weapons permit or a concealed security weapons permit. Additional hours are required to be documented for officers issuing public or private tickets as well as officers that will be using batons, pepper spray or tasers.

Virginia Security officers in Virginia are required to be licensed by DCJS (Department of Criminal Justice Services). To be licensed as an unarmed security officer one must go through 18 hours of classroom training from a licensed instructor in order to obtain this card and it must be done by the end of their 90 days after hire with a Security company. Every two years the card must be renewed, by completing an inservice with a licensed instructor. To be licensed as an armed security officer one must complete an additional 16 hours of firearms training, 6 hours of training in conducting a lawful arrest, and qualification with the type and caliber of weapon they intend to carry.

Firearms endorsements must be renewed annually by completing an inservice and passing a firearms qualification. Licensed armed security officers are authorized under state code to arrest for any offense committed in their presence while they are on duty at the location they are hired to protect. They may also be granted the authority by the chief law enforcement officer in their jurisdiction to issue summons to appear in court for felonies and misdemeanors.For more information on DCJS codes and regs click here.

St Louis, Missouri Security officers are required to be licensed by the St Louis County Police or St Louis City Police. St Louis County Security Officer training is a two day class and yearly renewal class. Armed officers must shoot bi-annually to keep their 'armed' status. County license is called a Metropolitan License meaning to is good for St Louis City and County. More Info for St Louis County License is available though the County website posted here: St Louis City Web site has all the info regarding licensing requirements due to fact they are the same in city and county.The City web site is posted here. Readers should note that this only applys to persons working in security in St Louis City or St Louis County

Security Officers and the Police

Security personnel are not police officers, unless they are security police, but are often identified as such due to similar uniforms and behaviors, especially on private property. Security personnel in the U.S. derive their powers from state laws, that allow them a contractual arrangement with clients that give them Agent of the Owner powers.

This includes a nearly unlimited power to question with the absence of probable cause requirements that frequently dog public law enforcement officers, provided that the security officer does not tread on the rights and liberties of others as guaranteed by the United States Constitution.

Some jurisdictions do commission or deputize security officers and give them limited additional powers, particularly when employed in protecting public property such as mass transit stations. This is a special case that is often unique to a particular jurisdiction or locale. Additionally, security officers may also be called upon to act as an agent of law enforcement if a police officer, sheriff's deputy, etc. is in immediate need of help and has no available backup.

Some security officers do reserve police powersand are typically employed directly by governmental agencies. Typically, these are sworn law enforcement personnelwhose duties primarily involve the security of a government installation, and are also a special case.

Other local and state governments occasionally enter into special contracts with security agencies to provide patrol services in public areas.These personnel are sometimes referred to as "private police officers."

Sometimes police officers work as security personnel while not on duty. This is usually done for extra income, and work is particularly done in hazardous jobs such as bodyguard work and bouncers outside nightclubs.

Police are called in when a situation warrants a higher degree of authorityto act upon reported observations that security does not have the authority to act upon, however, some states allow Licensed Security Officer the full arrest powers equal to that of a Sheriff Deputy.

In 1976, the Law Enforcement Assistance Administration's National Advisory Commission on Criminal Justice Standards and Goals reported:

'One massive resource, filled with significant numbers of personnel, armed with a wide array of technology, and directed by professionals who have spent their entire adult lifetimes learning how to prevent and reduce crime, has not been tapped by governments in the fight against criminality. The private security industry, with over one million workers, sophisticated alarm systems and perimeter safeguards, armored trucks, sophisticated mini-computers, and thousands of highly skilled crime prevention experts, offers a potential for coping with crime that can not be equalled by any other remedy or approach.

Underutilized by police, all but ignored by prosecutors and the judiciary, and unknown to corrections officials, the private security professional may be the only person in this society who has the knowledge to effectively prevent crime.'

In New York, the Area Police/Private Security Liaison program was organized in 1986 by the NYPD commissioner and four former police chiefs working in the private security industry to promote mutual respect, cross-training, and sharing of crime-related information between public police and private security.

Trends

Australia

Private Security personnel initially outnumbered police. From the Australian Bureau of Statistics Report in 2006 there were 52,768 full-time security officers in the security industry compared to 44,898 police officers. But since Security Industry Regulation Act 2007 it has droped to less than half that.

UK

The trend in the UK at the time of writing (March 2008) is one of polarisation. The market in Manned Guarding (the security industry term for the security guards most people are familiar with) is diverging toward two opposite extremes; one typified by a highly trained and well paid security officer; the other with security officers on or about minimum wage with only the minimum training required by law.

Within the 'in-house' sector, where security personnel are not subject to licensing under the Private Security Industry Act 2001, the same divergence can be seen; with some companies opting for in-house security to maintain control of their standards, whilst others use it as a route to cheaper, non-regulated, security.

USA

Economist Robert B. Reich, in his 1991 book The Work of Nations, stated that in the United States, the number of private security guards and officers was comparable to the number of publicly paid police officers. He used this phenomenon as an example of the general withdrawal of the affluent from existing communities where governments provide public services.

Instead, the wealthy pay to provide their own premium services, through voluntary, exclusive associations. As taxpayer resistance has limited government budgets, and as the demand for secure homes in gated communities has grown, these trends have continued in the 1990s and 2000s.

In the aftermath of 9/11, the trend in the US is one of a quiet transformation of the role of security guards into first responders in case of a terrorist attack or major disaster. This has resulted in longer guard instruction hours, extra training in Terrorism tactics and increased laws governing private security companies in some states.

History

The vigiles were soldiers assigned to guard the city of Rome, often credited as the origin of both security personnel and police, although their principal duty was as a fire brigade. There have been night watchmen since at least the Middle Ages in Europe; walled cities of ancient times also had watchmen. A special chair appeared in Europe sometime in the late Middle Ages, called the watchman's chair; this unupholstered wooden chair had a forward slanting seat to prevent the watchman from dozing off during his watch.

Notable Security Guards

- The security guard Frank Wills detected the Watergate burglars, ultimately leading to the resignation of Richard M. Nixon as President of the United States.
- Christoph Meili, night guard at a Swiss bank, became a whistle blower in 1997. He told about the bank destroying records related to funds of Holocaust victims, whose money the bank was supposed to return to their heirs.
- In 1999, Pierlucio Tinazzi rescued 10 victims from the Mont Blanc Tunnel Fire, before dying while trying to rescue an 11th.
- In 2001, Gary Coleman, former child actor, was employed as a shopping mall security guard in the Los Angeles area. Whilst shopping for a bullet-proof vest for his job, Coleman assaulted a female autograph collector. Coleman said he felt "threatened by her insistence" and punched her in the head. He was later charged for the assault and ordered to pay her $1,665 for hospital bills.
- Derrick Brun, an unarmed security guard employed by the Red Lake School District in Minnesota, was praised by President Bush for his heroic role in protecting children during the 2005 Red Lake High School Massacre: "Derrick's bravery cost him his life, and all Americans honor him".
- In 2007, Matthew Murray fatally shot two and wounded two others at the Youth With A Mission retreat center in Arvada Colorado. A few hours later he fatally shot two others and wounded another three in the New Life Church parking lot. When Murray entered the church, he was met by armed security guard Jeanne Assam, who ordered him to drop his weapon. Assam shot and wounded Murray when he failed to comply. The pastor of New Life Church credited Assam with saving over 100 lives.

UNIONIZATION

Canada

Many security guards in Canada are unionized. The primary unions which represent security guards in Canada are the United Food and Commercial Workers (UFCW), Local 333, and the Canadian branch of the United Steelworkers (USW). In contrast to the legal restrictions in the United States, Canadian labor relations boards will certify bargaining units of security guards for a Canadian Labour Congress (CLC)-affiliated union or in the same union with other classifications of employees.

United States

In June, 1947, the United States Congress passed the Taft-Hartley Act placing many restrictions on labor unions. Section 9 (B) (3) of the act prevents the National Labor Relations Board (NLRB) from certifying for collective bargaining any unit which mixes security employees with non-security employees. This restricts the ability of security employees to join any union that also represents other types of employees.

They may be part of an independent, "security-only" union, not affiliated with any coalition of other types of labor unions such as the American Federation of Labor and Congress of Industrial Organizations (AFL-CIO). A union which also represents non-security employees may also represent and bargain on behalf of security employees with the employer's consent.

Two of the largest security unions are the Security, Police, and Fire Professionals of America (SPFPA) and the United Government Security Officers of America (UGSOA).

SECURITY, POLICE, AND FIRE PROFESSIONALS OF AMERICA

In 1948 with the Taft-Hartley restrictions well into effect, the Detroit, Michigan area security guards of United Auto Workers (UAW) Amalgamated Local 114 were forced to break away and start a separate "Plant Guards Organizing Committee". The NLRB ruled that as an affiliate of the CIO, the committee was indirectly affiliated with production unions and therefore ineligible for certification under the new restrictions.

The committee was then forced to completely withdraw from the CIO and start the independent United Plant Guard Workers of America. By the 1990s, this union had evolved to include many other types of security officers and changed its name to the SPFPA.

United Government Security Officers of America

In 1992, the USGOA was formed. It specializes in organizing federal, state, and local government security officers, but since May, 2000 has been open to representing other types of security personnel as well.

Others

The Service Employees International Union (SEIU) has also sought to represent security employees, although its efforts have been complicated by the Taft-Harley Act because the SEIU also represents janitors, trash collectors, and other building service employees.

Hazards in the Industry

Security personnel often are exposed to physical and physiological trauma that can have lasting effects. This has always been an issue but the 21st century's more violent and angry culture combined with drug and alcohol related violence results in more instances of security personnel being physically or verbally abused.

Other contributing factors are high workload, long hours, low pay, boredom and disregard of industry standards by employers and clients e.g. break times, access to bathrooms and facilities ECT.

Another problem particularly in NSW Australia is the severe security officer shortage brought on by the rushed Security Industry Regulation Act 2007 (which has been nicknamed the Crimpers act).This act was approved by David Andrew Campbell who at the time was Minister for Illawarra and acting police commissioner and had signed the Act for both parties.

Airport Security

Airport security refers to the techniques and methods used in protecting airports and aircraft from crime. Large numbers of people pass through airports. This presents potential targets for terrorism and other forms of crime due to the number of people located in a small area. Similarly, the high concentration of people on large airliners, the potential high death rate with attacks on aircraft, and the ability to use a hijacked airplane as a lethal weapon may provide an alluring target for terrorism.

Airport security attempts to prevent would-be attackers from bringing weapons or bombs into the airport. If they can succeed in this, then the chances of these devices getting on to aircraft are greatly reduced. As such, airport security serves several purposes: To protect the airport from attacks and crime and to protect the aircraft from attack, and to reassure the travelling public that they are safe.

Monte R. Belger of the U.S. Federal Aviation Administration notes "The goal of aviation security is to prevent harm to aircraft, passengers, and crew, as well as support national security and counter-terrorism policy."

While some countries may have an agency that protects all of their airports (such as Australia, where the Australian Federal Police is responsible for security at major airports), in other countries like the United States, the protection is controlled at the state or local level. The primary personnel will vary and can include:

- A police force hired and dedicated to the airport
- A branch (substation) of the local police department stationed at the airport
- Members of the local police department assigned to the airport as their normal patrol area
- Members of a country's military
- Members of a country's airport protection service

- Police dog services for explosive detection, drug detection and other purposes

Other resources may include:

- Security guards
- Paramilitary forces
- Military forces

Process and equipment

Some incidents have been the result of travelers being permitted to carry either weapons or items that could be used as weapons on board aircraft so that they could hijack the plane. Travelers are screened by metal detectors. Explosive detection machines used include X-ray machines and explosives trace-detection portal machines (a.k.a. "puffer machines"). Explosive detection machines can also be used for both carry on and checked baggage. These detect volatile compounds given off from explosives using gas chromatography.

A recent development is the controversial use of backscatter X-rays to detect hidden weapons and explosives on passengers. These devices, which use Compton scattering, require that the passenger stand close to a flat panel and produce a high resolution image. A technology released in Israel in early 2008 allows passengers to pass through metal detectors without removing their shoes, a process required as walk-though gate detectors are not reliable in detecting metal in shoes or on the lower body extremities. Alternately, the passengers step fully shod onto a device which scans in under 1.2 seconds for objects as small as a razor blade. In some countries, specially trained individuals may engage passengers in a conversation to detect threats rather than solely relying on equipment to find threats.

Generally people are screened through airport security into areas where the exit gates to the aircraft are located. These areas are often called "secure", "sterile" and airside. Passengers are discharged from airliners into the sterile area so that they usually will not have to be re-screened if disembarking from a domestic flight; however they are still subject to search at any time. Airport food outlets have started using plastic glasses and utensils as opposed to glasses made out of glass and utensils made out of metal to reduce the usefulness of such items as weapons.

In the United States non-passengers were once allowed on the concourses to meet arriving friends or relatives at their gates, but this is greatly restricted now in the United States. Non-passengers must obtain a gate pass to enter the secure area of the airport. The most common reasons that a non-passenger may obtain a gate pass is to assist children and the elderly as well as for attending business meetings that take place in the secure area of the airport. In the United States, at least 24 hours notice is generally required for those planning to attend a business meeting inside the secure area of the airport. Other countries, such as Australia do not yet restrict non-travellers from accessing the airside area, however non-travellers are typically subject to the same security scans as travellers.

Sensitive areas in airports, including airport ramps and operational spaces, are restricted from the general public. Called a SIDA (Security Identification Display Area), these spaces require special qualifications to enter.

Throughout the world, there have been a few dozen airports that have instituted a version of a 'trusted traveler program'. Proponents argue that security screening can be made more efficient by detecting the people that are threats, and then searching them. They argue that searching trusted, verified individuals should not take the amount of time it does. Critics argue that such programs decrease security by providing an easier path to carry contraband through.

Another critical security measure utilised by several regional and international airports is the use of fiber optic perimeter intrusion detection systems. These security systems allow airport security to locate and detect any intrusion on the airport perimeter, ensuring real-time, immediate intrusion notification that allows security personnel to assess the threat and track movement and engage necceassary security procedures. This has notably been utilised at Dulles International Airport and U.S. Military JFPASS.

Notable Incidents

The world's first terrorist attack intending to indiscriminately kill civilians while in flight was Cubana Flight 455. It was a Cubana flight from Barbados to Jamaica that was brought down by a terrorist attack on October 6, 1976, killing 73 people. Evidence implicated several Central Intelligence Agency-linked anti-Castro Cuban exiles and members of the Venezuelan secret police DISIP, including Luis Posada Carriles.

The single deadliest airline catastrophe resulting from the failure of airport security to detect an on board bomb was Air India Flight 182 in 1985, which killed 329 people.

Another notable failure was the 1994 bombing of Philippine Airlines Flight 434, which turned out to be a test run for a planned terrorist attack called Operation Bojinka. The explosion was small, killing one person, and the plane made an emergency landing. Operation Bojinka was discovered and foiled by Manila police in 1995.

On May 30, 1972 three members of the Japanese Red Army undertook a terrorist attack, popularly called the Lod Airport massacre, at the Lod Airport, now known as the Ben Gurion International Airport, in Tel Aviv. Firing indiscriminately with automatic firearms and throwing grenades, they managed to kill 24 people and injure 78 others before being neutralized (one of them through suicide). One of the three terrorists, Kozo Okamoto, survived the incident.

The Rome and Vienna airport attacks in December 1985 were two more instances of airport security failures. The attacks left 20 people dead when gunmen threw grenades and opened fire on travelers at El Al airline ticket counters.

On July 5, 2002, a gunman opened fire at Los Angeles International Airport (Israel's El Al Ticket Counter). The shooter killed two people and injured four.

On August 10, 2006, security at airports in the United Kingdom, Canada, and the United States was raised significantly due to the uncovering by British authorities of a terror plot aimed at detonating liquid explosives on flights originating from these countries. This is also notable as it was the first time the U.S. Terror Alert Level ever reached "red". The incident also led to tighter restrictions on carrying liquids and gels in hand luggage in the EU, Canada, and the United States.

AIRPORT SECURITY BY COUNTRY

Canada

All restrictions involving airport security are determined by Transport Canada and are enforced by the Canadian Air Transport Security Authority (CATSA). Since the September 11, 2001 attacks, as well as the Air India bombing in 1985 and other incidents, airport security has tightened in Canada in order to prevent any attacks in Canadian Airspace.

CATSA uses x-ray machines to verify the contents of all carry-ons as well as metal detectors, explosive trace detection (ETD) equipment and random physical searches of passengers at the pre-board screening points. X-ray machines, CTX machines, high-resolution x-rays and ETDs are also used to scan checked bags. All checked baggage is always x-rayed at all major commercial airports.

CATSA also completed the first phase of its Restricted Area Identity Credential (RAIC) program in January 2007. This program replaces the old Airport Restricted Area Passes issued to airport employees after security checks by the Canadian Security Intelligence Service, the Royal Canadian Mounted Police (RCMP) and Transport Canada with new cards (issued after the same checks are conducted) that contain biometric information (fingerprints and iris scans) belonging to the person issued the RAIC.

The RAIC has yet to be extended to the security perimeter of Canadian airports for vehicles and persons entering from checkpoints not within airport terminals. As of September 2010 it is being tested at the Vancouver International Airport. Vehicles and personal entering near the domestic terminals from the YVR cargo and south side must drive through the new CATSA security screening booth.

While CATSA is responsible for pre-board passenger and random non-passenger screening, they contract out to third-party "service providers" such as Aeroguard and Garda to train, manage and employ the screening officers. In addition, individual airport authorities which were privatized in the 1990s by the Canadian Government are responsible for general airport security rather than CATSA and normally contract out to private companies and in the case of large airports, pay for a small contingent of local police officers to remain on site as well.

European Union

Regulation (EC) No 300/2008 of the European Parliament and of the Council establishes common rules in the European Union to protect civil aviation against acts of unlawful interference. The regulation's provisions apply to all airports or parts of airports located in an EU country that are not used exclusively for military purposes. The provisions also apply to all operators, including air carriers, providing services at the aforementioned airports. It also applies to all entities located inside or outside airport premises providing services to airports.

The standards of regulation 300/2008 are implemented by Commission Regulation (EU) No 185/2010.

France

French security has been stepped up since terrorist attacks in France in 1986. In response France established the Vigipirate program. The program uses troops to reinforce local security and increases requirements in screenings and ID checks. Since 1996 security check-points have transferred from the Police Nationale/ Gendarmerie de l'Air to private companies hired by the airport authorities.

Spain

Airport security in Spain is provided by police forces, as well as private security guards. The Policía Nacional provides general security as well as passport (in international airports) and documentation checking. In Catalonia and Basque Country, the Mossos d'Esquadra and the Ertzaintza, respectively, have replaced the Policía Nacional except for documentation functions. The Guardia Civil handles the security and customs checking, often aided by private security guards. Local police provide security and traffic control outside the airport building.

Safety measures are controlled by the state owned company Aena, and are bound to European Commission Regulations, as in other European Union countries.

United Kingdom

The Department for Transport (DFT) is the heart of airport security in the United Kingdom. In September 2004, with the Home Office, DFT started an initiative called the "Multi Agency Threat and Risk Assessment" (MATRA), which was piloted at five of the United Kingdom's major airports - Heathrow, Birmingham, East Midlands, Newcastle and Glasgow. Following successful trials, the scheme has now been rolled out across 44 airports.

Since the September 11 attacks in New York, the United Kingdom has been assessed as a high risk country due to its support of the United States both in its invasion of Afghanistan and Iraq.

From January 7, 2000, travelers are no longer limited to a single piece of carry-on luggage at most of the UK's major airports Currently, hand luggage is not limited by size or weight by the DFT, although most airlines do impose their own rules.

Passengers are not permitted to take any liquids over 100 ml past security, although liquids in larger containers purchased in the secure area are allowed on flights. Any liquids under 100 ml must be placed in "a single, transparent, re-sealable plastic bag (about the size of a small freezer bag), which itself must not exceed 1 litre in capacity (approximately 20cm x 20cm)".

All bags are screened via X-ray before being put on the plane. All passengers must walk through metal detectors. Human airport security has also been increased and people are highly likely to be searched. There are also the usual checks of passports and boarding cards.

The UK is considering controversial new methods of screening passengers to further improve airport security, such as backscatter X-ray machines that provide a 360-degree view of a person, as well as 'see' under clothes, right down to the skin and bones.

Hong Kong

The Hong Kong International Airport is secured by the Hong Kong Police Force and Aviation Security Company (AVSECO). Within the police force, the Airport District is responsible for the safety and security of the airport region. Airport Security Unit are deployed around the airport and are armed with H&K MP5 A3 Submachine Gun and Glock 17 handgun. The security of the restricted area is the responsibility of the police and AVSECO.

While the airport is under the control of the Airport Authority Hong Kong (AAHK), the security power has been delegated to the AVSECO staffs. All persons and baggages carried by them must be X-Rayed and checked at the security screening points of the AVSECO (with a few exceptions at the Tenant Restricted Area).

The Immigration Department will check incomers passport and other identities, while the Customs and Excise Department will check passengers and crews' luggages to discourage smuggling of drugs and contraband from entering Hong Kong.

India

India stepped up its airport security after the 1999 Kandahar hijacking. The Central Industrial Security Force, a paramilitary organisation is in charge of airport security under the regulatory frame work of the Bureau of Civil Aviation Security(Ministry of Civil Aviation Security). CISF formed an Airport Security Group to protect Indian airports. Every airport has now been given an

APSU (Airport Security Unit), a trained unit to counter unlawful interference with civil aviation. Apart from the CISF, every airline has an aviation security force which is a separate department.

Terrorist threats and narcotics are the main threats in Indian airports. Another problem that some airports face is the proliferation of slums around the airport boundaries in places like Mumbai. Before boarding, additional searching of hand luggage is likely.

Israel

El Al Airlines is headquartered in Israel. The last hijacking occurred on July 23, 1969, and no plane departing Ben Gurion Airport, just outside Tel Aviv, has ever been hijacked.

It was in 1972 that terrorists from the Japanese Red Army launched an attack that led to the deaths of at least 24 people at Ben Gurion. Since then, security at the airport relies on a number of fundamentals, including a heavy focus on what Raphael Ron, former director of security at Ben Gurion, terms the "human factor", which may be generalized as "the inescapable fact that terrorist attacks are carried out by people who can be found and stopped by an effective security methodology."

On December 27, 1985, terrorists simultaneously attacked El Al ticket counters at the Rome, Italy and Vienna, Austria airports using machine guns and hand grenades. Nineteen civilians were killed and many wounded. In response, Israel developed further methods to stop such massacres and drastically improved security measures around Israeli airports and even promised to provide plainclothes armed guards at each foreign airport. The last successful airline-related terrorist attack was in 1986, when a security agent found a suitcase full of explosives during the initial screening process. While the bag did not make it on board, it did injure 13 after detonating in the terminal.

As part of its focus on this so-called "human factor," Israeli security officers interrogate travelers using racial profiling, singling out those who appear to be Arab based on name or physical appearance. Additionally, all passengers, even those who do not appear to be of Arab descent, are questioned as to why they are traveling to Israel, followed by several general questions about the trip in order to search for inconsistencies. Although numerous civil rights groups have demanded an end to the profiling, Israel maintains that it is both effective and unavoidable. As stated by Ariel Merari, an Israeli terrorism expert, "it would be foolish not to use profiling when everyone knows that most terrorists come from certain ethnic groups. They are likely to be Muslim and young, and the potential threat justifies inconveniencing a certain ethnic group."

Passengers leaving Israel are checked against a computerized list. The computers, maintained by the Israeli Ministry of Interior, are connected to the Israeli police and Interpol in order to catch suspects or others leaving the country illegally.

Despite such tight security, an incident occurred on November 17, 2002 in which a man apparently slipped through airport security at Ben Gurion Airport with a pocketknife and attempted to storm the cockpit of El Al Flight 581 en route from Tel Aviv to Istanbul, Turkey. While no injuries were reported and the attacker was subdued by guards hidden among the passengers 15 minutes before the plane landed safely in Turkey, authorities did shut down Ben Gurion for some time after the attack to reassess the security situation and an investigation was opened to determine how the man, an Israeli Arab, managed to smuggle the knife past the airport security.

At a conference in May 2008, the United States Department of Homeland Security Secretary Michael Chertoff told Reuters interviewers that the United States will seek to adopt some of the Israeli security measures at domestic airports. He left his post in January 2009, a mere 6 months after this statement, which may or may not have been enough time to implement them.

On a more limited focus, American airports have been turning to the Israeli government and Israeli-run firms to help upgrade security in the post-9/11 world. Israeli officials toured Los Angeles Airport in November 2008 to re-evaluate the airport after making security upgrade recommendations in 2006, and Ron's company,

New Age Security Solutions, based in Washington, D.C., consults on aviation security at Boston's Logan International Airport. Calling Ben Gurion "the world's safest airport," Antonio Villaraigosa, mayor of Los Angeles, has implemented the Israeli review in order to bring state-of-the-art technology and other tactical measures to help secure LAX, considered to be the state's primary terrorist target and singled out by the Al Qaeda network.

Other U.S. airports to incorporate Israeli tactics and systems include Port of Oakland and the San Diego County Regional Airport Authority. "The Israelis are legendary for their security, and this is an opportunity to see firsthand what they do, how they do it and, as importantly, the theory behind it," said Steven Grossman, director of aviation at the Port of Oakland. He was so impressed with a briefing presented by the Israelis that he suggested a trip to Israel to the U.S. branch of Airports Council International in order to gain a deeper understanding of the methods employed by Israeli airport security and law enforcement.

Singapore

Security for the country's two international passenger airports comes under the purview of the Airport Police Division of the Singapore Police Force, although resources are concentrated at Singapore Changi Airport where scheduled passenger traffic dominate. Seletar Airport, which specializes in handling non-scheduled and training flights, is seen as posing less of a security issue. Since the September 11, 2001 attacks, and the naming of Changi Airport as a terrorism target by the Jemaah Islamiyah, the airport's security has been stepped up. Roving patrol teams of two soldiers and a police officer armed with machine guns patrol the terminals at random. Departing passengers are checked at the entrance of the gate rather than after immigration clearance like Hong Kong International Airport. This security measure is easily noticed by the presence of X-Ray machines and metal detectors at every gate which is not normally seen at other airports.

Assisting the state organizations, are the security services provided by the ground handlers, namely that of the ((Certis

CISCO)), Singapore Airport Terminal Services's SATS Security Services, and the Aetos Security Management Private Limited, formed from a merger of the Changi International Airport Services's airport security unit and that of other companies to become a single island-wide auxiliary police company. These officers duties include screening luggage and controlling movement into restricted areas.

Since 2005, an upgrade in screening technology and rising security concerns led to all luggage-screening processes to be conducted behind closed-doors. Plans are also in place to install over 400 cameras to monitor the airport, to discourage bomb attacks similar to the 2005 Songkhla bombings in Southern Thailand where Hat Yai International Airport was targeted. Tenders to incorporate such a system were called in late September 2005.

United States

Prior to the 1970s American airports had minimal security arrangements to prevent aircraft hijackings. Measures were introduced starting in the late 1960s after several high-profile hijackings.

Sky marshals were introduced in 1970, but there were insufficient numbers to protect every flight and hijackings continued to take place. Consequently in late 1972, the Federal Aviation Administration required that all airlines begin screening passengers and their carry-on baggage by January 5, 1973. This screening was generally contracted to private security companies. Private companies would bid on these contracts. The airline that had operational control of the departure concourse controlled by a given checkpoint would hold that contract. Although an airline would control the operation of a checkpoint, oversight authority was held by the FAA. C.F.R. Title 14 restrictions did not permit a relevant airport authority to exercise any oversight over checkpoint operations.

The September 11 attacks prompted even tougher regulations, such as limiting the number of and types of items passengers could carry on board aircraft and requiring increased screening for passengers who fail to present a government issued photo ID.

The Aviation and Transportation Security Act generally required that by November 19, 2002 all passenger screening must be conducted by Federal employees. As a result, passenger and baggage screening is now provided by the Transportation Security Administration (TSA), part of the Department of Homeland Security. Provisions to improve the technology for detecting explosives were included in the Terrorism Prevention Act of 2004. Often, security at category X airports, the U.S. largest and busiest as measured by volume of passenger traffic, are provided by private contractors. Because of the high volume of passenger traffic, category X airports are considered vulnerable targets for terrorism.

Noticing the demand for new technology in airport security, General Electric (GE) started to develop the Secure Registered Traveler System. The new system would use newly developed technology such as automated carry-on scanning, automatic biological pathogen detection, millimeter-wave full body scanning and a quadruple resonance carpet that would detect threats in shoes without having to take them off. The SRT program also works with smartcard technology along with fingerprint technology to help verify passengers. The fingerprint scanner also detects for explosive material traces on the person's fingers.

With the increase in security screening, some airports saw long queues for security checks. To alleviate this, airports created Premium lines for passengers traveling in First or Business Class, or those who were elite members of a particular airline's Frequent Flyer program.

The "screening passengers by observation techniques" (SPOT) program is operating at some U.S. airports.

United States Incidents

On February 27, 2006, at the Will Rogers World Airport in Oklahoma City, in an airliner cargo area (accessible only to authorized personnel), threatening graffiti was found.

On March 6, 2006 at John F. Kennedy International Airport in New York, an elderly man drove his car onto the runway through two security gates. He made it to an active runway where an Air France aircraft was preparing to land. The man drove around for approximately 23 minutes before being stopped. On the same day a man made it on to the runway by running through a secure gate while it was being opened at Midway International Airport in Chicago. The man made it through one of the three perimeter entrances that did not have a camera, resulting in four different runways being closed down. This incident led to 222 aviation security officers being retrained and a redesign of all perimeter gates.

On March 11, 2006, after four years of continuous security breaches and staffing problems news reports indicated that federal officials removed the head of security at Newark Liberty International Airport.

Chapter-4

Engineering Operations

Hotels are much more extensive and demanding. The engineering department has the responsibility for everything in the building as well. Depending on the organizational structure of the hotel, some elements are assigned to other departments. The Security or Loss Prevention department may take on the task of fire systems but ultimately this is the responsibility of the engineering department as the building operators to monitor for regulatory compliance.

The role and mandate of any property engineering department is the protection of the building's/owner's assets; the structure from the façade or building envelope, to the integrity of the floors, walls, ceilings and all of the furniture, fixtures, and equipment (FF&E) contained therein. This includes the electrical transformers and the distribution throughout, the domestic water distribution and sewage, the heating-ventilation-air conditioning system, (HVAC), the fire alarm system and fire safety components, the vertical transportation system (elevators), the property surroundings like parking and landscaping and pest control. Utility management such as electrical, gas, steam, water. Kitchen and laundry equipment. Lighting and sound systems and on and on.

The items in the preceding paragraph we like to refer to as the base building system or the physical plant as these components form the basis of all properties whether office or hotel or apartment block. A building is a building. The end use or purpose of the building is what differentiates how the engineering department is managed, and indeed, how the building is operated.

Aside from the base building, office buildings are quite easier to maintain. Generally, offices and shops within commercial buildings are subject to various lease arrangements, with the tenant often being responsible for all maintenance and repairs within their space and proportionate costs of the utilities and taxes . The property operators are usually only responsible for the base building and common areas. The same concept being applied to apartments and condominiums.

The important element here is what is contained within the lease or rental agreement. Office building hours are usually fixed, say, from 7:00 am to 6:00 pm; electronically controlled locks securing every outside door and alarm systems readied by time clocks. Security guards sweeping all areas at random and responding to any alarm calls. Weekends are generally in lock-down mode 24hrs a day. The after hours involvement of building staff are the building cleaners, normally contracted, however, engineering is rarely called for after hour situations. Tenants that would use their offices during off base building hours may contract for HVAC services and pay for the cost.

HOTEL ROOM SAFES

There are few companies in the world who manufacture of highest quality safes to be used in hotels. The strong boxes designed to protect the valuables of hotel guests against theft, are called "hotel in room safes". The world's leading hotels buy hotel safes for each room they have. The safes are installed in each hotel rooms for the best privacy of guests. The guests use hotel safes to store their travel documents and valuables while they are in the room or not.

Today's businessmen also expect hotel rooms with hotel safes to protect their notebooks, cellular phones, and work documents. Hotel safes with friendly usage is preferable among leading hotels and companies in hotel supplies business.

The first step is to determine who or where you will buy your safe from. There are many places to buy a safe today, you can buy from a "big box store", an office supply store, a furniture store, a hardware store, online, or even from a professional safe retailer or locksmith.

With any other than the safe retailer or locksmith you run the very real chance of not being able to get qualified advice as to what you need, not being able to arrange service or repair should the need arise. When you buy from a professional safe retailer or professional locksmith who also sells safes, you are likely to be dealing with someone who knows which safe will best fill your unique needs, these people make their living by selling safes, they know how a particular type or model will perform, they know the features and benefits, and what they are meant to protect. Being the experts they are, they also offer service, repair and delivery services.

Would you really trust the protection of your priceless valuables to the advise you will receive from a minimum wage stockperson at a "big box store"?

What do you want to protect and what do want to protect it against? Cash, jewelry, guns, important papers, or computer media could all require a completely different kind of safe.

Modern safes are manufactured specifically to protect against specific threats, a safe meant to guard against burglary, may not protect papers from fire. A fire safe, because of how it works, may actually destroy computer media or video tapes.

Burglary and jewelry safes are tested and labeled by a testing group according to how long it would take an expert thief, with all of the proper tools to break into the safe. The more time it would take, the more you have to pay for that safe. Contact your professional safe retailer for a complete discussion on burglary ratings.

Modern fire safes manufactured in the United States are tested and rated to keep the interior temperature below 350 degrees Fahrenheit for a specific amount of time, usually expressed in hours. The char point of paper is 405 degrees Fahrenheit, so therefore would be protected from burning. This is accomplished by the fill material in the safe releasing trapped moisture in the form of steam to keep the temperature within the proper range and seal entry points against heat and flame. This release of steam could destroy video tapes, photographs, and computer media.

Modern media safes are constructed using a dry fill that does not release moisture. These safes are usually much more expensive.

With the opening of world trade, and markets in the last few years, there are many safes being sold that are built in other countries, and some of them are labeled by groups other than UL?. Some of these safes are very well constructed, some are very poorly constructed. The problem is that the testing standards are not the same, the construction requirements are not the same. It takes real diligence to be sure you are getting the protection you think you are getting. This is another reason you need to seek out a professional safe retailer.

Next you should decide what size safe you need, be very honest with yourself when estimating what will be kept in your safe, it may only be a little more expensive to buy a larger safe than you need today. Having to buy a new larger safe could be much more expensive.

If you buy a properly rated safe, built to protect what you are putting in it, could result in homeowners insurance savings, check with your insurance agent. Be sure that you follow whatever requirements they may have, failure to do so could result in no coverage.

Hotels have often been given the analogy of a cruise ship or a hospital in that the operation is 24 - 7. Twenty-four hours a day and seven days a week. When the guests are sound asleep the systems of the building continue to operate. The heating and ventilation units are running, the domestic hot water is being heated, the laundry may be operating, the night cleaners making their rounds, desk clerks and night auditors all doing what they have to do. Behind the scenes, there is a flurry of activity, and everything has to work so that everyone can do their jobs and the guests are safe and comfortable.

Without minimizing the contribution of other departments, of which there may be as many as ten or more, the bottom line is if there is no engineering department there is no hotel. Take away those services like hot water or elevators, heating or cooling, electricity, kitchen equipment, laundry equipment etc, you simply would have no customers. When everything is working the next most significant department of course is housekeeping whose efforts keep the property clean and attractive, tending to the guests comfort in their rooms. Removing a restaurant from the system will not close the hotel, or closing the bar or lounge will not cause the hotel to cease operations. Again, all departments should contribute to a seamless operation where the guest comfort and safety and satisfaction are paramount.

The pages following will attempt to shed some light on the various segments of hotel engineering although some aspects are interrelated and not really separable. Hopefully, by narrowing the focus the reader will gain a rudimentary or cursory understanding of the role of the engineering department.

STAFFING

Staffing levels are going to be dictated by quite a number of variables. The variable that seems to pre-empt all others is the financial performance of the property, although manipulating the contribution or size of the engineering department will only defer more costs to further down the road. Factors other than financial can be building specific; the amount of rooms, meeting space, grounds, age of building, available talent pool, plant size (boiler room etc.) swimming pools and peripheral equipment.

The class of hotel also influences the caliber of maintenance. You can repair everything with sticky tape and glue, or you can do it right and replace the part. Scheduling plays a role depending on how busy it can be on any given shift. Hotels can be very busy in the evenings after dinner when guests return to their rooms and start using all equipment. More engineering staff may be required on the afternoon shift. Does the hotel require a midnight or graveyard shift?

The general rule/formula for the staffing level or department size is expounded by Frank D. Borsenik, a professor of engineering at an American University who gives a relatively accurate basis around which to set parameters. Reviewing my notes from the School of Hotel Administration at Cornell University compliment his opinion. When all the operating equipment, systems, building surfaces, are taken into consideration it is determined by following manufacturer's recommendations and current best methods, that in the areas of preventive maintenance and frequencies of maintenance required, the formula is 3.1 engineering full time equivalents per 100 available rooms.

That means that a hotel of 500 rooms would have 15.5 FTE's to properly maintain a hotel building in a state of good repair. Some hotels have other "appendages" such as retail and commercial, residential, or convention or marinas, which will add to the maintenance requirements. Mistakes are made in dismissing these areas as "self maintained" because of triple-net leases, where the tenants handle their own maintenance. This is not to be confused with a building of unitary function as previously mentioned, such as, office buildings, apartment buildings, factory or retail malls.

Forgotten behind the scenes is that the plumbing, ventilation and virtually all systems are sized larger and are generally more extensive in providing services to these locations. The tenants themselves have requests of maintenance and their own work has to be approved and monitored. The common areas still have to be maintained. Adjustments to the recommended number of FTE's are feasible if the work is contracted out. Unionized properties may or may not have issues with contracting out.

The formula of 3.1/100 available rooms is arbitrary as the physical property will dictate the staff required to maintain a building in a state of good repair. The cyclical "financial pressure" that has plagued most building operators and the slash and burn mentality that prevails will have a negative impact on the quantity and quality of maintenance.

The hotel is a business, and the prudent operator should operate it as such, however, should be cognizant, that saving a dollar on maintenance today will cost him two dollars tomorrow. During the course of my thirty-seven years in the business of hotels, commercial, and residential I've seen all too often where managers have cut costs irregardless of financial performance but based on their own political ambitions. The other greatest folly is rewarding by way of bonus or other accolades the engineering manager for budget performance.

I have seen where engineering managers have received hefty bonuses at the end of the year and behind the scenes have left devastation. Fan damper motors tied together with coat hangars, leaking pipes with little wooden wedges hammered into the holes, fire dampers wedged open because the fusible links had failed. Had these things been repaired and money spent the bonus would have been less. Temporarily increasing profits may lead to a manager's promotion or transfer, and in a year or two they are gone leaving the successor holding the bag as the "deferred maintenance" comes back to haunt.

These temporary measures are sometimes necessary and a recent survey of several hotels has shown that the common level for engineering during a "crisis" period is 2.3/100 available rooms after cutbacks. This is crisis management. These levels of cut-backs should only be sustained for a number of weeks as guaranteed deterioration will make it difficult to catch up or recover.

Never, should it be expected that requests for projects or creating what never existed should be handled by in-house staff when a department is staffed at the lower level; a misconception is that it is business as usual and other departments wonder why it may take so long to honour their wish list.

Generally, without getting into specific trades, a smaller operation can do well with generalists. A person who is proficient in electrical, in plumbing, in mechanical, in carpentry, painting; suffice a person with the necessary mechanical aptitude and skill. Caution should be exercised in the level of repair that is undertaken by any one trade person so as not to exceed his or her expertise or to do work when a permit or license is required.

Local regulations and authorities having jurisdiction should be consulted to determine if there are any code violations. Depending on the staffing level you could hire a kitchen and or laundry mechanic, at minimum staffing levels - these could be contracted out. Generalists by nature can be quite proficient in a variety of trades and excel at either one or more and are usually less expensive.

To hire a licensed tradesperson is not feasible and hotels usually will not compete on a salary basis as it could cost as much as two or three times more what they would normally pay. The tradesperson would have little versatility outside their specific training and would only be suited to a larger hotel that had a sufficient amount of work to keep them fully occupied in that particular trade.

It would make no sense to hire an electrician for $75,000 a year unless that person would have sufficient volume of electrical work ($75,000 +) to make it cheaper to have one on staff. More often than not, if a licensed trade person is working for you it is only because they are between jobs and will leave when there is an opening elsewhere for their skills.

For the complexities of a building and its systems it normally takes a good year and sometimes more to learn where everything is and how everything works. From valve locations, breakers, systems layout to operating procedures. Seasonal layoffs should never be considered for a couple of reasons; one, a year or more has been spent in training the individual who may permanently leave.

This is not the same as a person trained as a server who is required to walk from the kitchen to a table. Secondly, the hotel's off-peak season is the engineering departments busiest time as they are now able to access low or non-occupied areas. Managers of other departments having little to do often invent or create make-work projects for engineering which effectively competes for the time and dollars from the areas that have been deferred.

COMMUNICATION

The most disruptive method of communication for maintenance requests is VERBAL.

Normally when an engineer is sighted on route to a job site it inevitably happens that someone "Could you fix this?" I suppose it's normal for everyone to take the easiest route or the path of least resistance. When an engineering person is on route to a job they generally have brought the tools and materials for that particular job and are while on route forming a plan of attack in troubleshooting. I recall sending an individual on a job that would have taken thirty minutes including travel time, to come back an hour and a half later because he was interrupted with other jobs while on the way. Verbal requests should not only be avoided, they should be refused.

The best way of communicating maintenance requests has always been to fill out the appropriate maintenance request form and submit for action. Each area department head should inspect their areas daily, making out request forms as they go. Managers work in their area every day but seem oblivious to deficiencies. It is not nor should it be the responsibility of the engineering department to inspect or maintain areas that are managed by others.

Walkthroughs are another good method of keeping on top of the property's condition. A walkthrough should be conducted monthly of all public or common areas. Public or common areas are those areas of the building that do not specifically come under the jurisdiction of any one department or department head; such as lobby, grounds, public washrooms.

If walkthroughs are to be conducted of a restaurant or lounge or meeting room etc., the department head responsible should be held accountable for any deficiency and be able to produce a copy of the maintenance request form for that particular item. If the question is one of cleanliness, then again show a request of the housekeeping department to action. Too often, engineering will get a request for a burnt light or paint touchup just minutes before the guest arrives.

I read somewhere once "that lack of planning on your part shouldn't make it a crisis on my part". The message for other departments is to be a little pro-active. In just about every hotel that I have had the pleasure to work in, and in discussions with colleagues at other properties, the most offending department for unreported deficiencies and damage is banquets.

They usually are the ones to call ten minutes before a meeting starts to report a critical light burnt out or a piece of equipment not working. Meeting rooms will have holes poked into the ceiling or walls, doors knocked off their hinges. I have had scrapes in walls repaired only to see them damaged again within minutes. All hotels seem to have the same common challenge with the banquet department.

In their defense I have observed with banquets that it may be a staffing issue where part timers are only called in for the last minute for functions and they really don't care. Regular staff are too few to handle equipment properly as I see many a banquet person moving an eight-foot table by themselves and of course smacking into doors and walls. I never see supervisors "supervising" or inspecting vacant meeting rooms.

Lists of actions due to inspections are also good, however it then makes it incumbent on the engineering department to then write up maintenance request forms for assignment.

The maintenance request form is one of the most essential tools for which the engineering department operates. They are used to track trends, monitor inventory and labour and to ensure that things are not forgotten. Completed maintenance request forms should be sorted by type such as plumbing, electrical etc to indicate trends and frequencies. They can then be actioned in an attempt to eliminate repeating problems.

A good example of studying trends towards a solution is a hotel where I had started to work and it was mentioned to me that all guest room fan coil units leak condensation in the summer when the air conditioning is on. Too late to investigate and repair all four hundred and fifty units, we set up a room layout template and proceeded to chart each report of a leaking air conditioning unit during the summer season.

We would normally have liked to pre-empt any guest complaint but as this situation was happening for the previous twenty-five years that one more season wouldn't hurt. The survey indicated that 25% of the fan coil units had leaked and resulted in many repeat complaints exaggerating the extent of the problem. Unfortunately more that one hundred units were leaking but it went back to a construction deficiency where all the drain lines of these units were sloped uphill.

The fault was not only with the plumbers however; the drywall installers pushed up on the metal studs pushing up on the unit drain lines. The plumbing error is where they measured from the ceiling concrete slab to slant the drain line but the slab they measured from was poured on a slope as well. Engineering had one person of each shift who did nothing but drain these condensation pans daily to help prevent their leaking. They did this for twenty-five years! Now that the drains have been corrected and the problem resolved the engineers can go on to other things. Tracking request history is important.

Budgets

Budgets by and large are an interesting vehicle for fiscal manipulation. The engineering budget is split into two categories, heat light and power, and repair and maintenance. Depending on the location of the hotel the heat light and power budget might consume 4% or more of sales revenue with repairs and maintenance at about 5 or 6%. The combined average being about 10% of sales revenue. Note that a renowned consulting group determined, albeit 1991, that of full service hotels over 200 rooms and an average rate of $75.00 or more, it would cost about 10.3% of revenue.

It should be understood that HLP consumptions and costs are variable due to weather, room occupancy, restaurant and banquet covers, market price volatility. Predictability can only be assumed, however, baselines for utility consumption can be established to provide a relatively accurate consumption pattern for billing units. Regression analysis is one such method.

Keeping records of all utilities, heating degree-days, cooling degree-days, guests in house, covers, will provide background information to weigh against billing unit consumption. Meter information should be gathered on a daily basis to quickly diagnose any anomaly in consumption such as major leaks or equipment malfunction. The general ledger, chart of accounts will indicate each utility, i.e.; electricity, natural gas, steam, water and sewage etc.

Caution should be exercised when gathering utility history from P&L statements as these statements have sometimes gone through numerical gymnastics. I once had a utility budget pared down by a controller telling me to just say, "tell them the weather changed."

The repair and maintenance portion, R&M covers the balance of the engineering expenses such as labour, building, mechanical equipment repairs, kitchen repairs, uniforms and on and on, covering almost all repair contingencies.

What must be understood with any budget is that it is a guide only. Engineering budgets are best replicating historic data for that particular property. Zero-based budgeting is not possible, or at the least will not be accurate at year-end. When budgets are made it is only a foggy view of the next fiscal year.

An unexpected pump failure could cost $10,000.00 to name only one incident or the cost of natural gas go up 150% in one month. There are some hotels attempting at monthly forecasts that as a tool may arrive at some idea on how achievable the budget might be next month. Engineering forecasts are best kept to the weather.

Inevitably once the engineering manager submits the annual budget it is often "massaged" to placate corporate offices.

The end result of any budget is a reflection of management's commitment to the level of maintenance they would like to see in their property.

SCHEDULED MAINTENANCE

A plan to do maintenance work in the future is usually of two types and that is scheduled maintenance and preventive maintenance. Scheduled maintenance is that type of work that requires longer durations to complete, planning of manpower and tools and materials required, co-ordination with other trades and possibly outside contractors.

The timely replacement or maintenance on a major piece of equipment could involve shut downs of other departments or blocks of guest rooms. Projects such as building of walls or complete painting of areas could also come under scheduled maintenance. Indeed, any project requires scheduling and planning.

Preventive Maintenance, as it's name implies is the intent to perform timed inspections, minor adjustments, lubrication based on manufacture's recommendations with the ultimate goal of preventing unscheduled breakdowns and prolonging the life and efficiency of the equipment. During the course of the inspection if it is determined that major work may be required, then work orders are generated to schedule the maintenance.

Room Maintenance, both guest and meeting rooms again follows the above with inspections and generating work orders to schedule and correct deficiencies. The frequency of inspections should be determined to happen sometime before the area slow periods.

If guest rooms occupancy is peak in summer then schedule the inspection just prior to the downturn as it will give time to order necessary materials and schedule the labor to accomplish the tasks. The importance of inspections cannot be over emphasized because I have yet to see room attendants or banquet staff adequately report deficiencies.

Breakdown maintenance can be both negative and positive. Negative if it has an impact on guest comfort, safety, or is detrimental to the smooth flow of production that keeps other departments operational.

Breakdowns can be very expensive if it happens after hours and outside contractors are required, or if say the main chiller shuts down and all your guests walk out. Positive as you would not want to spend $100 a year on preventive maintenance on a blender worth $50. Also, in maintenance repairs don't waste $20 worth of time to repair something only worth $10.00.

Contract maintenance is mandated in some instances such as for elevator service, kitchen hood exhaust cleaning and fire systems. The reasoning behind this is to ensure that the work is performed by qualified technicians, and may also require licenses and special knowledge. Local regulations and insurance companies usually require these contracts. It also serves the purpose of making sure the work gets done irregardless of budget restraints. Maintenance contracts or contracting out is almost always necessary to complement an engineering department that is undersized.

Hiring

The hiring of engineering management personnel is unfortunately processed by persons without a technical and mechanical background. The difficulty with some properties is that they may not have the corporate resources to use a engineering person on staff, either at head office or a similar hotel in a chain. The benefit of experience and certification in property and hotel operation is apparent.

Often, again for the sake of the bottom line engineering management are hired based on little experience and know-how to save on dollars. There are some instances where power engineering 4th class or higher is required to satisfy boiler and pressure vessel regulations, however these only form the minimum entry level requirements of power plants in lumber mills and power process industries and may be necessary if the building has equipment with heating surfaces and refrigeration exceeding normal capacity.

Power Engineering does not confer on anyone the ability to operate buildings, especially hotels but could be an indicator of mechanical aptitude. There are other preferred courses in property management and building operations. Like anything else, you get what you pay for!

Electrical safety is everyone's responsibility. Electrical safety should be observed every time you even think about touching something connected to an electrical circuit. With the invention of electrical testers, circuits are easy to test and with circuit breakers and fuses, circuits can be shut off to avoid contact with electricity all together. Electrical safety often comes into play when bad weather strikes. Tornadoes, hurricanes, flooding, and ice storms bring a vast array of dangerous conditions. In this informative piece, you'll find some great tips to keep you safe when working with electricity.

Weather-Related Electrical Safety

The weather plays havoc on your electrical system, its components, and everything that is connected to them. Thunderstorms bring wild weather with lightning that can send a jolt to you electrical service. This can damage the electrical system itself and everything connected to it. Flooding rains can get into your house, cause electrocution hazards, damage electrical connections, and leave the devices it touched unsafe. Hurricanes and ice storms can take down power lines and leave electrocution hazards laying around everywhere.

This is a sensible look at preventing electrical shock. These tips will help keep you safe.

1. **Be Safety Conscious**—Working with electrical circuits can be dangerous if you don't take certain safety precautions. Electrical shock can not only injure you but also kill you. Practice safety when working on any circuit and slow down! When you hurry through a project, there is a greater chance for an accident to occur.

2. **Shut the Power Off**—Always shut off the power to a circuit or device that you will be working on. This is the first thing you should do before working on any electrical circuit. I don't know anyone who has been shocked by a circuit that is not energized.

3. Test the Circuit—After turning a circuit off, it's a good idea to check it with a tester to be sure that, indeed, it is off. Never assume that the circuit is off!

4. Ladders—Ladders are necessary to accomplish some electrical jobs. Never use an aluminum ladder on any electrical project. Always use an insulated fiberglass ladder to keep you safe.

5. Wet Locations—Avoid wet areas when working with or on anything electrical. If there is a reason that you have to be in that situation, wear rubber boots and gloves to lesson your chance of getting shocked. Tools and appliances should be plugged into a GFCI outlet or GFCI extension cord.

Don't forget to dry your hands before grabbing any cord to plug it in or unplug it. Wet hands and a frayed cord don't mix. You reach down to grab the cord and just like that, you've been shocked! Believe it or not, it happens.

6. Warning Labels—Finally, if you are working on the service panel or a circuit, be sure to place a warning label on the face of the panel. This will warn someone not to turn on the circuit that you are working on. There's nothing worse than turning off the power, checking that it's off and starting to work on the circuit, only to have someone come behind you and turn the circuit back on. Always think and ask questions before turning on a breaker that is shut off. Maybe someone is working on the other end.

PAT Testing

Portable Appliance Testing is a process in the United Kingdom, New Zealand and Australia by which electrical appliances are routinely checked for safety. The correct term for the whole process is In-service Inspection & Testing of Electrical Equipment.

When people work with electrical appliances, health and safety regulations state that the appliance must be safe, to prevent harm to the workers. Many types of equipment require testing at regular intervals to ensure continual safety; the interval between tests depending on both the type of appliance and the environment it is used in.

Evidence of testing is clearly visible to workers in the form of 'Passed' , 'Tested For Electrical Safety' and 'DO NOT USE after' labels affixed to various parts of the electrical equipment they use.

Portable appliance testing and inspection however was conducted on a 3 month (high risk) and 6 month (low risk) cycle from the early 1960s onwards in government departments under the control of the Department of the Environment Property and Services Agency (circa 1970 to 2000) as the DOEPSA was known and prior to that as the Ministry of Public Buildings and Works (MoPBW) until about 1970.

Extensive record keeping was made into log-books and generally the equipment used was an insulation resistance tester, simple hand tools and visual inspection. This testing and inspection was done under a planned maintenance scheme and predated both the Health and Safety at Work Act 1974 and the Electricity at Work Act 1990 that are frequently quoted as the reason that PAT inspection is done.

In reality neither act nor their corresponding regulations detail PAT inspection as an obligation but rather state a requirement of maintenance of safety and evidence of routine maintenance of all hand-held, portable and plug-in equipment.

It seemed inevitable with the increasing amounts of such equipment in domestic, commercial and industrial environments that the system employed for all government departments would become more formalized and adopted as a method for assuring safety of appliances in the world beyond the civil service departments.

Testing equipment specifically designed for PAT inspections was developed as mobile versions of the equipment used by manufacturers for testing their equipment at the end of the manufacturing process to ensure compliance with the relevant or corresponding BS (British Standard Code of Practice) for that type of appliance.

One other check carried out on high risk equipment such as hand held electrical mains drills class I equipment when issued from a government department stores was the Earth Yeading Test. This test passed a current of 25 A down the earth conductor (the c.p.c. circuit protective conductor as it is currently named) to substantiate that the earth was a sound and valid connection for safe disconnection in the event of a fault occurring.

Portable Appliance Testing is abbreviated to PAT. The phrase PAT Testing is in fact a tautology, in the same way that some people say "LCD Display" (see also RAS syndrome). However, the phrase is commonly used in the industry, even though most people realise it is incorrect. The correct term for the whole process is In-service Inspection & Testing of Electrical Equipment (as defined by IET/IEE and City and Guilds).

Legal

Regulations on who must have their Equipment PAT Tested

The Electricity at Work Regulations (1989) requires "All electrical systems shall be maintained so as to prevent, so far as is reasonably practicable, any danger". This is interpreted as covering the fixed electrical installation as well as portable and transportable equipment connected to it. The Regulations also state "It is the duty of every employer and self employed person to comply with the provision of these Regulations."

British law (the Electricity at Work Regulations 1989 in particular) requires that all electrical systems (including electrical appliances) are maintained (so far as is reasonably practicable) to prevent danger. Guidance from the Institution of Engineering and Technology (IET, published under the IEE brand) and the Health and Safety Executive (HSE) suggest initial intervals for combined inspection and testing that range from three months (for construction equipment) to one year for inspection and, in many cases, longer periods for testing (certain types of appliance in schools, hotels, offices and shops).

Electrical systems refer to the installation as well as all the appliances connected to it. A qualified electrician or someone that has PAT testing training must inspect the installation annually in any public building and/or a place that people work, private houses do not need this test. The maintenance of the appliances can largely be carried out in-house in many organisations. This can result in cost savings and more flexibility in when PAT testing is carried out.

The European Low Voltage Directive governs the manufacture or importation of electrical appliances. Compliance to this has to be declared and indicated by the display of the CE mark on the product. The responsibility for this lies with the manufacturer or the importer and is policed by the Trading Standards. However, it is important to have a maintenance regime for electrical appliances. The Electricity at Work Regulations (1989) requires that electrical appliances be maintained so that they remain safe during use. The implementation of this is up to employers. The HSE or the local authority is responsible for the policing of this.

Who can PAT test

It is a legal requirement to have attended a course or gained a qualification in order to PAT Test in Australia. If you are a competent person and have a basic knowledge of electricity then you can be perfectly capable of testing appliances for electrical safety. It is, however, recommended that an individual wanting to PAT Test attends a course related to the subject matter. There can be much confusion on what needs PAT Testing, what class an appliance is (and therefore which areas to test), and how often appliances legally need to be tested.

Proof of a company's competence in PAT Testing is usually found in the form of a course certificate or qualification. A formal examination process for the topic is operated in collaboration with EAL or City and Guilds (the awarding body) under the authority of the QCA (The Qualifications and Curriculum Authority) who validate and authorise the qualification.

In the UK, There is no formal qualification for persons carrying out PAT Testing. The Electricity at Work regulations of 1989 simply state that inspecting and testing must be carried out by a competent person, however does not mention a benchmark for competency. It has become accepted practice, however, for individuals operating as PAT Testers to hold a City and Guilds qualification. PAT Testers in the UK do not need to be electricians or have a background in the electrical industry.

Carrying out PAT Testing

This can be done by hiring an external company to test all the electrical products in a business or it can be done in-house by someone who has had some PAT training, either by an official qualification or by attending a health and safety course offered by some electrical health and safety companies.

The following steps are taken when testing a business' electrical equipment.

User Checks

Advising the user of potential danger signs can result in problems being picked up before they can result in any danger. For example, if the power cable is frayed or the plug is cracked, users need to be advised NOT TO USE the appliance and report the fault to a supervisor. This information can be put across, say by the use of a poster or in a memo. User checks are always carried out before operation, and the results are generally not recorded, unless a defect is identified.

Formal Visual Inspections

This is a process of simply inspecting the appliance, the cable and the plug for any obvious signs of damage. According to the HSE, this process can find more than 90% of faults.

Combined Inspections and PAT Testing

At periodic intervals, it is essential to test the portable appliances to measure that the degree of protection to ensure that it is adequate. At these intervals, a formal visual inspection is carried out and then followed by PAT testing. Note the inside of the plug MUST be checked unless it is moulded or there is an unbroken seal covering the screws (bad internal wiring or an unsuitable fuse would cause the item to be classed as dangerous).

The tests that an individual must carry out to declare an item electrically safe is dependant on the class of construction (shown below). Some of these tests are:

- Earth Continuity
- Insulation Resistance
- Polarity of Wiring

Class of Construction

Electrical appliances are differentiated by a series of IEC protection classes. In PAT Testing it is essential for the person PAT Testing to know the difference in classes and therefore what checks must be completed before declaring the item electrically safe.

Class I - Single insulated wiring, which requires an earth connection. There is no symbol for a Class I product so if a rating plate has no symbol on it then it is usually Class I.

Class II - Double insulated wiring, therefore no need for a earth lead. Class II is indicated by double box.

Class III - These are appliances that are supplied at a low voltage (usually called Separated Extra Low Voltage) which must be less than 50 V. These appliances are supplied with a transformer supply that is also marked.

Other

Class 0 - Non-earthed metal appliance with two core cable. Sales of these items have been banned since 1975.

Class 01 - As Class 0 but appliance has an earth terminal which is unused since two core cable is used.

PAT Training and Qualifications

It is not stated in the health and safety regulations for an individual to have any qualifications to PAT Test but it does state that it must be done by a competent person who has been given instruction - i.e. Someone who understands the process and can perform the necessary checks in a safe manner.

It is therefore generally recommended that if a company wishes to PAT Test in-house then they have the person who will be doing the testing attend a portable appliance testing training course so as to fully understand what it is they are checking for.

The only nationally recognized qualification of competence in PAT is offered by City & Guilds: 'Code of Practice for In-service Inspection and Testing of Electrical Equipment - Vocational 3 (No. 2377)'. although many other non-recognized PAT training courses are available.

TYPES OF PAT TESTERS

There are many different types of PAT testers available. The main kind for businesses are simple PASS/FAIL PAT testers that are very easy to use, and are aimed at in-house PAT testing. To use the majority of them, one does not require a high level of electrical skill.

There are also advanced PAT Testers, which give much more information and testing features but are mainly aimed at competent persons qualified to City & Guilds 2377 or EAL . To use the majority of these testers, one does require a higher level of electrical skill.

Pass / fail PAT Testers

These are the simple-to-use and comparatively much cheaper Portable Appliance Testers for most businesses who will test in-house to carry out the testing and suitable for a wide range of businesses. They simply say PASS or FAIL when a test is carried out. Battery operated PAT testers are particularly useful in getting into those awkward spaces to PAT Test. As with any inspections, it is important the test results are recorded onto a record sheet,or computer database, and stored in a safe place.

At the basic level PAT test instruments are relatively simple to operate devices that carry out basic safety checks. Most are equipped with an earth continuity test, insulation resistance test and the ability to check the wiring of detachable mains cords. They do not however include tests which inolve applying mains power to the appliance under test, for example, a protective conductor current or touch current tests.

Mains Powered Pass/fail PAT Testers

The powered Pass / Fail PAT testers are the standard for most businesses who test in-house. It is ideal for those wanting to carry out in-house testing of electrical appliances in offices, hotels, schools, nursing homes, factories and construction sites. You usually get test result labels, which are attached to the electrical equipment that is being tested with a date stamp to show when the item next needs to be tested. The simplicity of these devices make them very popular with small businesses simply because of the PASS or FAIL display when a test is done. These testers are also safe for use on PCs and other IT equipment.

The newer battery powered testers offer much more flexibility as the tester can be moved to the equipment as opposed to the other way round.

Battery Powered pass / fail PAT Testers

These are the newer and more convenient pass / fail PAT testers, which you can take to the appliance to be tested making testing multiple items in a business much quicker. They usually come with rechargeable batteries

The battery powered testers are fast replacing the older powered units.

The newer battery powered PAT testers have a simple "lights" system. They have a "Pass" light , a "Fail" light, options for Class I metal / plastic or Class II. They also will show:

- Earth Continuity
- Insulation Resistance
- Polarity

Advanced PAT Testers (electricians' PAT testers)

These PAT Testers give the actual readings from the PAT tester in Ohms (or Mohms) for the person testing to interpret. A knowledge of electrical readings is required hence why these type of PAT Testers are designed for use by an electrician / someone with electrical qualifications. Also some hybrid designs will have the electrical readings along with a PASS / FAIL option.

Advanced PAT Testers

These are PAT Testers designed to display more information than just pass or fail. As well as giving the Pass / Fail results it will give readings for the tester to interprete. Some of these include:

- Earth Continuity Resistance (aka Earth Bond) tests with a measurement range of 0 - 1.99 ? at high test currents (usually 8 A, 10 A or 25 A) and lower test currents (in the range 20 mA to 200 mA), enabling a complete range of appliances including personal computers to be tested.
- Insulation Resistance tests at test voltages of 500 V DC or 250 V DC.
- Protective Conductor/Touch Current measurement (sometimes referred to as Earth Leakage tests on some older PAT units).
- Fuse test.
- Lead Polarity
- Some units incorporate an RCD test function.
- Testing both 230 V and 110 V appliances

Advanced PAT testers are also much more effective as facilities management tools because of their ability to log, capture and record the location and test status of electrical equipment and appliances.

RCD Testing

In the most modern PAT testers RCD testing is now included in the suite of test options available. This follows the inclusion of new advice in the IEE Code of Practice that when an extension lead or multiway adaptor is fitted with an RCD, the operation of the RCD should be checked to determine that the trip time is within specified limits.

Modern PAT Testers Include an RCD Test

Computerised PAT Testers

Also some advanced PAT testers have the capability of downloading the information to a pc or laptop for recordings (examples are shown below left and right).

Bluetooth enabled computerised PAT testers make the two way transfer of test data between the tester and PC-based record keeping systems much simpler.

In addition, PAT testers equipped with Bluetooth means that connectivity with other test accessories such as label printers can also be made without having to use cable connection.

Calibration of PAT Testers

As PAT Testers are sophisticated instruments, it is important to make sure that they are continuing to measure correctly. If a company fails to check and maintain calibration, it could face difficulty substantiating any measurements in the event of a claim. It is usually recommended that calibration is carried out annually on a PAT testing unit.

When a PAT Tester is calibrated it is re-configuring it to match the original specification. This includes:

- Calibrating the unit back to National Standards. This is best performed by the product manufacturer (if they offer a calibration service) or a laboratory accredited by UKAS
- If it is mains powered, then a safety test must be carried out.
- A calibration certificate should be issued to prove the PAT unit has been electrically tested.

Dual purpose checkboxes have also been introduced which are capable of validating the accuracy of both electrical installation testers and portable appliance testers.

A list of simple ways householders can save on their electricity bills.

Energy costs are rising and there's no reason to think that trend will change in the near future. The summer of 2000 saw Arab Sultanates manipulating the cost of crude oil for their own sake and not yours. California experienced electrical deregulation with household bills doubling in some areas.

In the future, energy companies may compete for your business the way that long distance companies do now. For now, however, the only way to save energy is to use less of it.

Some of us are reluctant to try to conserve energy because we believe the savings will be minor. Others associate energy conservation with poverty.

Energy conservation saves real dollars and preserves a public resource. Here are some ways to cut energy costs without compromising your lifestyle too much.

Control Heating and Cooling Costs

In some climates, heating and cooling represent the largest part of household energy use. In many climates, running your air conditioner at 78 instead of 72 will save 40% of your cooling bill. You don't have to freeze or roast to death in order to save money. Here are a few tips:

* Make sure your filters are clean. Check with the manufacturer of your equipment or with your utility company to see how often filters on your units need to be cleaned.
* Don't heat or cool when no one is home. If you are going to be gone for more than a half an hour, you can turn your heating or cooling off or down. Don't turn off the heat in a cold climate, however, if that will result in the pipes breaking.
* Supplement your main unit with portable units Running a fan can help you use less air conditioning. Using portable

heaters when you are asleep or otherwise staying in one room can mean less use of heat if it means that you don't have to use the main unit.

* Try setting your thermostat to run less frequently Turn your air conditioner up a degree or two or your heater down a degree or two and see if you still can be

Time your opening and closing of windows and drapes to reduce heading and cooling costs. On cold, sunny days, opening curtains and drapes while leaving windows closed will help you heat your home. Opening the windows on summer nights helps cool your home. Buying storm windows in some climates reduces heating costs.

* Check for holes in your roof and in your pipes. This can help save up to 10% of your heating and cooling costs.

Get Ideas from your Utility Company

Several years ago my electric company put extra insulation in all the units of my condominium complex to help us save electricity. At that time they also offered sizeable rebates to people who bought more energy efficient air conditioners and water heaters.

Utility companies are among the few businesses who hope that you use less of their product. Most power companies are anxious to postpone construction of new power plants, so they strongly encourage customers to use less power.

Utility companies offer energy audits, tips, and other help for customers who want to save energy. Call your local utility or log onto their website to see what they have to offer.

Other Tips

* Consider energy efficiency when buying appliances Appliances are labeled with energy usage comparison tables. Look at these figures. Also, you may be able to buy an adapter to make your older appliances more energy efficient.

* Turn off appliances that no one is using Turning off TV's, lamps, computers, VCR's, ovens, and other appliances that no one is using can save electricity. Even turning them off for short periods can produce noticeable results.
* See if an alternative energy company is available In California, electrical deregulation is beginning to result in alternative providers for electricity. This is a trend that should increase nationally. See if that option is available to you.
* Install low-flow showerheads. Also, check your water heater's temperature and set it for 120 degrees. Putting insulation over your water heater and pipes can also help.
* Wash and dry only full loads of clothing or dishes

Saving energy won't make you rich, but it will help you cut down some on your costs and will help prevent blackouts and power shortages in your community.

CHAPTER–5

MARKETING

Marketing is the process of performing market research, selling products and/or services to customers and promoting them via advertising to further enhance sales. It generates the strategy that underlies sales techniques, business communication, and business developments. It is an integrated process through which companies build strong customer relationships and create value for their customers and for themselves.

Marketing is used to identify the customer, to satisfy the customer, and to keep the customer. With the customer as the focus of its activities, it can be concluded that marketing management is one of the major components of business management. Marketing evolved to meet the stasis in developing new markets caused by mature markets and overcapacities in the last 2-3 centuries. The adoption of marketing strategies requires businesses to shift their focus from production to the perceived needs and wants of their customers as the means of staying profitable. The term marketing concept holds that achieving organizational goals depends on knowing the needs and wants of target markets and delivering the desired satisfactions. It proposes that in order to satisfy its organizational objectives, an organization should anticipate the needs and wants of consumers and satisfy these more effectively than competitors.

Marketing is defined by the American Marketing Association (AMA) as "the activity, set of institutions, and processes for creating, communicating, delivering, and exchanging offerings that have value for customers, clients, partners, and society at large. Marketing is a product or service selling related overall activities.

The term developed from an original meaning which referred literally to going to a market to buy or sell goods or services. Seen from a systems point of view, sales process engineering marketing is "a set of processes that are interconnected and interdependent with other functions, whose methods can be improved using a variety of relatively new approaches."

The Chartered Institute of Marketing defines marketing as "the management process responsible for identifying, anticipating and satisfying customer requirements profitably." A different concept is the value-based marketing which states the role of marketing to contribute to increasing shareholder value. In this context, marketing is defined as "the management process that seeks to maximise returns to shareholders by developing relationships with valued customers and creating a competitive advantage."

Marketing practice tended to be seen as a creative industry in the past, which included advertising, distribution and selling. However, because the academic study of marketing makes extensive use of social sciences, psychology, sociology, mathematics, economics, anthropology and neuroscience, the profession is now widely recognized as a science, allowing numerous universities to offer Master-of-Science (MSc) programmes.

The overall process starts with marketing research and goes through market segmentation, business planning and execution, ending with pre- and post-sales promotional activities. It is also related to many of the creative arts. The marketing literature is also adept at re-inventing itself and its vocabulary according to the times and the culture.

An orientation, in the marketing context, related to a perception or attitude a firm holds towards its product or service, essentially concerning consumers and end-users. Throughout history, marketing has changed considerably in time with consumer tastes.

CONTEMPORARY APPROACHES

Recent approaches in marketing include relationship marketing with focus on the customer, business marketing or industrial marketing with focus on an organization or institution and social marketing with focus on benefits to society. New forms of marketing also use the internet and are therefore called internet marketing or more generally e-marketing, online marketing, search engine marketing, desktop advertising or affiliate marketing.

It attempts to perfect the segmentation strategy used in traditional marketing. It targets its audience more precisely, and is sometimes called personalized marketing or one-to-one marketing. Internet marketing is sometimes considered to be broad in scope, because it not only refers to marketing on the Internet, but also includes marketing done via e-mail and wireless media.

CUSTOMER ORIENTATION

A firm in the market economy survives by producing goods that persons are willing and able to buy. Consequently, ascertaining consumer demand is vital for a firm's future viability and even existence as a going concern. Many companies today have a customer focus (or market orientation). This implies that the company focuses its activities and products on consumer demands. Generally, there are three ways of doing this: the customer-driven approach, the market change identification approach and the product innovation approach.

In the consumer-driven approach, consumer wants are the drivers of all strategic marketing decisions. No strategy is pursued until it passes the test of consumer research. Every aspect of a market offering, including the nature of the product itself, is driven by the needs of potential consumers. The starting point is always the consumer.

The rationale for this approach is that there is no reason to spend R&D funds developing products that people will not buy. History attests to many products that were commercial failures in spite of being technological breakthroughs.

A formal approach to this customer-focused marketing is known as SIVA (Solution, Information, Value, Access). This system is basically the four Ps renamed and reworded to provide a customer focus. The SIVA Model provides a demand/customer-centric alternative to the well-known 4Ps supply side model (product, price, placement, promotion) of marketing management.

Product ? Solution

Price ? Value

Place ? Access

Promotion ? Information

If any of the 4Ps were problematic or were not in the marketing factor of the business, the business could be in trouble and so other companies may appear in the surroundings of the company, so the consumer demand on its products will decrease.

ORGANIZATIONAL ORIENTATION

In this sense, a firm's marketing department is often seen as of prime importance within the functional level of an organization. Information from an organization's marketing department would be used to guide the actions of other departments within the firm. As an example, a marketing department could ascertain (via marketing research) that consumers desired a new type of product, or a new usage for an existing product. With this in mind, the marketing department would inform the R&D department to create a prototype of a product/service based on consumers' new desires.

The production department would then start to manufacture the product, while the marketing department would focus on the promotion, distribution, pricing, etc. of the product. Additionally, a firm's finance department would be consulted, with respect to securing appropriate funding for the development, production and promotion of the product. Inter-departmental conflicts may occur, should a firm adhere to the marketing orientation. Production may oppose the installation, support and servicing of new capital stock, which may be needed to manufacture a new product. Finance may oppose the required capital expenditure, since it could undermine a healthy cash flow for the organization.

Herd Behavior

Herd behavior in marketing is used to explain the dependencies of customers' mutual behavior. The Economist reported a recent conference in Rome on the subject of the simulation of adaptive human behavior. It shared mechanisms to increase impulse buying and get people "to buy more by playing on the herd instinct."

The basic idea is that people will buy more of products that are seen to be popular, and several feedback mechanisms to get product popularity information to consumers are mentioned, including smart card technology and the use of Radio Frequency Identification Tag technology. A "swarm-moves" model was introduced by a Florida Institute of Technology researcher, which is appealing to supermarkets because it can "increase sales without the need to give people discounts."

Other recent studies on the "power of social influence" include an "artificial music market in which some 19,000 people downloaded previously unknown songs" (Columbia University, New York); a Japanese chain of convenience stores which orders its products based on "sales data from department stores and research companies;" a Massachusetts company exploiting knowledge of social networking to improve sales; and online retailers who are increasingly informing consumers about "which products are popular with like-minded consumers" (e.g., Amazon, eBay).

Further Orientations

- An emerging area of study and practice concerns internal marketing, or how employees are trained and managed to deliver the brand in a way that positively impacts the acquisition and retention of customers, see also employer branding.

- Diffusion of innovations research explores how and why people adopt new products, services, and ideas.
- With consumers' eroding attention span and willingness to give time to advertising messages, marketers are turning to forms of permission marketing such as branded content, custom media and reality marketing.

Marketing Research

Marketing research involves conducting research to support marketing activities, and the statistical interpretation of data into information. This information is then used by managers to plan marketing activities, gauge the nature of a firm's marketing environment and attain information from suppliers. Marketing researchers use statistical methods such as quantitative research, qualitative research, hypothesis tests, Chi-squared tests, linear regression, correlations, frequency distributions, poisson distributions, binomial distributions, etc. to interpret their findings and convert data into information.

The marketing research process spans a number of stages, including the definition of a problem, development of a research plan, collection and interpretation of data and disseminating information formally in the form of a report. The task of marketing research is to provide management with relevant, accurate, reliable, valid, and current information.

A distinction should be made between marketing research and market research. Market research pertains to research in a given market. As an example, a firm may conduct research in a target market, after selecting a suitable market segment. In contrast, marketing research relates to all research conducted within marketing. Thus, market research is a subset of marketing research.

Market segmentation pertains to the division of a market of consumers into persons with similar needs and wants. For instance, Kellogg's cereals, Frosties are marketed to children. Crunchy Nut Cornflakes are marketed to adults. Both goods denote two products which are marketed to two distinct groups of persons, both with similar needs, traits, and wants.

Market segmentation allows for a better allocation of a firm's finite resources. A firm only possesses a certain amount of resources. Accordingly, it must make choices (and incur the related costs) in servicing specific groups of consumers. In this way, the diversified tastes of contemporary Western consumers can be served better. With growing diversity in the tastes of modern consumers, firms are taking note of the benefit of servicing a multiplicity of new markets.

Market segmentation can be defined in terms of the STP acronym, meaning Segment, Target and Position.

Types of Marketing Research

Marketing research, as a sub-set aspect of marketing activities, can be divided into the following parts:

- Primary research (also known as field research), which involves the conduction and compilation of research for a specific purpose.
- Secondary research (also referred to as desk research), initially conducted for one purpose, but often used to support another purpose or end goal.

By these definitions, an example of primary research would be market research conducted into health foods, which is used solely to ascertain the needs/wants of the target market for health foods. Secondary research in this case would be research pertaining to health foods, but used by a firm wishing to develop an unrelated product.

Primary research is often expensive to prepare, collect and interpret from data to information. Nevertheless, while secondary research is relatively inexpensive, it often can become outdated and outmoded, given that it is used for a purpose other than the one for which it was intended.

Primary research can also be broken down into quantitative research and qualitative research, which, as the terms suggest, pertain to numerical and non-numerical research methods and techniques, respectively. The appropriateness of each mode of research depends on whether data can be quantified (quantitative research), or whether subjective, non-numeric or abstract concepts are required to be studied (qualitative research).

There also exist additional modes of marketing research, which are:

- Exploratory research, pertaining to research that investigates an assumption.
- Descriptive research, which, as the term suggests, describes "what is".
- Predictive research, meaning research conducted to predict a future occurrence.
- Conclusive research, for the purpose of deriving a conclusion via a research process.

Marketing Planning

The marketing planning process involves forging a plan for a firm's marketing activities. A marketing plan can also pertain to a specific product, as well as to an organization's overall marketing strategy. Generally speaking, an organization's marketing planning process is derived from its overall business strategy. Thus, when top management are devising the firm's strategic direction or mission, the intended marketing activities are incorporated into this plan. There are several levels of marketing objectives within an organization. The senior management of a firm would formulate a general business strategy for a firm. However, this general business strategy would be interpreted and implemented in different contexts throughout the firm.

Marketing Strategy

The field of marketing strategy encompasses the strategy involved in the management of a given product. A given firm may hold numerous products in the marketplace, spanning numerous and sometimes wholly unrelated industries. Accordingly, a plan is required in order to effectively manage such products. Evidently, a company needs to weigh up and ascertain how to utilize its finite resources.

For example, a start-up car manufacturing firm would face little success should it attempt to rival Toyota, Ford, Nissan, Chevrolet, or any other large global car maker. Moreover, a product may be reaching the end of its life-cycle. Thus, the issue of divest, or a ceasing of production, may be made. Each scenario requires a unique marketing strategy. Listed below are some prominent marketing strategy models.

Marketing Specializations

With the rapidly emerging force of globalization, the distinction between marketing within a firm's home country and marketing within external markets is disappearing very quickly. With this in mind, firms need to reorient their marketing strategies to meet the challenges of the global marketplace, in addition to sustaining their competitiveness within home markets.

Buying Behaviour

A marketing firm must ascertain the nature of customers' buying behavior if it is to market its product properly. In order to entice and persuade a consumer to buy a product, marketers try to determine the behavioral process of how a given product is purchased. Buying behavior is usually split into two prime strands, whether selling to the consumer, known as business-to-consumer (B2C), or to another business, known as business-to-business (B2B).

B2C Buying Behaviour

This mode of behaviour concerns consumers and their purchase of a given product. For example, if one imagines a pair of sneakers, the desire for a pair of sneakers would be followed by an information search on available types/brands. This may include perusing media outlets, but most commonly consists of information gathered from family and friends. If the information search is insufficient, the consumer may search for alternative means to satisfy the need/want.

In this case, this may mean buying leather shoes, sandals, etc. The purchase decision is then made, in which the consumer actually buys the product. Following this stage, a post-purchase evaluation is often conducted, comprising an appraisal of the value/utility brought by the purchase of the sneakers. If the value/utility is high, then a repeat purchase may be made. This could then develop into consumer loyalty to the firm producing the sneakers.

B2B Buying Behaviour

Relates to organizational/industrial buying behavior. "B2B" stands for Business to Business. B2B marketing involves one business marketing a product or service to another business. B2C and B2B behavior are not precise terms, as similarities and differences exist, with some key differences listed below:

In a straight re-buy, the fourth, fifth and sixth stages are omitted. In a modified re-buy scenario, the fifth and sixth stages are precluded. In a new buy, all stages are conducted.

Use of Technologies

Marketing management can also rely on various technologies within the scope of its marketing efforts. Computer-based information systems can be employed, aiding in better processing and storage of data. Marketing researchers can use such systems to devise better methods of converting data into information, and for the creation of enhanced data gathering methods. Information technology can aid in enhancing an MKIS' software and hardware components, and improve a company's marketing decision-making process.

In recent years, the netbook personal computer has gained significant market share among laptops, largely due to its more user-friendly size and portability. Information technology typically progresses at a fast rate, leading to marketing managers being cognizant of the latest technological developments. Moreover, the launch of smartphones into the cellphone market is commonly derived from a demand among consumers for more technologically advanced products. A firm can lose out to competitors should it ignore technological innovations in its industry.

Technological advancements can lessen barriers between countries and regions. Using the World Wide Web, firms can quickly dispatch information from one country to another without much restriction. Prior to the mass usage of the Internet, such transfers of information would have taken longer to send, especially if done via snail mail, telex, etc.

Services Marketing

Services marketing relates to the marketing of services, as opposed to tangible products. A service (as opposed to a good) is typically defined as follows:

- The use of it is inseparable from its purchase (i.e., a service is used and consumed simultaneously)
- It does not possess material form, and thus cannot be touched, seen, heard, tasted, or smelled.
- The use of a service is inherently subjective, meaning that several persons experiencing a service would each experience it uniquely.

For example, a train ride can be deemed a service. If one buys a train ticket, the use of the train is typically experienced concurrently with the purchase of the ticket. Although the train is a physical object, one is not paying for the permanent ownership of the tangible components of the train.

Services (compared with goods) can also be viewed as a spectrum. Not all products are pure goods, nor are all pure services. An example would be a restaurant, where a waiter's service is intangible, but the food is tangible.

Marketing through the Internet opened new frontiers for advertisers and contributed to the "dot-com" boom of the 1990s. Entire corporations operated solely on advertising revenue, offering everything from coupons to free Internet access. At the turn of the 21st century, a number of websites including the search engine Google, started a change in online advertising by emphasizing contextually relevant, unobtrusive ads intended to help, rather than inundate, users. This has led to a plethora of similar efforts and an increasing trend of interactive advertising.

The share of advertising spending relative to GDP has changed little across large changes in media. For example, in the US in 1925, the main advertising media were newspapers, magazines, signs on streetcars, and outdoor posters. Advertising spending as a share of GDP was about 2.9 percent. By 1998, television and radio had become major advertising media. Nonetheless, advertising spending as a share of GDP was slightly lower-about 2.4 percent.

A recent advertising innovation is "guerrilla marketing", which involve unusual approaches such as staged encounters in public places, giveaways of products such as cars that are covered with brand messages, and interactive advertising where the viewer can respond to become part of the advertising message.Guerrilla advertising is becoming increasing more popular with a lot of companies.

This type of advertising is unpredictable and innovative, which causes consumers to buy the product or idea. This reflects an increasing trend of interactive and "embedded" ads, such as via product placement, having consumers vote through text messages, and various innovations utilizing social network services such as Facebook.

Public Service Advertising

The advertising techniques used to promote commercial goods and services can be used to inform, educate and motivate the public about non-commercial issues, such as HIV/AIDS, political ideology, energy conservation and deforestation.

Advertising, in its non-commercial guise, is a powerful educational tool capable of reaching and motivating large audiences. "Advertising justifies its existence when used in the public interest-it is much too powerful a tool to use solely for commercial purposes." Attributed to Howard Gossage by David Ogilvy.

Public service advertising, non-commercial advertising, public interest advertising, cause marketing, and social marketing are different terms for (or aspects of) the use of sophisticated advertising and marketing communications techniques (generally associated with commercial enterprise) on behalf of non-commercial, public interest issues and initiatives.

In the United States, the granting of television and radio licenses by the FCC is contingent upon the station broadcasting a certain amount of public service advertising. To meet these requirements, many broadcast stations in America air the bulk of their required public service announcements during the late night or early morning when the smallest percentage of viewers are watching, leaving more day and prime time commercial slots available for high-paying advertisers.

Public service advertising reached its height during World Wars I and II under the direction of more than one government. During WWII President Roosevelt commissioned the creation of The War Advertising Council (now known as the Ad Council) which is the nation's largest developer of PSA campaigns on behalf of government agencies and non-profit organizations, including the longest-running PSA campaign, Smokey Bear.

Marketing Mix

The marketing mix has been the key concept to advertising. The marketing mix was suggested by professor E. Jerome McCarthy in the 1960s. The marketing mix consists of four basic elements called the four P's Product is the first P representing the actual product. Price represents the process of determining the value of a product.

Place represents the variables of getting the product to the consumer like distribution channels, market coverage and movement organization. The last P stands for Promotion which is the process of reaching the target market and convincing them to go out and buy the product.

Advertising Theory

- Hierarchy of effects model

It clarifies the objectives of an advertising campaign and for each individual advertisement. The model suggests that there are six steps a consumer or a business buyer moves through when making a purchase. The steps are:

1. Awareness
2. Knowledge
3. Liking
4. Preference
5. Conviction
6. The actual purchase

- Means-End Theory

This approach suggests that an advertisement should contain a message or means that leads the consumer to a desired end state.

- Leverage Points

It is designed to move the consumer from understanding a product's benefits to linking those benefits with personal values.

- Verbal and Visual Images

Types of Advertising

Virtually any medium can be used for advertising. Commercial advertising media can include wall paintings, billboards, street furniture components, printed flyers and rack cards, radio, cinema and television adverts, web banners, mobile telephone screens, shopping carts, web popups, skywriting, bus stop benches, human billboards, magazines, newspapers, town criers, sides of buses, banners attached to or sides of airplanes ("logojets"), in-flight advertisements on seatback tray tables or overhead storage bins, taxicab doors, roof mounts and passenger screens, musical stage shows, subway platforms and trains, elastic bands on disposable diapers,doors of bathroom stalls, stickers on apples in supermarkets, shopping cart handles (grabertising), the opening section of streaming audio and video, posters, and the backs of event tickets and supermarket receipts. Any place an "identified" sponsor pays to deliver their message through a medium is advertising.

DIGITAL ADVERTISING

Television Advertising/Music in Advertising

The TV commercial is generally considered the most effective mass-market advertising format, as is reflected by the high prices TV networks charge for commercial airtime during popular TV events. The annual Super Bowl football game in the United States is known as the most prominent advertising event on television. The average cost of a single thirty-second TV spot during this game has reached US$3 million (as of 2009). The majority of television commercials feature a song or jingle that listeners soon relate to the product. Virtual advertisements may be inserted into regular television programming through computer graphics. It is typically inserted into otherwise blank backdrops or used to replace local billboards that are not relevant to the remote broadcast audience.

More controversially, virtual billboards may be inserted into the background where none exist in real-life. This technique is especially used in televised sporting events. Virtual product placement is also possible. Infomercials: An infomercial is a long-format television commercial, typically five minutes or longer. The word "infomercial" combining the words "information" & "commercial".

The main objective in an infomercial is to create an impulse purchase, so that the consumer sees the presentation and then immediately buys the product through the advertised toll-free telephone number or website. Infomercials describe, display, and often demonstrate products and their features, and commonly have testimonials from consumers and industry professionals.

Radio Advertising

Radio advertising is a form of advertising via the medium of radio. Radio advertisements are broadcast as radio waves to the air from a transmitter to an antenna and a thus to a receiving device. Airtime is purchased from a station or network in exchange for airing the commercials. While radio has the obvious limitation of being restricted to sound, proponents of radio advertising often cite this as an advantage.

Online Advertising

Online advertising is a form of promotion that uses the Internet and World Wide Web for the expressed purpose of delivering marketing messages to attract customers. Examples of online advertising include contextual ads that appear on search engine results pages, banner ads, in text ads, Rich Media Ads, Social network advertising, online classified advertising, advertising networks and e-mail marketing, including e-mail spam.

Product Placements

Covert advertising, also known as guerrilla advertising, is when a product or brand is embedded in entertainment and media. For example, in a film, the main character can use an item or other of a definite brand, as in the movie Minority Report, where Tom Cruise's character John Anderton owns a phone with the Nokia logo clearly written in the top corner, or his watch engraved with the Bulgari logo. Another example of advertising in film is in I, Robot, where main character played by Will Smith mentions his Converse shoes several times, calling them "classics," because the film is set far in the future. I, Robot and Spaceballs also showcase futuristic cars with the Audi and Mercedes-Benz logos clearly displayed on the front of the vehicles. Cadillac chose to advertise in the movie The Matrix Reloaded, which as a result contained many scenes in whieh Cadillac cars were used. Similarly, product placement for Omega Watches, Ford, VAIO, BMW and Aston Martin cars are featured in recent James Bond films, most notably Casino Royale. In "Fantastic Four: Rise of the Silver Surfer", the main transport vehicle shows a large Dodge logo on the front. Blade Runner includes some of the most obvious product placement; the whole film stops to show a Coca-Cola billboard.

Press Advertising

Press advertising describes advertising in a printed medium such as a newspaper, magazine, or trade journal. This encompasses everything from media with a very broad readership base, such as a major national newspaper or magazine, to more narrowly targeted media such as local newspapers and trade journals on very specialized topics.

A form of press advertising is classified advertising, which allows private individuals or companies to purchase a small, narrowly targeted ad for a low fee advertising a product or service. Another form of press advertising is the Display Ad, which is a larger ad (can include art) that typically run in an article section of a newspaper.

Billboard Advertising

Billboards are large structures located in public places which display advertisements to passing pedestrians and motorists. Most often, they are located on main roads with a large amount of passing motor and pedestrian traffic; however, they can be placed in any location with large amounts of viewers, such as on mass transit vehicles and in stations, in shopping malls or office buildings, and in stadiums.

Mobile Billboard Advertising

Mobile billboards are generally vehicle mounted billboards or digital screens. These can be on dedicated vehicles built solely for carrying advertisements along routes preselected by clients, they can also be specially equipped cargo trucks or, in some cases, large banners strewn from planes. The billboards are often lighted; some being backlit, and others employing spotlights.

Some billboard displays are static, while others change; for example, continuously or periodically rotating among a set of advertisements. Mobile displays are used for various situations in metropolitan areas throughout the world, including: Target advertising, One-day, and long-term campaigns, Conventions,

Sporting events, Store openings and similar promotional events, and Big advertisements from smaller companies.

In-store Advertising

In-store advertising is any advertisement placed in a retail store. It includes placement of a product in visible locations in a store, such as at eye level, at the ends of aisles and near checkout counters, eye-catching displays promoting a specific product, and advertisements in such places as shopping carts and in-store video displays.

Coffee Cup Advertising

Coffee cup advertising is any advertisement placed upon a coffee cup that is distributed out of an office, café, or drive-through coffee shop. This form of advertising was first popularized in Australia, and has begun growing in popularity in the United States, India, and parts of the Middle East.

Street Advertising

This type of advertising first came to prominence in the UK by Street Advertising Services to create outdoor advertising on street furniture and pavements. Working with products such as Reverse Graffiti and 3d pavement advertising, the media became an affordable and effective tool for getting brand messages out into public spaces.

Celebrity Branding

This type of advertising focuses upon using celebrity power, fame, money, popularity to gain recognition for their products and promote specific stores or products. Advertisers often advertise their products, for example, when celebrities share their favorite products or wear clothes by specific brands or designers. Celebrities are often involved in advertising campaigns such as television or print adverts to advertise specific or general products.

The use of celebrities to endorse a brand can have its downsides, however. One mistake by a celebrity can be detrimental to the public relations of a brand. For example, following his performance of eight gold medals at the 2008 Olympic Games in Beijing, China, swimmer Michael Phelps' contract with Kellogg's was terminated, as Kellogg's did not want to associate with him after he was photographed smoking marijuana.

Sales Promotions

Sales promotions are another way to advertise. Sales promotions are double purposed because they are used to gather information about what type of customers you draw in and where they are, and to jumpstart sales. Sales promotions include things like contests and games, sweepstakes, product giveaways, samples coupons, loyalty programs, and discounts. The ultimate goal of sales promotions is to stimulate potential customers to action.

Media and Advertising Approaches

Increasingly, other media are overtaking many of the "traditional" media such as television, radio and newspaper because of a shift toward consumer's usage of the Internet for news and music as well as devices like digital video recorders (DVRs) such as TiVo.

Advertising on the World Wide Web is a recent phenomenon. Prices of Web-based advertising space are dependent on the "relevance" of the surrounding web content and the traffic that the website receives.

Digital signage is poised to become a major mass media because of its ability to reach larger audiences for less money. Digital signage also offer the unique ability to see the target audience where they are reached by the medium. Technological advances have also made it possible to control the message on digital signage with much precision, enabling the messages to be relevant to the target audience at any given time and location which in turn, gets more response from the advertising. Digital signage is being successfully employed in supermarkets. Another successful use of digital signage is in hospitality locations such as restaurants and malls.

E-mail advertising is another recent phenomenon. Unsolicited bulk E-mail advertising is known as "e-mail spam". Spam has been a problem for email users for many years.

Some companies have proposed placing messages or corporate logos on the side of booster rockets and the International Space Station. Controversy exists on the effectiveness of subliminal advertising, and the pervasiveness of mass messages (see propaganda).

Unpaid advertising (also called "publicity advertising"), can provide good exposure at minimal cost. Personal recommendations ("bring a friend", "sell it"), spreading buzz, or achieving the feat of equating a brand with a common noun (in the United States, "Xerox" = "photocopier", "Kleenex" = tissue, "Vaseline" = petroleum jelly, "Hoover" = vacuum cleaner, "Nintendo" (often used by those exposed to many video games) = video games, and "Band-Aid" = adhesive bandage) - these can be seen as the pinnacle of any advertising campaign. However, some companies oppose the use of their brand name to label an object. Equating a brand with a common noun also risks turning that brand into a genericized trademark - turning it into a generic term which means that its legal protection as a trademark is lost.

As the mobile phone became a new mass media in 1998 when the first paid downloadable content appeared on mobile phones in Finland, it was only a matter of time until mobile advertising followed, also first launched in Finland in 2000. By 2007 the value of mobile advertising had reached $2.2 billion and providers such as Admob delivered billions of mobile ads.

More advanced mobile ads include banner ads, coupons, Multimedia Messaging Service picture and video messages, advergames and various engagement marketing campaigns. A particular feature driving mobile ads is the 2D Barcode, which replaces the need to do any typing of web addresses, and uses the camera feature of modern phones to gain immediate access to web content. 83 percent of Japanese mobile phone users already are active users of 2D barcodes.

A new form of advertising that is growing rapidly is social network advertising. It is online advertising with a focus on social networking sites. This is a relatively immature market, but it has shown a lot of promise as advertisers are able to take advantage of the demographic information the user has provided to the social networking site. Friendertising is a more precise advertising term in which people are able to direct advertisements toward others directly using social network service.

From time to time, The CW Television Network airs short programming breaks called "Content Wraps," to advertise one company's product during an entire commercial break. The CW pioneered "content wraps" and some products featured were Herbal Essences, Crest, Guitar Hero II, CoverGirl, and recently Toyota.

Recently, there appeared a new promotion concept, "ARvertising", advertising on Augmented Reality technology.

Chapter—6

Financial Control

Financial controls are a set of procedures (a financial control system) for setting financial objectives or targets, monitoring financial outcomes against those objectives by means of accounting, and analysing the differences (variances) with a view to finding explanations for them. In terms of control theory or cybernetics, budgeting or financial planning represents feed forward control, while accounting statements and variance analysis represent feedback control and are provided by the organisation's management accounting. Variances between targets and outcomes may be used as financial performance indicators.

Financial controls are only part of an organisation's planning and control systems, being directly concerned only with financial targets and outcomes (such as hotel sales revenue, profit margins, cost levels and returns on capital) rather than other key success variables such as product or service quality, staff turnover and market share (see marketing). In general, achievement of financial targets will be associated with meeting other key targets.

However, in the short term tourism and other managers may be able to achieve a financial target such as profit or return on capital by reducing expenses in ways that adversely affect quality. A well-designed financial control system will make it hard for managers to resort to this type of short-termism, for example by monitoring the expenses that are critical to quality against budgeted amounts. Financial controls may be applied at various organisational levels within the tourism industry. At the overall or corporate level, top management will be concerned that the organisation as a whole is performing financially in line with management's own published forecasts for such matters as earnings (or net profit) per share.

Florida's tourism industry serves an estimated 40 million visitors annually. More than 50% of these visitors are hotel guests during some or all of their stay. The waste generated by these guests constitutes a large portion of the state's commercial waste stream. A hotel waste audit showed that majority of waste in a hotel is not produced in the rooms, but in the Food and Beverage Department. If a hotel's waste is not reduced or recycled, it contributes to the state's environmental problems.

Reducing the amount and/or toxicity of materials entering the solid waste stream prior to recycling, treatment, or disposal is waste reduction. This resource management technique can save the hotel and motel industry money while helping the environment. In Florida, over 15 million tons of garbage is landfilled annuallyl despite aggressive statewide, city and county, commercial and residential recycling programs.

Reducing materials at their source, coupled with recovery, reuse and recycling prevents pollution and reduces or eliminates treatment and disposal cost. Recycling should be incorporated into daily operations along with staff training. Each hotel/motel recycling program must be specifically designed to accommodate the hotel's procedures of operation, hotel activities and structural design. A large property can generate as much as 8 tons of waste per day. Up to 60% of this waste is recyclable.2

Many hotels and motels already have some sort of recycling, reduction, reuse program established. A study by the Southern Waste Information Exchange in 2000 revealed that the materials most recovered are:

- 93% corrugated cardboard
- 68% office paper
- 63% printer cartridges
- 54% newspaper

- 49% telephone books
- 42% linens/towels and plastic bottles
- 27% yard waste and magazines
- 25% furniture
- 23% steel cans and scrap metal
- 21% aluminum cans
- 12% computers and televisions
- 10% or less wood and food waste

Florida's hotel/motel industry has been a nationwide leader in resource management, actively participating since the early 1980s.

A characterization of the waste stream of the Wyndham Anatole Hotel in Dallas conducted by The Texas Natural Resource Conservation Commission showed three primary materials; paper was 40%, food waste was 30% and organics from grounds maintenance was nearly 25%.

Educating guests about recycling through guest books, media boards, and in-house television is a great public relations tool that is received favorably by guests. Many guests are familiar with recycling from home or work and are glad to continue the process when in a hotel.

The most effective method for reducing waste is to prevent it in the first place. Ecopurchasing can further reduce the hotel's waste stream. Reducing waste creates a more efficient management program.

How to Get Started

A little research will go a long way. First assess - What are you already doing to reduce, recycle and reuse?

To know this, it is recommended that your homework include the following:

1. Set up a waste reduction committee made up of staff members from each operational area

Explain your team goals and what you are trying to accomplish. Ask what procedures they are using for disposal, cleaning and training of personnel. This committee will gather the preliminary information which will help formulate recommendations and procedures. Appoint a waste reduction coordinator to provide a central point for leadership for this initiative. Reach out to all employees in the early stages of the recycling program and include on-going training. Some of the best ideas will come from your employees.

2. Conduct a waste audit of each operational area

Do a walk through of each area. Identify the recyclable material, source of material and the quantity of the recyclable materials currently being collected or thrown away. This audit will help identify opportunities to reduce waste, conserve water and electricity. Consideration should be given to:

- o Who collects the waste?
- o What type of waste is generated?
- o When is the waste collected?
- o Where is the waste stored until collection?
- o How is the waste collected at the source and diverted to recycling?

This analysis of the composition of waste from a hotel will serve as a valuable planning tool for its waste reduction program.

3. Conduct a waste evaluation

Learn about your waste and do a waste evaluation, which includes examining current and perspective purchasing and disposal cost records. Research your waste disposal costs, options, and alternatives.

4. Evaluate your waste recycler's contract

Insure invoices match written negotiated prices. Have more than just verbal agreements, do written contracts. Some items to consider for the service:

- o What material do you collect?

- o What size container is needed?
- o Do you supply containers?
- o Is there a charge for these containers?
- o Is there a minimum volume or weight requirement for pickup frequency?
- o What are the charges for collection?
- o How frequent is collection?

Most recyclers base charges on operational cost and require a minimum quantity of material. This can create storage issues for back of the house operation. Consider storage when deciding what materials to collect and how materials are collected. Also consider that when fees for recycling and land filling are low, incentives to recycle and practice waste reduction may decrease, whereas increased tipping fees promote waste reduction and recycling.

5. Determine the composition of your waste stream

Classify materials for recycling and initiate other waste reduction activities by determining the composition of your waste stream. Selection of materials disposal method is one of the key considerations before designing a recycling program.

6. Have an auditor evaluate your facility if necessary

Solicit help from the city or county recycling coordinator or contact the Florida Department of Environmental Protection (FDEP) Waste Reduction or Pollution Prevention Program in Tallahassee to have an auditor come out to evaluate your facility.

7. Find out what materials are recycled in your area

Go to Earth 911 (www.earth911.com) and enter your zip code to obtain information about recycling in your area. Most communities have a recycling coordinator that is available to assist or contact FDEP for a list of recyclers.

8. Practice eco-purchasing

Examine the current buying practices. Are you just buying a product because that is the way it has always been done?

Ecopurchasing involves evaluating practices and products not only on price and quality but also on durability, reusability, recyclability and content. This strategy calls for business consumers to think first before purchasing any material or service. It may require changing the way things are done or how a product is packaged. Work with your vendors to get the best value.

9. Design a materials flow plan

A materials flow plan identifies materials, collection, container size and placement, recycling, reuse and disposal.

10. Inform hotel owners and/or corporate management of your recycling initiative

Keep owners and corporate management informed about your waste stream and recycling opportunities that will save time and money. Let them know what you are trying to achieve and ask for their support.

11. Establish an accounting system that reflects monthly waste management costs

Formulate a monthly report for tracking waste disposal and reduction information.

12. Set goals and objectives based on a realistic time line

Working with the committee, set goals and objectives based on a realistic time line. Map out action plans to reach these goals and objectives and assign responsible parties. Practical reduction programs must be periodically evaluated in relationship to the overall economic benefits and impacts to time and manpower usage. Consider sharing recycling with neighboring facilities. Monitor, measure and report progress.

Construction and Demolition (C&D) Waste

Hotels produce large volumes of C&D materials, especially during renovations. These materials are often recyclable depending on the availability of recycling program operated by local, county or city agencies. In particular, clean rubble, concrete, plastics, ferrous metals, drywall, and wood can all be recovered in a C&D

recycling program that includes a program plan with established markets. The opportunities and methods for reducing your C & D waste are:

1. Evaluate options for reducing and recycling C&D waste

Hotels and motels have a variety of options for reducing and recycling C&D waste. Green building techniques may be used in renovation and construction of a hotel. For example, a contractor can reduce wood waste by taking time to measure wood accurately before cutting or donating excess wood material to a local reuse building organization. Untreated wood waste can be collected for composting or mulched and used on site.

2. Contact deconstruction or salvage companies prior to the project to inspect items to be salvaged and determine interest

Some items that could be reused or recycled are wood, light fixtures, ballast, concrete, drywall, doors, and bathroom fixtures.

3. Donate items

Consider donating old or unwanted furniture, light fixtures, bathroom fixtures, doors, drapes, and appliances to a charity or thrift store or make them available to employees. Carpet companies now offer recycling of old carpets and pads if you purchase from them.

4. Reduce excess material

Buy only what is needed and be mindful of dimensions to reduce excess material.

5. Remove unused chemicals and unnecessary items from facility

Have the local chemical waste disposal services remove unused chemicals and unnecessary items from hotel premises.

E-Waste

E-Waste is waste generated from electronic equipment. New technology is making E-waste the fastest growing waste stream in the country. Most items that we have today will be obsolete in three to five years. Some of the items that fall in to this category are land-line telephones, PDAs, cellular phones, computers, keyboards, monitors, hand-held video games, calculators, TVs, VCRs, DVD players, tape recording machines, cameras, video cameras, two-way radios, fax machines, copiers and printers. The following are opportunities and methods for reducing your e-waste:

1. Develop a waste reduction plan for electronics

Electronics are potentially recyclable but contain lead, which can be harmful to the environment if disposed of improperly. All motels and hotels have at least one television in each guest room and many have two. There are additional televisions in lobbies, guest and employee lounges, laundry rooms, bars, restaurants and in-house gyms. Many of the facilities lease their televisions and phone systems that may be connected to providing the cable, satellite service or internet service. This option takes the burden from the hotel and shifts it back to the leasing company. The leasing company recycles these items to other properties or they are sold at the end of the lease (three to five years). Beach hotels may have to replace televisions more often because the salt air tends to corrode the internal components.

2. Recycle or donate used electronics

Most electronics that are placed with the garbage are collected by local junkmen before the collector arrives. Many properties have a system to sell items to their own employees or local residents. Others denote to local charities.

3. Find out about e-waste recycling opportunities in your area

Several stores have recycling opportunities for cell phones. Many counties and cities also have electronic recycling days for their communities. For large quantity recycling, contact your local recycling coordinator to find out what is being done in your area.

Training

Staff training is one of the most important keys to making it all work. You have to train current staff and new staff on the overall program. Short frequent refresher training programs are encouraged. Monitoring is necessary and receiving feed back from personnel is also important to find out what is working and what is not. Quality education and clear communication will result in higher participation.

1. Appoint a person responsible for separating waste for recycling

For general waste disposal, appoint a responsible person to make sure items are separated as they go into dumpsters or main collection containers. This monitoring will help with a load not being rejected due to contamination and incurring a higher disposal cost. It has been demonstrated that the closer the waste generation was monitored, the less the hotels paid for disposal.

2. Provide opportunities for regular feedback

Communication is the key and regular feedback will be necessary to keep a program going. Consider using a newsletter which can get information out to more than one employee at a time. Include how much and what materials are being recovered as well as information on any new efforts to reduce waste further.

3. Determine collection areas

Many hotels have implemented recycling programs, which include collection in the guest room as well as containers in the pool area, lobby, meeting rooms, and other common areas.

Internal Control

In accounting and auditing, internal control is defined as a process effected by an organization's structure, work and authority flows, people and management information systems, designed to help the organization accomplish specific goals or objectives. It is a means by which an organization's resources are directed, monitored, and measured. It plays an important role in preventing and detecting fraud and protecting the organization's resources, both physical (e.g., machinery and property) and intangible (e.g., reputation or intellectual property such as trademarks).

At the organizational level, internal control objectives relate to the reliability of financial reporting, timely feedback on the achievement of operational or strategic goals, and compliance with laws and regulations. At the specific transaction level, internal control refers to the actions taken to achieve a specific objective (e.g., how to ensure the organization's payments to third parties are for valid services rendered.) Internal control procedures reduce process variation, leading to more predictable outcomes.

Internal control is a key element of the Foreign Corrupt Practices Act (FCPA) of 1977 and the Sarbanes-Oxley Act of 2002, which required improvements in internal control in United States public corporations. Internal controls within business entities are also referred to as operational controls.

Internal controls have existed from ancient times. In Hellenistic Egypt there was a dual administration, with one set of bureaucrats charged with collecting taxes and another with supervising them. In the Republic of China, the Control Yuan, one of the five branches of government, is an investigatory agency that monitors the other branches of government.

There are many definitions of internal control, as it affects the various constituencies (stakeholders) of an organization in various ways and at different levels of aggregation.

Under the COSO Internal Control-Integrated Framework, a widely-used framework in the United States, internal control is broadly defined as a process, effected by an entity's board of directors, management, and other personnel, designed to provide reasonable assurance regarding the achievement of objectives in the following categories: a) Effectiveness and efficiency of operations; b) Reliability of financial reporting; and c) Compliance with laws and regulations.

COSO defines internal control as having five components:

1. Control Environment-sets the tone for the organization, influencing the control consciousness of its people. It is the foundation for all other components of internal control.

2. Risk Assessment-the identification and analysis of relevant risks to the achievement of objectives, forming a basis for how the risks should be managed
3. Information and Communication-systems or processes that support the identification, capture, and exchange of information in a form and time frame that enable people to carry out their responsibilities
4. Control Activities-the policies and procedures that help ensure management directives are carried out.
5. Monitoring-processes used to assess the quality of internal control performance over time.

The COSO definition relates to the aggregate control system of the organization, which is composed of many individual control procedures.

Discrete control procedures, or controls are defined by the SEC as: "...a specific set of policies, procedures, and activities designed to meet an objective. A control may exist within a designated function or activity in a process. A control's impact...may be entity-wide or specific to an account balance, class of transactions or application.

Controls have unique characteristics - for example, they can be: automated or manual; reconciliations; segregation of duties; review and approval authorizations; safeguarding and accountability of assets; preventing or detecting error or fraud. Controls within a process may consist of financial reporting controls and operational controls (that is, those designed to achieve operational objectives)."

BUDGET AND PLANNING

More generally, setting objectives, budgets, plans and other expectations establish criteria for control. Control itself exists to keep performance or a state of affairs within what is expected, allowed or accepted. Control built within a process is internal in nature. It takes place with a combination of interrelated components - such as social environment effecting behavior of employees, information necessary in control, and policies and procedures. Internal control structure is a plan determining how internal control consists of these elements.

The concepts of corporate governance also heavily rely on the necessity of internal controls. Internal controls help ensure that processes operate as designed and that risk responses (risk treatments) in risk management are carried out. In addition, there needs to be in place circumstances ensuring that the aforementioned procedures will be performed as intended: right attitudes, integrity and competence, and monitoring by managers.

ROLES AND RESPONSIBILITIES

According to the COSO Framework, everyone in an organization has responsibility for internal control to some extent. Virtually all employees produce information used in the internal control system or take other actions needed to affect control. Also, all personnel should be responsible for communicating upward problems in operations, noncompliance with the code of conduct, or other policy violations or illegal actions. Each major entity in corporate governance has a particular role to play:

Management: The Chief Executive Officer (the top manager) of the organization has overall responsibility for designing and implementing effective internal control. More than any other individual, the chief executive sets the "tone at the top" that affects integrity and ethics and other factors of a positive control environment. In a large company, the chief executive fulfills this duty by providing leadership and direction to senior managers and reviewing the way they're controlling the business.

Senior managers, in turn, assign responsibility for establishment of more specific internal control policies and procedures to personnel responsible for the unit's functions. In a smaller entity, the influence of the chief executive, often an owner-manager, is usually more direct. In any event, in a cascading responsibility, a manager is effectively a chief executive of his or her sphere of responsibility. Of particular significance are financial officers and their staffs, whose control activities cut across, as well as up and down, the operating and other units of an enterprise.

Board of Directors: Management is accountable to the board of directors, which provides governance, guidance and oversight. Effective board members are objective, capable and inquisitive. They also have a knowledge of the entity's activities and environment, and commit the time necessary to fulfill their board responsibilities.

Management may be in a position to override controls and ignore or stifle communications from subordinates, enabling a dishonest management which intentionally misrepresents results to cover its tracks. A strong, active board, particularly when coupled with effective upward communications channels and capable financial, legal and internal audit functions, is often best able to identify and correct such a problem.

Auditors: The internal auditors and external auditors of the organization also measure the effectiveness of internal control through their efforts. They assess whether the controls are properly designed, implemented and working effectively, and make recommendations on how to improve internal control. They may also review Information technology controls, which relate to the IT systems of the organization. There are laws and regulations on internal control related to financial reporting in a number of jurisdictions.

In the U.S. these regulations are specifically established by Sections 404 and 302 of the Sarbanes-Oxley Act. Guidance on auditing these controls is specified in PCAOB Auditing Standard No. 5 and SEC guidance, further discussed in SOX 404 top-down risk assessment. To provide reasonable assurance that internal controls involved in the financial reporting process are effective, they are tested by the external auditor (the organization's public accountants), who are required to opine on the internal controls of the company and the reliability of its financial reporting.

Limitations

Internal control can provide reasonable, not absolute, assurance that the objectives of an organization will be met. The concept of reasonable assurance implies a high degree of assurance, constrained by the costs and benefits of establishing incremental control procedures.

Effective internal control implies the organization generates reliable financial reporting and substantially complies with the laws and regulations that apply to it. However, whether an organization achieves operational and strategic objectives may depend on factors outside the enterprise, such as competition or technological innovation.

These factors are outside the scope of internal control; therefore, effective internal control provides only timely information or feedback on progress towards the achievement of operational and strategic objectives, but cannot guarantee their achievement.

Internal controls may be described in terms of: a) the objective they pertain to; and b) the nature of the control activity itself.

Objective Categorization

Internal control activities are designed to provide reasonable assurance that particular objectives are achieved, or related progress understood. The specific target used to determine whether a control is operating effectively is called the control objective. Control objectives fall under several detailed categories; in financial auditing, they relate to particular financial statement assertions, but broader frameworks are helpful to also capture operational and compliance aspects:

1. Existence (Validity): Only valid or authorized transactions are processed (i.e., no invalid transactions)
2. Occurrence (Cutoff): Transactions occurred during the correct period or were processed timely.
3. Completeness: All transactions are processed that should be (i.e., no omissions)

4. Valuation: Transactions are calculated using an appropriate methodology or are computationally accurate.
5. Rights & Obligations: Assets represent the rights of the company, and liabilities its obligations, as of a given date.
6. Presentation & Disclosure (Classification): Components of financial statements (or other reporting) are properly classified (by type or account) and described.
7. Reasonableness-transactions or results appears reasonable relative to other data or trends.

For example, a control observices received." This is a validity objective. A typical control procedure designed to achieve this objective is: "The accounts payable system compares the purchase order, receiving record, and vendor invoice prior to authorizing payment."

Management is responsible for implementing appropriate controls that apply to transactions in their areas of responsibility. Internal auditors perform their audits to evaluate whether the controls are designed and implemented effectively to address the relevant objectives.

Activity Categorization

Control activities may also be explained by the type or nature of activity. These include (but are not limited to):

- Segregation of duties - separating authorization, custody, and record keeping roles of fraud or error by one person.
- Authorization of transactions - review of particular transactions by an appropriate person.
- Retention of records - maintaining documentation to substantiate transactions.
- Supervision or monitoring of operations - observation or review of ongoing operational activity.
- Physical safeguards - usage of cameras, locks, physical barriers, etc. to protect property, such as merchandise inventory.

- Top-level reviews-analysis of actual results versus organizational goals or plans, periodic and regular operational reviews, metrics, and other key performance indicators (KPIs).
- IT Security - usage of passwords, access logs, etc. to ensure access restricted to authorized personnel.
- Top level reviews-Management review of reports comparing actual performance versus plans, goals, and established objectives.
- Controls over information processing-A variety of control activities are used in information processing. Examples include edit checks of data entered, accounting for transactions in numerical sequences, comparing file totals with control accounts, and controlling access to data, files and programs.

Control Precision

Control precision describes the alignment or correlation between a particular control procedure and a given control objective or risk. A control with direct impact on the achievement of an objective (or mitigation of a risk) is said to be more precise than one with indirect impact on the objective or risk. Precision is distinct from sufficiency; that is, multiple controls with varying degrees of precision may be involved in achieving a control objective or mitigating a risk.

Precision is an important factor in performing a SOX 404 top-down risk assessment. After identifying specific financial reporting material misstatement risks, management and the external auditors are required to identify and test controls that mitigate the risks. This involves making judgments regarding both precision and sufficiency of controls required to mitigate the risks.

Risks and controls may be entity-level or assertion-level under the PCAOB guidance. Entity-level controls are identified to address entity-level risks. However, a combination of entity-level and assertion-level controls are typically identified to address assertion-level risks. The PCAOB set forth a three-level hierarchy for considering the precision of entity-level controls. Later guidance by the PCAOB regarding small public firms provided several factors to consider in assessing precision.

Fraud and Internal Control

Internal control plays an important role in the prevention and detection of fraud. Under the Sarbanes-Oxley Act, companies are required to perform a fraud risk assessment and assess related controls. This typically involves identifying scenarios in which theft or loss could occur and determining if existing control procedures effectively manage the risk to an acceptable level. The risk that senior management might override important financial controls to manipulate financial reporting is also a key area of focus in fraud risk assessment.

The AICPA, IIA, and ACFE also sponsored a guide published during 2008 that includes a framework for helping organizations manage their fraud risk.

Internal Controls and Improvement

If the internal control system is implemented only to prevent fraud and comply with laws and regulations, then an important opportunity is missed. The same internal controls can also be used to systematically improve businesses, particularly in regard to effectiveness and efficiency.

Continuous Controls Monitoring

Advances in technology and data analysis have led to the development of numerous tools which can automatically evaluate the effectiveness of internal controls. Used in conjunction with continuous auditing, continuous controls monitoring provides assurance on financial information flowing through the business processes.

Risk Management

The strategies to manage risk include transferring the risk to another party, avoiding the risk, reducing the negative effect of the risk, and accepting some or all of the consequences of a particular risk.Certain aspects of many of the risk management standards have come under criticism for having no measurable improvement on risk even though the confidence in estimates and decisions increase.

Risk management is the identification, assessment, and prioritization of risks followed by coordinated and economical application of resources to minimize, monitor, and control the probability and/or impact of unfortunate events or to maximize the realization of opportunities.

Risks can come from uncertainty in financial markets, project failures, legal liabilities, credit risk, accidents, natural causes and disasters as well as deliberate attacks from an adversary. Several risk management standards have been developed including the Project Management Institute, the National Institute of Science and Technology, actuarial societies, and ISO standards.

Methods, definitions and goals vary widely according to whether the risk management method is in the context of project management, security, engineering, industrial processes, financial portfolios, actuarial assessments, or public health and safety.

In ideal risk management, a prioritization process is followed whereby the risks with the greatest loss and the greatest probability of occurring are handled first, and risks with lower probability of occurrence and lower loss are handled in descending order. In practice the process can be very difficult, and balancing between risks with a high probability of occurrence but lower loss versus a risk with high loss but lower probability of occurrence can often be mishandled.

Intangible risk management identifies a new type of a risk that has a 100% probability of occurring but is ignored by the organization due to a lack of identification ability. For example, when deficient knowledge is applied to a situation, a knowledge risk materializes. Relationship risk appears when ineffective collaboration occurs. Process-engagement risk may be an issue when ineffective operational procedures are applied. These risks directly reduce the productivity of knowledge workers, decrease cost effectiveness, profitability, service, quality, reputation, brand value, and earnings quality. Intangible risk management allows risk management to create immediate value from the identification and reduction of risks that reduce productivity.

Risk management also faces difficulties in allocating resources. This is the idea of opportunity cost. Resources spent on risk management could have been spent on more profitable activities. Again, ideal risk management minimizes spending and minimizes the negative effects of risks.

Method

For the most part, these methods consist of the following elements, performed, more or less, in the following order.

1. identify, characterize, and assess threats
2. assess the vulnerability of critical assets to specific threats
3. determine the risk (i.e. the expected consequences of specific types of attacks on specific assets)
4. identify ways to reduce those risks
5. prioritize risk reduction measures based on a strategy

Principles of Risk Management

The International Organization for Standardization (ISO) identifies the following principles of risk management:

Risk management should:

- create value
- be an integral part of organizational processes
- be part of decision making
- explicitly address uncertainty

- be systematic and structured
- be based on the best available information
- be tailored
- take into account human factors
- be transparent and inclusive
- be dynamic, iterative and responsive to change
- be capable of continual improvement and enhancement

Process

According to the standard ISO 31000 "Risk management -- Principles and guidelines on implementation," the process of risk management consists of several steps as follows:

Establishing the Context

Establishing the context involves:

1. Identification of risk in a selected domain of interest
2. Planning the remainder of the process.
3. Mapping out the following:
   - o the social scope of risk management
   - o the identity and objectives of stakeholders
   - o the basis upon which risks will be evaluated, constraints.
4. Defining a framework for the activity and an agenda for identification.
5. Developing an analysis of risks involved in the process.
6. Mitigation or Solution of risks using available technological, human and organizational resources.

Identification

After establishing the context, the next step in the process of managing risk is to identify potential risks. Risks are about events that, when triggered, cause problems. Hence, risk identification can start with the source of problems, or with the problem itself.

- Source analysis Risk sources may be internal or external to the system that is the target of risk management.

Examples of risk sources are: stakeholders of a project, employees of a company or the weather over an airport.

- Problem analysis Risks are related to identified threats. For example: the threat of losing money, the threat of abuse of privacy information or the threat of accidents and casualties. The threats may exist with various entities, most important with shareholders, customers and legislative bodies such as the government.

When either source or problem is known, the events that a source may trigger or the events that can lead to a problem can be investigated. For example: stakeholders withdrawing during a project may endanger funding of the project; privacy information may be stolen by employees even within a closed network; lightning striking an aircraft during takeoff may make all people onboard immediate casualties.

The chosen method of identifying risks may depend on culture, industry practice and compliance. The identification methods are formed by templates or the development of templates for identifying source, problem or event. Common risk identification methods are:

- Objectives-based risk identification Organizations and project teams have objectives. Any event that may endanger achieving an objective partly or completely is identified as risk.
- Scenario-based risk identification In scenario analysis different scenarios are created. The scenarios may be the alternative ways to achieve an objective, or an analysis of the interaction of forces in, for example, a market or battle. Any event that triggers an undesired scenario alternative is identified as risk - see Futures Studies for methodology used by Futurists.
- Taxonomy-based risk identification The taxonomy in taxonomy-based risk identification is a breakdown of

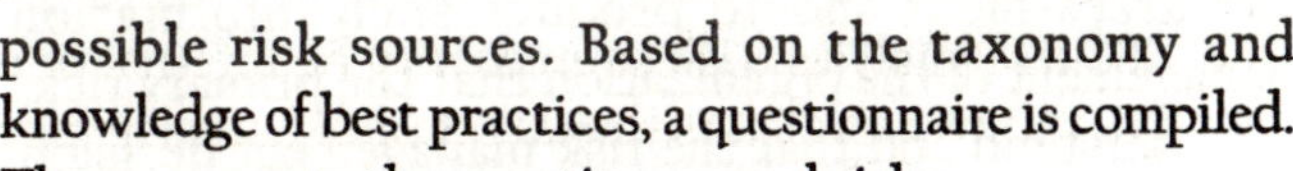

possible risk sources. Based on the taxonomy and knowledge of best practices, a questionnaire is compiled. The answers to the questions reveal risks.

- Common-risk checking In several industries, lists with known risks are available. Each risk in the list can be checked for application to a particular situation.
- Risk charting This method combines the above approaches by listing resources at risk, Threats to those resources Modifying Factors which may increase or decrease the risk and Consequences it is wished to avoid. Creating a matrix under these headings enables a variety of approaches. One can begin with resources and consider the threats they are exposed to and the consequences of each. Alternatively one can start with the threats and examine which resources they would affect, or one can begin with the consequences and determine which combination of threats and resources would be involved to bring them about.

Assessment

Once risks have been identified, they must then be assessed as to their potential severity of loss and to the probability of occurrence. These quantities can be either simple to measure, in the case of the value of a lost building, or impossible to know for sure in the case of the probability of an unlikely event occurring. Therefore, in the assessment process it is critical to make the best educated guesses possible in order to properly prioritize the implementation of the risk management plan.

The fundamental difficulty in risk assessment is determining the rate of occurrence since statistical information is not available on all kinds of past incidents. Furthermore, evaluating the severity of the consequences (impact) is often quite difficult for immaterial assets. Asset valuation is another question that needs to be addressed. Thus, best educated opinions and available statistics are the primary sources of information. Nevertheless, risk assessment should produce such information for the management of the organization that the primary risks are easy to understand and that the risk management decisions may be prioritized. Thus, there have been several theories and attempts to quantify risks. Numerous different risk formulae exist, but perhaps the most widely accepted formula for risk quantification is:

Risk Avoidance

This includes not performing an activity that could carry risk. An example would be not buying a property or business in order to not take on the legal liability that comes with it. Another would be not flying in order not to take the risk that the airplane were to be hijacked.

Avoidance may seem the answer to all risks, but avoiding risks also means losing out on the potential gain that accepting (retaining) the risk may have allowed. Not entering a business to avoid the risk of loss also avoids the possibility of earning profits.

Hazard Prevention

Hazard prevention refers to the prevention of risks in an emergency. The first and most effective stage of hazard prevention is the elimination of hazards. If this takes too long, is too costly, or is otherwise impractical, the second stage is mitigation.

Risk Reduction

Risk reduction or "optimization" involves reducing the severity of the loss or the likelihood of the loss from occurring. For example, sprinklers are designed to put out a fire to reduce the risk of loss by fire. This method may cause a greater loss by water damage and therefore may not be suitable. Halon fire suppression systems may mitigate that risk, but the cost may be prohibitive as a strategy.

Acknowledging that risks can be positive or negative, optimising risks means finding a balance between negative risk and the benefit of the operation or activity; and between risk reduction and effort applied. By an offshore drilling contractor effectively applying HSE Management in its organisation, it can optimise risk to achieve levels of residual risk that are tolerable.

Modern software development methodologies reduce risk by developing and delivering software incrementally. Early methodologies suffered from the fact that they only delivered software in the final phase of development; any problems encountered in earlier phases meant costly rework and often jeopardized the whole project. By developing in iterations, software projects can limit effort wasted to a single iteration.

Outsourcing could be an example of risk reduction if the outsourcer can demonstrate higher capability at managing or reducing risks. For example, a company may outsource only its software development, the manufacturing of hard goods, or customer support needs to another company, while handling the business management itself. This way, the company can concentrate more on business development without having to worry as much about the manufacturing process, managing the development team, or finding a physical location for a call center.

Risk Sharing

The term of 'risk transfer' is often used in place of risk sharing in the mistaken belief that you can transfer a risk to a third party through insurance or outsourcing. In practice if the insurance company or contractor go bankrupt or end up in court, the original risk is likely to still revert to the first party.

As such in the terminology of practitioners and scholars alike, the purchase of an insurance contract is often described as a "transfer of risk." However, technically speaking, the buyer of the contract generally retains legal responsibility for the losses "transferred", meaning that insurance may be described more accurately as a post-event compensatory mechanism.

Some ways of managing risk fall into multiple categories. Risk retention pools are technically retaining the risk for the group, but spreading it over the whole group involves transfer among individual members of the group. This is different from traditional insurance, in that no premium is exchanged between members of the group up front, but instead losses are assessed to all members of the group.

Risk Retention

Involves accepting the loss, or benefit of gain, from a risk when it occurs. True self insurance falls in this category. Risk retention is a viable strategy for small risks where the cost of insuring against the risk would be greater over time than the total losses sustained. All risks that are not avoided or transferred are retained by default. This includes risks that are so large or catastro

War is an example since most property and risks are not insured against war, so the loss attributed by war is retained by the insured. Also any amounts of potential loss (risk) over the amount insured is retained risk. This may also be acceptable if the chance of a very large loss is small or if the cost to insure for greater coverage amounts is so great it would hinder the goals of the organization too much.

Create a Risk Management Plan

Select appropriate controls or countermeasures to measure each risk. Risk mitigation needs to be approved by the appropriate level of management. For instance, a risk concerning the image of the organization should have top management decision behind it whereas IT management would have the authority to decide on computer virus risks.

The risk management plan should propose applicable and effective security controls for managing the risks. For example, an observed high risk of computer viruses could be mitigated by acquiring and implementing antivirus software. A good risk management plan should contain a schedule for control implementation and responsible persons for those actions.

Implementation

Implementation follows all of the planned methods for mitigating the effect of the risks. Purchase insurance policies for the risks that have been decided to be transferred to an insurer, avoid all risks that can be avoided without sacrificing the entity's goals, reduce others, and retain the rest.

Review and Evaluation of the Plan

Initial risk management plans will never be perfect. Practice, experience, and actual loss results will necessitate changes in the plan and contribute information to allow possible different decisions to be made in dealing with the risks being faced.

Risk analysis results and management plans should be updated periodically. There are two primary reasons for this:

1. to evaluate whether the previously selected security controls are still applicable and effective, and
2. to evaluate the possible risk level changes in the business environment. For example, information risks are a good example of rapidly changing business environment.

Limitations

If risks are improperly assessed and prioritized, time can be wasted in dealing with risk of losses that are not likely to occur. Spending too much time assessing and managing unlikely risks can divert resources that could be used more profitably. Unlikely events do occur but if the risk is unlikely enough to occur it may be better to simply retain the risk and deal with the result if the loss does in fact occur. Qualitative risk assessment is subjective and lacks consistency. The primary justification for a formal risk assessment process is legal and bureaucratic.

Prioritizing the risk management processes too highly could keep an organization from ever completing a project or even getting started. This is especially true if other work is suspended until the risk management process is considered complete.

It is also important to keep in mind the distinction between risk and uncertainty. Risk can be measured by impacts x probability.

Areas of Risk Management

As applied to corporate finance, risk management is the technique for measuring, monitoring and controlling the financial or operational risk on a firm's balance sheet. See value at risk.

The Basel II framework breaks risks into market risk (price risk), credit risk and operational risk and also specifies methods for calculating capital requirements for each of these components.

Enterprise Risk Management

In enterprise risk management, a risk is defined as a possible event or circumstance that can have negative influences on the enterprise in question. Its impact can be on the very existence, the resources (human and capital), the products and services, or the customers of the enterprise, as well as external impacts on society, markets, or the environment. In a financial institution, enterprise risk management is normally thought of as the combination of credit risk, interest rate risk or asset liability management, market risk, and operational risk.

In the more general case, every probable risk can have a pre-formulated plan to deal with its possible consequences. From the information above and the average cost per employee over time, or cost accrual ratio, a project manager can estimate:

- the cost associated with the risk if it arises, estimated by multiplying employee costs per unit time by the estimated time lost (cost impact, C where C = cost accrual ratio * S).
- the probable increase in time associated with a risk (schedule variance due to risk, Rs where Rs = P * S):

  Sorting on this value puts the highest risks to the schedule first. This is intended to cause the greatest risks to the project to be attempted first so that risk is minimized as quickly as possible.

  This is slightly misleading as schedule variances with a large P and small S and vice versa are not equivalent. (The risk of the RMS Titanic sinking vs. the passengers' meals being served at slightly the wrong time).

- the probable increase in cost associated with a risk (cost variance due to risk, Rc where Rc = P*C = P*CAR*S = P*S*CAR)

  sorting on this value puts the highest risks to the budget first.

  see concerns about schedule variance as this is a function of it, as illustrated in the equation above.

Risk in a project or process can be due either to Special Cause Variation or Common Cause Variation and requires appropriate treatment. That is to re-iterate the concern about extremal cases not being equivalent in the list immediately above.

Risk Management Activities as Applied to Project Management

In project management, risk management includes the following activities:

- Planning how risk will be managed in the particular project. Plans should include risk management tasks, responsibilities, activities and budget.
- Assigning a risk officer - a team member other than a project manager who is responsible for foreseeing potential project problems. Typical characteristic of risk officer is a healthy skepticism.
- Maintaining live project risk database. Each risk should have the following attributes: opening date, title, short description, probability and importance. Optionally a risk may have an assigned person responsible for its resolution and a date by which the risk must be resolved.
- Creating anonymous risk reporting channel. Each team member should have possibility to report risk that he/she foresees in the project.
- Preparing mitigation plans for risks that are chosen to be mitigated. The purpose of the mitigation plan is to describe how this particular risk will be handled - what, when, by

who and how will it be done to avoid it or minimize consequences if it becomes a liability.

Risk Management for Megaprojects

Megaprojects (sometimes also called "major programs") are extremely large-scale investment projects, typically costing more than US$1 billion per project. Megaprojects include bridges, tunnels, highways, railways, airports, seaports, power plants, dams, wastewater projects, coastal flood protection schemes, oil and natural gas extraction projects, public buildings, information technology systems, aerospace projects, and defence systems. Megaprojects have been shown to be particularly risky in terms of finance, safety, and social and environmental impacts. Risk management is therefore particularly pertinent for megaprojects and special methods and special education have been developed for such risk management.

Risk Management of Information Technology

IT risk is a risk related to information technology. This relatively new term due to an increasing awareness that information security is simply one facet of a multitude of risks that are relevant to IT and the real world processes it supports. A number of methodologies have been developed to deal with this kind of risk.

Risk Management Techniques in Petroleum and Natural Gas

For the offshore oil and gas industry, operational risk management is regulated by the safety case regime in many countries. Hazard identification and risk assessment tools and techniques are described in the international standard ISO 17776:2000, and organisations such as the IADC (International Association of Drilling Contractors) publish guidelines for HSE Case development which are based on the ISO standard.

Further, diagrammatic representations of hazardous events are often expected by governmental regulators as part of risk management in safety case submissions; these are known as bow-tie diagrams. The technique is also used by organisations and regulators in mining, aviation, health, defence, industrial and finance.

Risk Management and Business Continuity

Risk management is simply a practice of systematically selecting cost effective approaches for minimising the effect of threat realization to the organization. All risks can never be fully avoided or mitigated simply because of financial and practical limitations. Therefore all organizations have to accept some level of residual risks.

Whereas risk management tends to be preemptive, business continuity planning (BCP) was invented to deal with the consequences of realised residual risks. The necessity to have BCP in place arises because even very unlikely events will occur if given enough time. Risk management and BCP are often mistakenly seen as rivals or overlapping practices. In fact these processes are so tightly tied together that such separation seems artificial. For example, the risk management process creates important inputs for the BCP (assets, impact assessments, cost estimates etc.).

Risk management also proposes applicable controls for the observed risks. Therefore, risk management covers several areas that are vital for the BCP process. However, the BCP process goes beyond risk management's preemptive approach and assumes that the disaster will happen at some point.

Risk Communication

Risk communication is a complex cross-disciplinary academic field. Problems for risk communicators involve how to reach the intended audience, to make the risk comprehensible and relatable to other risks, how to pay appropriate respect to the audience's values related to the risk, how to predict the audience's response to the communication, etc. A main goal of risk communication is to improve collective and individual decision making. Risk communication is somewhat related to crisis communication.

Bow Tie Diagrams

A popular solution to the quest to communicate risks and their treatments effectively is to use bow tie diagrams. These have been effective, for example, in a public forum to model perceived risks and communicate precautions, during the planning stage of offshore oil and gas facilities in Scotland.

Equally, the technique is used for HAZID (Hazard Identification) workshops of all types, and results in a high level of engagement. For this reason (amongst others) an increasing number of government regulators for major hazard facilities (MHFs), offshore oil & gas, aviation, etc. welcome safety case submissions which use diagrammatic representation of risks at their core.

Communication advantages of bow tie diagrams:

- Visual illustration of the hazard, its causes, consequences, controls, and how controls fail.
- The bow tie diagram can be readily understood at all personnel levels.
- "A picture paints a thousand words."

Seven cardinal rules for the practice of risk communication

- Accept and involve the public/other consumers as legitimate partners.
- Plan carefully and evaluate your efforts with a focus on your strengths, weaknesses, opportunities, and threats.
- Listen to the public's specific concerns.
- Be honest, frank, and open.
- Coordinate and collaborate with other credible sources.
- Meet the needs of the media.
- Speak clearly and with compassion.

Communications and Information Department

Hospitality communication in the workplace is always an important issue which is constantly addressed by employers and staff alike. Excellent communication is a vital issue, because customers are paying not only for the product - the food, the room or the facilities - they are also paying for the service. And service is just as much about communication as it is about skill.

When speaking of hospitality, people have very high standards. Even if you have the very best hotel in Philadelphia it will not make a difference if you can't establish to your customers that they are important to you. Every faculty member that you employ has to be happy to take the individual whims of each one walking through the door into consideration. If they don't do a good job of presenting the business then it can be in dire straits soon.

Proper training is important in the hospitality industry. Those that aren't up to par shouldn't be working in it. If they have the right idea about what is expected of them though most will do a remarkable job. Don't assume they know or leave things open to interpretation. Of course there are situations that come up that they will not know how to deal with. When that comes about they need to have a chain of command to go through in order to get a resolution that that client is going to be happy with.

There are various hotels to choose from, and most of them offer similar prices and accommodations in Philadelphia. It is the personalized services that are going to make a large difference in someone experience. When a guest needs help with transportation, directions, or needs information about an activity in town they should be able to get that information from the hotel.

When your guests want to be able to get fantastic food to eat it should be offered to them. If the hotel doesn't have a restaurant, then a list of delivery locations or restaurants in the area should be provided. Assistance with luggage, internet connections, and anything else that may be of use all needs to be made available.

In order for the hospitality industry public relations to work effectively, it has to be continually updated and adapted. Being able to get the very best information when they need it makes guests feel great in your ability to cater to them. If they need something like extra towels in their room it shouldn't be complicated to get. It also should be taken care of immediately because their time is important.

The demand for conference rooms is common at Philadelphia hotels. Most of the people hosting them won't be coming to the area until the days right before the event. They need to be confident who they speak with on the phone or via email is handling their needs effectively. Everything should be taken care of so that the host can just show up and use those facilities as they need to.

More weight is placed on the hospitality aspects of any hotel in Philadelphia than you might think. The information is going to get out there to the public regarding how great an event is handled or what is lacking. Do your part to make sure the information circulating about you is very positive. It is a good idea to check out that information from time to time as well. If you find that information isn't' what you would like it to be, take steps to make improvements. Utilizing this information should help you have a better grasp on the need of well managed public relations in the hospitality field.

Hospitality communication covers two important areas: customer service, and 'behind the scenes' staff and management interaction. Good communication in both areas is essential for the high standards of operation everyone expects in the industry.

The ability to communicate is the primary factor that distinguishes human beings from animals. And it is the ability to communicate well that distinguishes one individual from another.

The fact, is that apart from the basic necessities, one needs to be equipped with habits for good communication skills, as this is what will make them a happy and successful social being. In order to develop these habits, one needs to first acknowledge the fact that they need to improve communication skills from time to time.

They need to take stock of the way they interact and the direction in which their work and personal relations are going. The only constant in life is change, and the more one accepts one's strengths and works towards dealing with their shortcomings, especially in the area of communication skills, the better will be their interactions and the more their social popularity.

The dominating question that comes here is: How to improve communication skills? Well, the answer is simple. One can find plenty of literature on this. There are also experts, who conduct workshops and seminars based on communication skills of men and women. In fact, a large number of companies are bringing in trainers to regularly conduct sessions on the subject, in order to help their work force maintain better interpersonal work relations.

Today, effective communication skills has become a predominant factor even while recruiting employees. While interviewing candidates, most interviewers judge them on the basis of the way they communicate. They believe that skills can be improvised on the job; but ability to communicate well is important, as every employee becomes the representing face of the company.

There are trainers, who specialize in delivering custom-made programs on the subject. Through the session they not only facilitate better skills in the department of communications, but also look into the problems that come in the way of being able to convey messages effectively. They discuss these issues with the management and then sought to design programs accordingly.

For instance, time mismanagement becomes a cause for stress and frustration, which then hampers the possibility of healthy communications at work. Then in weeks to come the company organizes a program on time management. Thus, a workshop on communication skills helps the management t to deal with the finer employee nuances about which they lack awareness.

Designing quality service is an important issue in today's world of competition in the tourism industry and in particular in the hotel sector. Although numerous resources are available on the subject of service quality design, only a few have provided a comprehensive framework and rarely have taken customer point of view in their studies. This study attends to propose a comprehensive framework for designing hotel service quality from customer's point of view. Hospitality firms, such as hotels, are an ideal example of a market which could benefit from the implementation of service innovation. First, from a customer's perspective, the hospitality market is perpetually inundated by many similar, often easily substitutable service offerings. This can cause difficulties for hotel managers as they attempt to differentiate an individual hotel from its competitors.

One solution to this challenge may be to offer new and innovative features to customers. Secondly, the hospitality industry is rapidly changing due to accelerations in information technology. This research try to show the importance of service quality management for providing better service in hotels to the guests, based on guests points of view.

The benefits of offer higher service quality have influence on both hotel sector and customers. Some of these advantages are, competitive advantages, management leadership, productivity improvement, work development, reduce costs and economic profits, employees satisfaction and increase their working value, staff empowerment, involvement, communication and teamwork, commitment on the different parts of management, customer satisfaction, customer loyalty, the benefit of this resources has influence on hotel sector and guests, innovation is an important value.

The Importance of Hospitality Communication in the Customer Service Level:

A client may have a bad day, or be in a bad mood, but a genuine smile from the receptionist and a warm welcome from all the staff might just change their outlook for the rest of that day and the days to come.

The same applies for the waitperson at the restaurant, the housekeeping or maintenance staff, or any other employee that comes in contact with the guests. A caring, positive atmosphere makes the difference between just a place you pass through and a place your guests will remember.

Employees in the hospitality industry must remember that "service with a smile" is not just a logo - it's what clients expect. It requires a positive attitude 100% of the time, even if you are having a bad day or you are tired - the customer is paying for your smile, not your frown. It requires patience when dealing with customers from overseas who have a hard time making themselves understood in English.

It requires 'putting up' with grumpy people or ones who's manners are not always impeccable - because, up to a certain point, 'the customer is always right'. These are situations that staff learn to deal with and they take pride in the professional manner in which they handle 'difficult customers'.

Other important aspect of hospitality communication with customers is providing clear and useful information when asked by customers. Restaurant staff should know the menu inside out, understand special dietary requirements, know about the source of the ingredients they are serving, etc.

Reception staff at the hotel should be up-to-date not only with the facilities and services that the hotel offers, but also with all the other information travellers need: activities, transport, eating and entertainment, and opening hours of shops and agencies. It is part of the service, and guests appreciate well-informed and courteous staff - it can make a difference between "just another day" and a memorable day.

Importance of Hospitality Communication between Staff and Management:

Employers should take the time to explain and train their employees to always maintain a warm, welcoming and professional environment in the workplace, not only where customers are concerned, but also among the staff themselves.

An employer can do a lot to promote a positive atmosphere for the staff; a nice staff room with facilities for workers to relax during their breaks will let them know they are valued, that the boss cares about them. This small investment will pay off by having loyal staff who are willing to give a little extra because they feel it is appreciated.

Good communication between management and staff will be passed down the line in the form of good communication between staff and guests. Making sure that staff has all the 'tools of their trade' to do their job to the highest standards is a two-way thing - employees have to communicate clearly and on time what they need, and management should listen and make sure they are well informed of all their staff's requirements and needs.

Smiling, happy staff is one of management's most important assets in the hospitality industry. Therefore, people who are looking at a career in this sector should know that the skills required include 'people skills' - understanding, patience, the ability to perform well as a team, and, above all, a positive disposition. Bad tempered people have no place in the hospitality industry - it's a place where people come to relax and enjoy themselves. A happy and relaxed atmosphere is what anyone entering the facility should immediately feel, and if staff and management can communicate this at all times, they can be assured that their guests will be coming back for more.

RECEPTIONIST

A receptionist is an employee taking an office/administrative support position. The work is usually performed in a waiting area such as a lobby or front office desk of an organization or business. The title 'receptionist' is attributed to the person who is specifically employed by an organization to receive or greet any visitors, patients, or clients and answer telephone calls.

The business duties of a receptionist may include answering visitors' inquiries about a company and its products or services, directing visitors to their destinations, sorting and handing out mail, answering incoming calls on multi-line telephones or, earlier in the 20th century, a switchboard, setting appointments, filing, records keeping, keyboarding/data entry and performing a variety of other office tasks, such as faxing or emailing. Some receptionists may also perform bookkeeping or cashiering duties. Some, but not all, offices may expect the receptionist to serve coffee or tea to guests, and to keep the lobby area tidy.

A receptionist may also assume some security guard access control functions for an organization by verifying employee identification, issuing visitor passes, and observing and reporting any unusual or suspicious persons or activities.

A receptionist is often the first business contact a person will meet at any organization. It is an expectation of most organizations that the receptionist maintains a calm, courteous and professional demeanor at all times regardless of the visitor's behavior.

Some personal qualities that a receptionist is expected to possess in order to do the job successfully include attentiveness, a well-groomed appearance, initiative, loyalty, maturity, respect for confidentiality and discretion, a positive attitude and dependability. At times, the job may be stressful due to interaction with many different people with different types of personalities, and being expected to perform multiple tasks quickly.

Depending upon the industry, a receptionist position can be considered a low-ranking, dead-end or servile position, or it could be perceived as having a certain veneer of glamor with opportunities for networking in order to advance to other positions within a specific field. Some people may use this type of job as a way to familiarize themselves with office work, or to learn of other functions or positions within a corporation. Some people use receptionist work as a way to earn money while pursuing further educational opportunities or other career interests such as in the performing arts or as writers.

While many persons working as receptionists continue in that position throughout their careers, some receptionists may advance to other administrative jobs, such as a customer service representative, dispatcher, interviewers, secretary, production assistant, personal assistant, or executive assistant.

In smaller businesses, such as a doctor's or a lawyer's office, a receptionist may also be the office manager who is charged with a diversity of middle management level business operations. For example, in the hotel industry, the night-time receptionist's role is almost always combined with performing daily account consolidation and reporting, more particularly known as night auditing.

When receptionists leave the job, they often enter other career fields such as sales and marketing, public relations or other media occupations.

A few famous people were receptionists in the beginning, such as Betty Williams, a co-recipient of the 1976 Nobel Peace Prize. A number of celebrities had worked as receptionists before they became famous, such as singer/songwriter Naomi Judd and the late entrepreneur/Beatle wife Linda McCartney. Other famous people who began their careers as receptionists or worked in the field include civil rights activist Rosa Parks and former Hewlett-Packard CEO Carly Fiorina.

The advancement of office automation has eliminated some receptionists' jobs. For example, a telephone call could be answered by an Automated attendant. However, a receptionist who possesses strong office/technical skills and who is also adept in courtesy, tact and diplomacy is still considered an asset to a company's business image, and is still very much in demand in the business world.

With the recent development in optical fiber technology, some small-to-medium-sized business owners hire a live remote receptionist in lieu of a full-time, in-house receptionist.

As the phrase itself suggests, a live remote receptionist deals with phone calls for a company in another location using telephony private branch exchange (PBX) servers. Often, the responsibilities of a live remote receptionist include, but are not limited to live phone answering, live call screening/forwarding, appointment scheduling, customized greetings, flexible call routing, email and fax services, order taking, voicemail services, and message taking.

INFORMATION MANAGEMENT

Information management (IM) is the collection and management of information from one or more sources and the distribution of that information to one or more audiences. This sometimes involves those who have a stake in, or a right to that information. Management means the organization of and control over the structure, processing and delivery of information.

Throughout the 1970s this was largely limited to files, file maintenance, and the life cycle management of paper-based files, other media and records. With the proliferation of information technology starting in the 1970s, the job of information management took on a new light, and also began to include the field of Data maintenance.

No longer was information management a simple job that could be performed by almost anyone. An understanding of the technology involved, and the theory behind it became necessary. As information storage shifted to electronic means, this became more and more difficult.

By the late 1990s when information was regularly disseminated across computer networks and by other electronic means, network managers, in a sense, became information managers. Those individuals found themselves tasked with increasingly complex tasks, hardware and software. With the latest tools available, information management has become a powerful resource and a large expense for many organizations.

In short, information management entails organizing, retrieving, acquiring and maintaining information. It is closely related to and overlapping with the practice of Data Management.

Information Management Concepts

Following the behavioral science theory of management, mainly developed at Carnegie Mellon University and prominently represented by Barnard, Richard M. Cyert, March and Simon, most of what goes on in service organizations is actually decision making and information processes. The crucial factor in the information and decision process analysis is thus individuals' limited ability to process information and to make decisions under these limitations.

According to March and Simon, organizations have to be considered as cooperative systems with a high level of information processing and a vast need for decision making at various levels. They also claimed that there are factors that would prevent individuals from acting strictly rational, in opposite to what has been proposed and advocated by classic theorists

Instead of using the model of the economic man, as advocated in classic theory, they proposed the administrative man as an alternative based on their argumentation about the cognitive limits of rationality.

While the theories developed at Carnegie Mellon clearly filled some theoretical gaps in the discipline, March and Simon did not propose a certain organizational form that they considered especially feasible for coping with cognitive limitations and bounded rationality of decision-makers. Through their own argumentation against normative decision-making models, i.e., models that prescribe people how they ought to choose, they also abandoned the idea of an ideal organizational form.

In addition to the factors mentioned by March and Simon, there are two other considerable aspects, stemming from environmental and organizational dynamics. Firstly, it is not possible to access, collect and evaluate all environmental information being relevant for taking a certain decision at a reasonable price, i.e., time and effort.

In other words, following a national economic framework, the transaction cost associated with the information process is too high. Secondly, established organizational rules and procedures can prevent the taking of the most appropriate decision, i.e., that a sub-optimum solution is chosen in accordance to organizational rank structure or institutional rules, guidelines and procedures, an issue that also has been brought forward as a major critique against the principles of bureaucratic organizations.

Environmental management. Instead of adapting to changing environmental circumstances, the organization can seek to modify its environment. Vertical and horizontal collaboration, i.e. cooperation or integration with other organizations in the industry value system are typical means of reducing uncertainty. An example of reducing uncertainty in relation to the prior or demanding stage of the industry system is the concept of Supplier-Retailer collaboration or Efficient Customer Response.

Creation of slack resources. In order to reduce exceptions, performance levels can be reduced, thus decreasing the information load on the hierarchy. These additional slack resources, required to reduce information processing in the hierarchy, represent an additional cost to the organization. The choice of this method clearly depends on the alternative costs of other strategies.

Creation of self-contained tasks. Achieving a conceptual closure of tasks is another way of reducing information processing. In this case, the task-performing unit has all the resources required to perform the task. This approach is concerned with task (de-)composition and interaction between different organizational units, i.e. organizational and information interfaces.

Creation of lateral relations. In this case, lateral decision processes are established that cut across functional organizational units. The aim is to apply a system of decision subsidiarity, i.e. to move decision power to the process, instead of moving information from the process into the hierarchy for decision-making.

Investment in vertical information systems. Instead of processing information through the existing hierarchical channels, the organization can establish vertical information systems. In this case, the information flow for a specific task (or set of tasks) is routed in accordance to the applied business logic, rather than the hierarchical organization.

Following the lateral relations concept, it also becomes possible to employ an organizational form that is different from the simple hierarchical information. The Matrix organization is aiming at bringing together the functional and product departmental bases and achieving a balance in information processing and decision making between the vertical (hierarchical) and the horizontal (product or project) structure. The creation of a matrix organization can also be considered as management's response to a persistent or permanent demand for adaptation to environmental dynamics, instead of the response to episodic demands.

Chief Communications Officer

The chief communications officer or CCO is a job title for the head of communications, public relations, social media and/or public affairs within an organization. Most typically, the CCO reports to the chief executive officer (CEO) of a corporate entity. The CCO is part of the executive team and typically reports to the CEO and is an advisor to the board. (see organizational structures at Fortune 500 companies including www.deere.com; www.walmart.com; www.pepsico.com;)

The CCO of a company is the corporate officer primarily responsible for managing the communications risks and opportunities of a business, both internally and externally. This executive is typically responsible for communications to a wide range of stakeholders, including but not limited to employees, shareholders, media, bloggers, influential members of the business community, the press, the community and the public.

Typically, the CCO may partner with others in the organization to communicate with investors, analysts, customers and company Board members. Most organizations will rely on the CCO to advise and participate in decisions that may impact the ongoing reputation of the firm.

The Chief Communications Officer role is further defined by the Arthur Page Society. This study indicates the importance in the role especially as a key advisor to the CEO. In addition to the Chief Communications Officer title, comparable titles include Vice President of Corporate Communications and Vice President of Public Affairs.

QUALIFICATIONS

Qualifications of the CCO typically include communications experience with multiple stakeholder groups. Early experience may include journalism, work in a public relations agency or an MBA-type background in strategy or business development. In many cases, the CCO will need to assume responsibility for plans and outcomes that are the result of actions by persons throughout the organization.

Korn/Ferry's Corporate Affairs Center of Expertise conducted a study of CCOs at 67 Fortune 200 companies in order to develop a current profile of the individuals who run the communications function at major global organizations. The survey reviewed how these executives are compensated, the size and scope of their responsibility and where they reside organizationally.

Developing good communication skills is an important part of living a fulfilled life. Effectively communicating your career, personal, and everyday needs in a way that comes across clearly, persuasively, and thoughtfully is crucial; and yet, not everyone knows how. It isn't innate, and many bright, talented, and dedicated people don't get where they should, all because they fail to adequately communicate their point.

Don't let that be your fate. No matter what your age, background, or experience, effective communication is a skill you can learn (no matter how you might feel about it now). With a little self-confidence and knowledge of the basics of good communications, you will be able to effectively communicate your message in both conversations and presentations, in all walks of life.

Communicating Through Body Language

Whatever we'd rather believe, people do judge by appearances. In terms of communicating effectively, this reality means that your body language matters as much as your speech.

1. Use facial expressions consciously. Aim to reflect passion and generate empathy with the listener by using soft, gentle, and aware facial expressions. Avoid negative facial expressions, such as frowns or raised eyebrows. What is or isn't negative is dependent on the context, including cultural context, so be guided by your situation. Be alert for unexpected behavior that suggests you're cross-culturally colliding, such as a clenched fist, a slouched posture, or even silence. If you don't know the culture, ask questions about communication challenges before you start to speak with people in their cultural context.

Communicate eye to eye. Eye contact establishes rapport, helps to convince that you're trustworthy, and displays interest. During a conversation or presentation, it is important to look into the other person's eyes if possible and maintain contact for a reasonable amount of time (but don't overdo it; just as much as feels natural, about 2-4 seconds at a time).

Remember to take in all of your audience. If you're addressing a boardroom, look every member of the board in the eye. Neglecting any single person can easily be taken as a sign of offense and could lose you business, admission, success, or whatever it is you are endeavoring to achieve. If you're addressing an audience, pause and make eye contact with a member of audience for up to two seconds before breaking away and resuming your talk. This helps to make individual members of the audience feel personally valued. Be aware that eye contact is culturally ordained. In some cultures it is considered to be unsettling, or inappropriate. Ask or research in advance.

Use breathing and pauses to your advantage. There is power in pausing. Siimon Reynolds says that pausing causes an audience to lean in and listen, their interest piqued; it helps you to emphasize your points, allowing the listener time to digest what has been said; it helps to make your communication come across as more compelling, and it makes your speech easier to listen to. To help improve your ability to make the most of pauses:

Take deep breaths to steady yourself before you begin communicating. Get into the habit of solid, regular breathing during a conversation that will help you to keep a steady, calm voice. It will also keep you more relaxed. Use pauses to take a breather in what you are saying. Use hand gestures carefully. Be conscious of what your hands are saying as you speak. Hand gestures can be divided into open gestures (positive responses) or closed/concealed gestures (negative responses).

Some hand gestures can be very effective in highlighting your points (open gestures), while others can be distracting or even offensive to some listeners, and can lead to the conversation or listening being closed down (closed gestures). Pay careful attention to the gestures as you make them; it also helps to watch other people's hand gestures to see how they come across to you.

Keep a check on other body language signals. Watch for wandering eyes, hands picking at fluff on your clothing, and constant sniffling. These small gestures add up and are all guaranteed to dampen the effectiveness of your message, and will result in your ceasing to engage your listeners.

Thoughtfulness When Communicating

1. Choose the right time. As the cliché states, there is a time and a place for everything, and communicating is no different. Avoid leaving discussions about heavy topics such as finances or

weekly planning until 10 pm at night, for example. That's going-to-bed time and few people will be thrilled to be faced with sorting out major issues when they're at their most tired. Instead, leave heavy topics for mornings and afternoon times, when people are alert, available, and more likely to be able to hear what is said and to respond with clarity.

Choose the right place. If you need to tell someone something that isn't going to be well received (such as news of a death, a breakup, a job loss, a change of plans, or a criticism of their efforts), don't do it in public, around colleagues, or near other people. Be respectful and mindful of the person receiving the communication, and communicate to them in a private place. This will also enable you to provide space to open dialog with them about the communication, and helps to ensure that the two-way process is occurring properly. If you're trying to give bad news in a cafe surrounded by loud chatting and reverberating sounds, the surroundings will affect the impact, and you will find it hard to know if your message has been understood. By the same token, if you are presenting to a group of people, be sure to check the acoustics beforehand, to practice projecting your voice clearly, and to use a microphone if needed to ensure that your audience can hear you.

Remove distractions. Turn off the cell phone, put away the iPod, tie your dog to a post. Do not allow external distractions to act as crutches that keep sidetracking your concentration. They will distract both you and your listener and they will also effectively kill the communication. Even if the communication that you are having is a difficult one, it will not help the effectiveness of your message if you are seeking comfort or respite through such distractions.

Thank the person or group for the time taken to listen and respond. No matter what the outcome of your communication, even if the response to your talk or discussion has been negative, it is good manners to end it politely and with respect for everyone's input and time.

CHAPTER-8

ROOM SERVICE MANAGEMENT

As you know when food and beverage items are served to guests in his or her room is called Room Service. It is an accommodation available at many hotels where workers at the hotel bring food and other items to hotel rooms, by request of the guest and usually for extra charge.

Take and Process Room Service Orders:

- The telephone is answered promptly and courteously accordance with enterprise procedures and customer service standards.
- The customer's name is checked and used in the interaction.
- Details of orders are clarified, repeated and checked with the guest.
- Suggestive selling techniques are used.
- Approximate time for delivery is advised to the customer.
- Orders are accurately recorded and the information is checked.
- Door knob dockets are correctly interpreted.
- Where necessary, orders are promptly transferred to the appropriate location for preparation.

Set Up Trays and Trolleys:

- Food and beverage items are correctly prepared for service periods.

- General room service equipment is prepared for use.
- Trays and trolleys are set up in accordance with enterprise standards for a range of meals including:
  - Breakfast
  - Lunch
  - Dinner
  - Complimentaries
  - Special requests
- Correct and sufficient service equipment is selected and checked for cleanliness, and damage.
- Trays and trolleys are set up so that they are balanced, safe and attractively presented.
- All food items and beverages are collected promptly and in the right order.
- Orders and trays are checked before leaving the kitchen and before entering the room.

Present Room Service Meals and Beverages:

- Rooms are approached and guests greeted in accordance with enterprise service standards.
- Customers are consulted about where trays or trolleys should be placed in the room and advised of potential hazards.
- Trays and trolleys are placed safely and conveniently.
- Furniture is correctly positioned where required.
- Meals and beverages are correctly served and placed if required by the customer and in accordance with enterprise procedures.

Present Room Service Accounts:

- The customers account is checked for accuracy and presented in accordance with enterprise procedures.
- Cash payments received are presented to the cashier.

- Charge accounts are presented to the guests for signing and charged to the account.

Clean Room Service Area:

- Floors are checked and promptly cleared of used room service trolleys and trays.
- trays and trolleys are returned to the room service area and dismantled / cleaned in accordance with enterprise procedures.
- Equipment and food and beverage items are re-stocked in accordance with enterprise procedures.

Generally, at the minimum, parking valets should be tipped a minimum of $1-2 when you leave your car and again $1-$2 when they get your car. However, depending on your location and the parking facility, valet tips could be much higher.

Nowadays, tips are more or less expected. Many service workers are paid minimum wage, and rely on tips to augment their earnings.

Here are some guidelines for tipping: Generally, salaried staff such as hotel managers or cruise captains are not tipped. Gratuities are given to service employees such as valets, waiters, housekeepers, taxicab drivers, airport porters, hairstylists, and tour guides.

Always carry smaller bills when going out to dinner or traveling, i.e. $1, $2, $5 bills. For example, when handing the gratuity to the valet fold the bill at least in half or thirds, and say thank you while handing it to them.

The amount of the tip is up to you. But, the following are some general gratuity amounts compiled from emilypost.com, Zappone from CNNMoney.com, insiderviewpoint.com, and cruise directonline.com.

AT THE RESTAURANT

Maitre d': $20 or more, if a special service is performed such as getting you a table when you have no reservation and the restaurant is full.

Waiters: 15-20% of the bill, unless a gratuity is already added to the bill. In the United States normally a gratuity is not automatically added unless you have a party of 6 or more. In a buffet restaurant, add 10% to the bill for gratuity, more if drinks are filled and plates removed. Many foreign countries automatically add gratuities, so check your bill carefully. Overseas, even if the gratuity is already added, some people like to leave some small change on the table.

Sommelier (Wine Steward): 15-20% percent of the bottle price

Cocktail Waitress or Bar Waiter: 15-20% of bill or $1 minimum whichever is greater (i.e. if a drink costs $5, then 15% is 75 cents, but leave at least $1).

Bartender: if you are served at the bar, 15-20% of the bill, or $1 minimum, whichever is greater.

Coat Check: $1 per coat

Restroom Attendants: $0.50-$1

Musician in Lounge: $1-$5.

AT THE HOTEL

Parking Valets: $1-$2 when you leave your car and again when they get your car.

Bell Hop: $1-$2 per bag plus a couple extra if he shows you the room.

Doorman: $1 for hailing a cab; if he helps with luggage, same as Bell Hop.

Concierge: nothing for simple questions. But, if they make restaurant reservations, obtain theater tickets for you, make travel arrangements, then $5-$10 per task performed. Put the gratuity in an envelope with a note of thanks and give to the concierge.

Room Service: 15-20% of the bill, unless a gratuity is already added, then no additional tip or $1 or $2. However, when ordering room service, make sure to inquire whether the server will actually receive the gratuity that has been added to the bill. If not, then tip accordingly.

Delivery to Room: if you requested something delivered such as a hairdryer: $1-$2.

Housekeepers (maids): $1-$2 per day left at the end of your stay.

Spa Services: 15-20%, if a service charge is not already included.

AT THE AIRPORT

Porters and Skycaps: $1-$2 per bag.

Shoeshine Person: $3-$5.

Cab Drivers: 15% of the bill or $2 minimum, whichever greater.

ON A CRUISE SHIP

Some cruise lines add the gratuity onto the payment for you, so check with the specific cruise ship on which you will be traveling. Otherwise, plan to include tipping as part of the cost of taking a cruise. Usually small envelopes are left in your cabin with suggestions for gratuity amounts.

Cabin Stewards and Waiters: $3-$4 each per guest per day.

Maitre d' and Busboy: $1.50-$2 each per guest per day. (Some suggest $10-$15 to Maitre d' for the week).

Hand out the gratuities in the envelopes to each person at the last evening meal, and to the cabin steward the day before the cruise ends. On a cruise ship, you don't need to tip your bartender, wine steward or bar waiter because a 15% surcharge has been added to every drink for gratuity. Some cruise lines may state tipping not required, but tips should still be given for good service.

OTHER SERVICES PROVIDED

Tour Guide: $2-$5 for a 1-2 hour sightseeing tour.

Pizza Delivery: $1 per pizza or 10% of the bill.

Furniture Delivery: $10 each person.

Hair stylist: $2 minimum or 15-20% of the bill, whichever is greater (i.e. if a haircut costs $10, then 15% is $1.50 but leave at least $2).

Blackjack Dealer: $2-$10 or minimum bet at the table, after you're through playing.

Change Person at Slot Machine: $1-$5, more if you hit a jackpot.

Few things seem more luxurious than having breakfast and the morning paper delivered to your hotel room. If you're wondering whether to include a tip for the room service attendant, there are a few things to remember about tipping etiquette when you're traveling.

Tips

1. Inquire about whether gratuities are part of the deal when you make your hotel reservation. A few upscale hotels add a daily fee to your bill to cover tips for the bellhops, concierge, room service attendants and housekeepers.
2. Learn to decipher the room service bill, and ask questions if you don't understand. Most hotels include a "service charge" to deliver to your room, often along with an added gratuity charge of 20 percent. The built-in gratuity is a tip that goes to the room service attendant.
3. Don't feel obligated to tip beyond the 20 percent delivery charge. Simply mark a line through the "tip" area, sign the bill and thank your server. If you wish to give the delivery person a small additional amount, $1 to $2 is sufficient.
4. Tip a standard 15 to 20 percent if there is no gratuity charge included in your bill. It is acceptable to add the tip to a credit card slip, or to use cash if you prefer. Remember, though, that tipping is discretionary and dependent upon service efficiency and friendliness.
5. Print out a free tip table at Tipping if numbers tax your brain.

Taking Guest Orders

Taking an order is a very skillful art which reflects efficiency and standard of both waiter and the establishment. Every Food &

Beverage Service staff should have good command over order taking skill to ensure that each guest gets proper food he ordered and importantly in right sequence.

Here are some food & beverage order taking tips:

1. First give time to guests after his arrival to feel comfortable with the environment.
2. After the guest is seated and feel comfortable then present the menu and stand away to give guests some time to decide what to order. Remember don't be hurry. Give proper time to the guest. Try to evaluate guest and understand when reaches to decision to order.
3. When you feel to that the guest wants to order then approach toward him and courteously ask this way 'May I take your order sir' or 'Would you like to order now?'
4. Before taking order first ensures that you are fully ready. You have to have a notepad, a pencil or a pen and an eraser to take notes.
5. Although ordering depends on guest but try to maintain sequence that means first convince the guest to give beverage order and then food.
6. Don't lean too close to the guest and especially the host is a lady guest and also don't keep one hand in your back. Just be smart, stand straight to the left side of the guest and bend slightly forward to guest.
7. Always focus on what guest order. It will make guest insulted if he has to repeat his order again or again or if your attitude shows that you are not concentrating to him fully.
8. It is must for a waiter or server to have full command on the menu items. Guest may ask different types of questions. So be prepared for that. You should know what are the ingredients of the foods you are offering, what is the special food of the day, which food is not suitable for vegetarians or different religious people etc.

9. Many times it may be happened that guest are uncertain what to order. In that case it is your time to show some expertise. You can give him some options to choose by asking this way "Do you like to have smoked English ham or roast beef with gravy " or "May I suggest you to have any Indian dishes "

10. It is very important to keep sequence while you present food. In your notepad you have to write down both the sequence of the food and the person who order. Generally it is done by clockwise direction. First take order from host and then start following to his right and give an identification number to each guest. Another way is to give number to the person who is sitting nearer to the service door. You should plan some coding method by your own so that you can easily understand who order which food. As a professional server you should not ask that "who order xyz " or it will look worse if you place wrong food in front of wrong guest.

11. Generally guest order appetizer, then beverages then main courses and at last some dessert items. So if guest order haphazardly, it is your duty to serve food according to the sequence.

12. Give proper time to guests to enjoy their beverage items. If the glass gets empty then you can graciously ask him whether he wants replenishment or not by saying this way "Would you like to replenish your glass, sir?"

13. If the guest is in hurry and seek your assistance then suggest him some "Ready to serve" food items rather "Cooked to order" items.

14. Suggestive selling is a good skill of a waiter but if your guest is a couple or student then it is advisable not to suggest hugely expensive foods. You have to keep increasing your sells but also remember not to lead your guest in an embracing situating. This may hamper repeat guest.

CHAPTER-9

RESERVATIONS

The reservation section in the front office, as mentioned before, is the nerve centre of the department where all requests of reservation are received and processed.

RESERVATION PROCESS

The reservation process has been produced to be easy and instinctive. Firstly you have to use the hotel search box and find the accommodation you like. Your reservation can be made in three easy steps only: you simply select which rooms you wish to book, number of rooms, enter your dates and guarantee the reservation.

Usually a higher number of rooms are available on request than online. In case of an on-request reservation, you do not have to guarantee your reservation immediately, just send us your order, specify in what time and how would you like us to respond.

SEARCHING

- Use the hotel search box on the main page or on the city pages. Enter the dates of your stay and preferences regarding hotel and hotel rooms and click "SHOW PRICES" button.
- Search results page will appear. All offered hotels will be shown on the same page - sorted according to price, the cheaper first. Click the "sort button" on the top of the page to sort hotels by price, name, location or size - as you prefer.

- Click at hotel names or hotel pictures to view hotel pages. Each hotel page has informative sub pages (general info, rooms&rates, hotel map, services & amenities, guest comments, photo gallery, similar hotels). Compare all hotels and find the one you like.

Requesting/Reserving

- Proceed to reservations either from the search results page or from any particular hotel page. Click on the word "book" and enter the number of rooms you need. The room type you wanted will have "1" in it, but you can change it for more rooms. You can easily select number of any room type you want to be reserved. Click "SUBMIT" and move to the booking /request form.
- Booking/request form shows which rooms you selected, with all their price details and the total price you are to pay. The system will tell you if the reservation will be processed immediately (online) or if this is an on-request reservation which requires an assistance from our reservation staff. You will also see the payment options (PAYMENT AT HOTEL or PREPAYMENT). Then you will be asked to submit your contact details. To do this you either log into your customer profile (customers who have booked with our updated system, received a log-in/ password) or enter your contact data when making the first request or reservation.

Confirming your Request

- If the booking cannot be processed immediately, our system will ask you how quickly do you want us to respond by email, telephone or fax and inform about the rooms availability. Then you wait for us to contact you. We will try to confirm the hotel you chose or offer the best alternative option.
- If you are satisfied with our offer, you will have a possibility to go immediately to the booking form and

secure your reservation either with credit card or prepayment. The booking form can be accessed either though a coded link in the response e-mail we will send you or easily by logging into your customer profile on STAYPOLAND. Both in the e-mail and in your customer profile you will be able to review the hotel (hotels) we are offering you in your dates.

- Wait for our staff to send you the confirmation letter.
- If you receive a confirmation letter or voucher from us, it means that we guarantee that the hotel holds a reservation for you - as shown in the document. We recommend to print your confirmation letter or voucher and have it with you when checking in the hotel.
- Three days after the departure day you will receive an automatic e-mail from our system asking to evaluate the hotel services.

How the Reservation with Bookings Works

By sending the reservation request via BOOKINGS you send the request for room reservation directly to the hotel. The reservation must be confirmed back by the hotel to be valid and final.

1. You select the hotel of your choice, and click the 'Request a reservation' link .
2. You select the arrival date, departure date, enter your Full Name, address, contacts, and Email, you can attach any comments that will be read by the hotel. Then you click the 'Submit Request' button.
3. The review screen appears, where you review your data and confirm these are correct. Then you click the 'Confirm' button.
4. Your reservation will be processed by the BOOKINGS system and sent directly to the hotel reception.
5. The details about your request are e-mailed to your contact email for future reference. Also a telephone number and the fax to the hotel is provided in case you need.

6. In a reasonable time period (from 1 hour up to 2 days) you should received the final confirmation from the hotel. From this moment you stay in touch directly with the hotel, in a case of difficulties please contact our support.
7. You might be requested the feedback about our service or the service of the hotel. For any details on your personal data please read our Privacy Statement.

Sources of Reservation

The usual sources from which reservation requests come are

- Airlines
- Wholesale tour operators
- Travel agents-local and foreign
- Free Individual Traveller (FIT)
- any person who makes a booking directly with a hotel and not through a travel agent
- Companies and commercial business houses
- Embassies/Consulates and Institutions

A source is classified as any individual or body that actually pays a hotel for services rendered.

Modes of Reservation Request

Requests for reservation may come by various modes:

- Letters
- Telex
- Telegrams
- Cables
- Telephones
- Personally

Types of Rooms

Each hotel has a variety of rooms to suit the needs of guests. Alone individual may prefer a single room while a couple would book a double room, or an executive may prefer a suite so that he can hold meetings or entertain privately. Appended below are typical rooms that hotels have. A reservation for a room would be made using the following terminology:

Single	Room with one normal-sized single bed
Double	One double bed
Studio	One single bed+one sofa cum bed
Twin	Two normal sized but separate single beds
Triplet	Twin+extra bed
Single suite	Single room+one living room
Double suite	Double room+one living room

Dupleix suite : Rooms spread over two floors with interconnecting staircase

Cabana : Room attached to the swimming pool with one sofa cum bed

Suites may be assigned other names, such as Presidential, Diplomatic, Special, etc. but they are basically similar to other suites in accommodation but may be more lavish in decor or appointments.

Types of Plans

A plan is a package proposal of rooms and meals. Whereas those who stay on a European Plan have the option to eat when and wherever they wish paying the listed price in the menu, the American plan is beneficial to economy tourists who may have fixed meals at fixed hours and thereby are restricted to fixed programmes in a day. The common plans in hotels are:

EP: European Plan: Room only

CP: Continental Plan: Room+continental breakfast

MAP: Modified American Plan: Room+breakfast+lunch or dinner (2 meals only)

AP: American Plan: Room+breakfast+lunch and dinner (3 meals)

Types of Room Rates

Hotels would normally have three types of rates for the same room; maximum, minimum and moderate. This is done to enable the hotel to sell a room to suit the budget of a guest. The right thing would be to give a slightly superior room in terms of location, decor, etc. to those paying a maximum price for the same type of room. Hotels offer other special rates, either extra or discounted, to suit the type of guest and his needs. Some of these rates are:

Crib rate: Applicable to children below five years

Extra bed: Generally one-fourth of maximum rate

Airlines: Contract rate-fixed discounted rate for a long period

Groups: Special rate-discounted rates applicable to groups only. A group consists of 15 people or more. Normally for every 30 people a free room is given to the tour leader.

Day rate: Part rate is charged for persons who want a room for day use only (Day use in hotel parlance refers to all check in and check out the same day between 6.00 A.M. to 9.00 P.M.)

Family rate:

(1) 2 adults+1 child below 5 years=1 double

(2) 2 adults+2 children below 12 years=1 double

(3) 2 adults+2 children below 12 in separate room =1 double+1 single.

Discounts and Allowances

Some of the discounts perceived in the hotel trade are:

- Airlines, 20%
- Travel agents, 20%
- UN employees, 10%
- Guaranteed company rate
- moderate rate

(Moderate rate is also given to individuals as per company policy)

- Travel writers, 20%
- Hotel federation members, 20% on room and food and beverage
- Top executives of travel agencies, 50%

Note: Discount rates are subject to revision on mutually agreed terms between parties. Therefore, the front office staff should check the discount rates from the Management and keep an updated information with them. Allowances are daily cash paid-outs given to airline crews. These allowances are fixed and predetermined by the airline and hotel to be later recovered by the hotel. Discounts are a percentage of charge off from a rack-rate offered to individuals and institutions in view of volume of business anticipated, and as a public relations gesture.

Group Reservation

A group is a body of 15 persons or more. Because it involves volume business, managements offer a special discount. The discount is given to tour operators who sell a total tourism package to customers which includes airfares, hotel accommodation, fees for sight seeing, etc. The saleability of the package depends on the discounts given by the airlines, hotels, etc. The amount of discount depends on the volume of groups sent and the frequency of visits organised by the tour operator. In addition to the group discounts there are special facilities for the tour leader.

Groups of 15-30, pax will earn their tour leader one complimentary room. Groups of 31-45, pax will earn their tour leader two complimentary rooms. Groups of 40 or more, will be governed by the discretion of the management as to how many complimentaries they wish to give.

Group reservations and correspondence assume great importance and must be dealt with quickly and accurately because.

1. groups form a major part of business,
2. the travel agent or tour operators' arrangements are dependent upon confirmation of accomodation,

3. group reservation demands blocking of a large number of rooms; thus, the hotel could suffer if the group is cancelled at the last minute,
4. a final confirmation of group booking takes longer to materialise.

It is prudent for a hotel to insist on a 30-day advance notice should a travel agent or tour operator wish to cancel a group. If a group cancels a booking within 30 days of their arrival it is acceptable to charge a retention equivalent to one night's stay of group. The principle behind a retention charge is to offset the inability to sell the booked rooms again, specially in the first few days of the groups intended stay. Charging retention is a normal practice which may be waived by the hotel depending upon:

- the size of the group,
- relation between the travel agent and the hotel,
- inconvenience caused to the hotel's management in terms of their inability to sell the rooms on the particular days and the consequent loss of revenue.

While handling the group reservation it is important to ensure the following:

1. The booking needs to be recorded accurately on the Reservation Chart.
2. A separate file needs to be opened for each group handled.
3. Room break-up.
4. Time of arrival and departure.
5. Name of tour leader so that all matters pertaining to the group arrival may be referred to him, and to award him a complimentary room as per rules.
6. Passport details (of foreigners) to complete all government formalities in advance.
7. Any other specific instructions.

The above information helps the front office to complete several formalities in advance and also to circulate the Group Meal Information Sheet to room service and restaurants.

Periodically statistics are made to ascertain the percentage of materialisation of booked groups from various travel agents. On the basis of these statistics future strategies are made, that is, which travel agent needs to be developed through public relations, which travel agent needs to be dropped in priority, which travel agent is unreliable and would thus have to pay a deposit in advance.

Forecasting Room Reservations

Forecasting is an important activity to ascertain the volume of business expected. It helps to coordinate a sales effort to sell days or weeks that are lean or to refuse booking on sold out days. On the basis of forecasting every hotel believes in a strategy of overbooking which is a percentage of rooms sold, over and above a full house. The percentage of overbooking is determined through experience. Calculated overbooking is safe as there are always last-minute cancellations or 'no shows'. Working on the premise that a room is a highly perishable commodity, overbooking offsets "no shows" or cancellations. Sometimes, forecasting can be affected by several factors:—

1. More cancellations than anticipated.
2. More 'no shows' than anticipated, referred to as mortality rate.
3. People wanting to check in without a prior reservation, referred to as 'walk-ins'.
4. Guests who overstay.
5. Rooms taken under repair.
6. Faulty overbooking.
7. Residents in the house.
8. Additions or reduction of guestrooms that affect the number of saleable rooms.

Forecasting may be done on a daily, weekly or monthly basis from the confirmed reservations on hand supported by the reservation chart plus 'waitlisted' and 'to be confirmed' bookings.

INSTANT RESERVATIONS

Instant reservation is a facility offered by large hotels or chain hotel operations whereby a customer anywhere may easily make a reservation at locations far away from the hotel itself. Basically, hotels feed information on room availability frequently so that the Instant Reservations (IR) can confirm the booking immediately. Sometimes, hotels give the IR the authority to confirm rooms upto a certain number.

TAKING A RESERVATION ON PHONE

Step 1 Answer the phone promptly and say:

"Good morning, Front Office Reservation, may I help you?" Meanwhile keep a blank Reservation Form and a pencil at hand to fill in the reservation request.

Step 2 As soon as the guest asks for rooms on certain dates look at the room status board (Plate 4) which will indicate the status of rooms on those days under one of the three categories-SOLD OUT, ON REQUEST, FREE SALE.

Step 3 If dates indicate SOLD OUT, politely inform the guest by saying: "I am sorry, the dates requested are all sold out". If dates indicate ON REQUEST, politely inform the guest by saying: "All bookings on the dates required by you are wait-listed. I shall take your reservation but would suggest that you check again closer to the date for a confirmation".

If dates indicate FREE SALE, say: "We will be pleased to reserve a room for you. May I have the following particulars?"

Then meticulously take down the following particulars on the reservation form:

- Name of the guest
- Type of room
- Number of persons
- Date of arrival
- Date of departure

- Who will pay the bill (billing instructions)
- Any special instructions
- Name of the person making the booking
- Telephone Number/ Address of person
- Date and time of booking made

Step 4 It is important to ask the party to send a written confirmation of reservation request. Billing instructions specially are never accepted verbally. Sometimes, a doubtful party, may be asked to give a deposit in advance which may be a certain part of the room rent for the reservation period. This is completely legal. Thank the guest.

Step 5 Type out a Reservation Slip in two copies. One goes to the reservation rack while the other is clipped with the reservation form and filed. The Reservation Rack is a series of racks displayed on the wall of a Reservation Office with carriers that hold the reservation slip.

A busy hotel would normally have a reservation rack divided into three main sections: (a) reservation slips under each day of the current month, (b) reservation slips under each month of the present year, and (c) reservation slips recorded for each of the future years. As each month becomes current, the reservation slips are re-distributed to each day of the month. Step 6 Block off the rooms on the reservation chart.

Processing Reservation Revisions/Cancellations

Often a guest may change his programmed visit to the hotel and may request for a revision or cancellation of reservation. The following steps would have to be taken:

Step 1 Take down necessary revisions and cancellations on the Revisions/ Cancellation forms

Step 2 Amend the Reservation Chart by removing the room allocation made of the earlier dates (allocating the rooms on the new dates in the case of a revision).

Step 3 Amend or remove the reservation slip from the rack. In case of amendments prepare a new reservation slip attaching the old and new slips with revision/cancellation forms to the appropriate correspondence and file.

Terms for the Payment of Hotel Bills

1. Hotels will have the right to call upon travel agents to settle bills either before or during the stay of their client. In any case travel agencies must settle the bill to the hotel within 30 days from the date of presentation of the bill in order claim 10% commission. In the event of payment not being made within the stipulated period, travel agencies run the risk of for feiture of their commission.
2. Hotels can insist for payment by giving 14 days notice from defaulting agencies. Despite this notice if an agency fails to settle account the hotel can take up the matter with the Travel Agents Association through the Hotel Federation.
3. Travel agents will submit their commission bill monthly for the bookings given to hotels which will be paid by the hotel within a fortnight from the date of receipt of bill.

Note: Under no circumstances will travel agents be permitted to deduct their commission from the hotel bill.

Chapter-10

Departure Procedure

Departure Procedure

Step 1 The bell desk will receive a phone call from the guest about his intention to check out. Write the room number carefully on the errand card, a stack of which is kept at the bell desk itself. Inform the Bell Captain and proceed to the room.

Step 2 Knock on the guest's door and announce yourself. Look around the room for any guest articles left, any damaged hotel property and switch off the airconditioning/ heating, lights, etc. Collect the room key and depart from the room letting the guest lead the way. Ensure that the guest room is locked. If the guest wants to carry the room key himself, permit him to do so.

Step 3 Place the baggage at the bell desk. Stick on any hotel stickers or publicity tags. Hand over the room key to the Information counter and errand card to the Front Office Cashier. Wait for the guest to pay the bill.

Step 4 The bell boy will receive an authorisation to take the baggage out of the hotel only after the Front Office cashier has signed that the guest has paid his bills, and the Receptionist that the room key has been received.

Step 5 Take the baggage to the car porch and load it to the transport.

Step 6 Report back to the bell desk and hand over the errand card with the authorisation signatures.

A DP is a preplanned, coded IFR departure route. It provides the following advantages:

a. Graphic portrayal of departure route.

b. Reduces time delays and radio communications required to issue clearances.

c. Provides approved ATC departure route clearance in the event of radio failure.

d. Can be designed to support noise abatement programs.

Planning for the route of flight is an integral part of preflight preparation. Once the appropriate DP has been selected, its name and number are entered in the route of flight block of the DD 175 Military Flight Plan. Approach plates provide a ready reference to departure plates at various airports. Always consult NOTAM for any changes. In most cases, the aircrew can expect ATC to issue the clearance as filed. Using a departure plate, it enables the aircrew to anticipate ATC instructions. The departure plate must be studied thoroughly for heading, courses, and altitude restrictions.

Departure Control

A guest departure is the most critical moment for the front office cashier. The cashier must ensure that the guest has paid his bill entirely or there is adequate information or authorisation to allow him to sign his bill. This is because the cashier is held responsible for any shortages which may be deducted from his salary. Some hotels insure cashiers to safeguard against shortages. Appended below is the procedure to handle guest departures.

1. Receive the intimation of a guest/ guests desire to leave the hotel from the lobby captain, or from the guest himself

over the telephone or in person, and pull out the folio from the pigeon hole.

2. Note down the reading of the telephone meter applicable to the room number of guest checking out.
3. Substract the initial telephone meter reading taken at the time of the guest's arrival from the final reading.
4. Multiply the total number of calls by the amount for an individual local call charge as laid down by the management.
5. Fill in a Telephone Charge Voucher (see Fig. 18.2).
6. Post these charges to the guest folio in the debit column.
7. Find out if there are any cheques/ vouchers pending in the counter, if so, post them to the folio.
8. Ask the guest if he/she has signed any bills/vouchers in any of the service areas immediately before departure. If so, ring up the area cashier and find out the amount of charges. Ask for the voucher/bill immediately and post it to the guest folio.
9. Put the folio at the printing table of the machine and print the total debit as well as credit balances.

   Work out on the machine total debit balances to be recovered from guest.
10. Present the bill to the guest at the front office cashier's cabin only (in no case bills can be taken to guest rooms or elsewhere).
11. Collect the total amount of charges from the guest.
12. Mark the folio with the 'PAID' stamp and put down your initials.
13. Return the correct amount of change to the guest.
14. Tear off the first page of the guest folio and present it to the guest.
15. Keep aside the paid folios together for further processing by accounts.

Payment by Personal Cheques

1. Inform the guest politely that normally payments by personal cheques are not entertained.
2. In case of further insistance from guests, ask them to contact the lobby manager for a written authorisation.
3. At the receipt of the authorisation from the lobby manager, give the Application for Payment by Personal Cheques Form (Fig. 20.1).
4. Check the details of the cheque and make sure that it has been marked 'A/ C payee only' and is duly filled.
5. Compare the signature on the cheque with that of the application form.

Payment by Travel Agency

Travel agency voucher indicates that the guest has pre-paid to the travel agent amounts for accomodation etc. and the recovery of such amounts are made from Voucher the travel agent not from the guest.

1. Receive the travel agency voucher and see if such billing instructions are mentioned in the folio.
2. Read the voucher carefully and determine whether it has been issued from a bonafide travel agency duly recognised by the hotel, by referring to the list of bonafide agencies as issued by the accounts department.
3. See whether all the expenses/charges are covered by the voucher: if not, open and process guest folios, posting miscellaneous charges not covered by the voucher.
4. If the voucher is from a foreign travel agency, get it authorised by the lobby manager.
5. Ask the guest/group leader to sign the folio.
6. Do not give copies of signed bills.
7. Attach the voucher and the folio(s) together.

Chapter-11

Cleaning Agents

Cleanliness is one of the most important features a hotel or motel can offer its guests. Housekeepers, also known as maids, are the staff members who perform cleaning duties in these establishments. Housekeepers may be assigned specialized cleaning duties. For example, most hotels have laundry facilities for cleaning towels, linen, bedding, and workers' uniforms. Some housekeepers work only in the laundry area, washing, drying, and folding these items and then stocking the linen storage rooms.

Other housekeepers only clean guest rooms. An especially thorough cleaning is done after the occupants of a room check out. Using a large wheeling cart to hold supplies, guest room housekeepers bring clean linen, bedding, cleansers, and all other necessary cleaning equipment to the rooms. The housekeepers replace soiled linen and towels; restock soap, tissues, and drinking glasses; disinfect bathroom surfaces; dust and polish the furniture; remove all trash; vacuum the carpet; and wash any uncarpeted floors. Before leaving, they check to make sure that the room is spotless and ready for new guests. If housekeepers notice anything in a room that is not working properly, they report it to their supervisor, the executive housekeeper. They also send to the lost-and-found department any articles that previous guests may have left in the rooms when they checked out.

Aside from doing laundry and cleaning guest rooms, housekeepers replace light bulbs, wash windows, empty ashtrays, and clean hallways and stairs. Some housekeepers make sewing repairs or upholster furniture. Others work in lobbies, lounges, and conference and banquet rooms, where they clean carpets and move and set up furniture. In small hotels housekeepers usually perform several of these tasks.

Cleaners perform a variety of heavy cleaning duties, such as cleaning floors, shampooing rugs, washing walls and glass, and removing trash. They may fix leaky faucets, empty trash cans, do painting and carpentry, replenish bathroom supplies, mow lawns, and see that heating and air-conditioning equipment works properly. On a typical day, janitors may wet- or dry-mop floors, clean bathrooms, vacuum carpets, dust furniture, make minor repairs, and exterminate insects and rodents. They may also clean snow or debris from sidewalks in front of buildings and notify management of the need for major repairs. While janitors typically perform most of the duties mentioned, cleaners tend to work for companies that specialize in one type of cleaning activity, such as washing windows.

Maids and housekeeping cleaners perform any combination of light cleaning duties to keep private households or commercial establishments, such as hotels, restaurants, hospitals, and nursing homes, clean and orderly. In private households, they dust and polish furniture; sweep, mop, and wax floors; vacuum; and clean ovens, refrigerators, and bathrooms. They also may wash dishes, polish silver, and change and make beds. Some wash, fold, and iron clothes; a few wash windows. General houseworkers also may take clothes and laundry to the cleaners, buy groceries, and perform other errands. In hotels, aside from cleaning and maintaining the premises, maids and housekeeping cleaners may deliver ironing boards, cribs, and rollaway beds to guests' rooms. In hospitals, they also may wash bed frames, make beds, and disinfect and sanitize equipment and supplies with germicides. Janitors, maids, and cleaners use many kinds of equipment, tools, and cleaning materials. For one job, they may need standard cleaning implements; another may require an electric floor polishing machine and a special cleaning solution. Improved building materials, chemical cleaners, and power equipment have made many tasks easier and less time consuming, but cleaning workers must learn the proper use of equipment and cleaners to avoid harming floors, fixtures, building occupants, and themselves.

Cleaning supervisors coordinate, schedule, and supervise the activities of janitors and cleaners. They assign tasks and inspect building areas to see that work has been done properly; they also issue supplies and equipment and inventory stocks to ensure that supplies on hand are adequate. They may be expected to screen and hire job applicants; train new and experienced employees; and recommend promotions, transfers, or dismissals. Supervisors may prepare reports concerning the occupancy of rooms, hours worked, and department expenses. Some also perform cleaning duties.

Building cleaning workers in large office and residential buildings, and more recently in large hotels, often work in teams consisting of workers who specialize in vacuuming, picking up trash, and cleaning restrooms, among other things. Supervisors conduct inspections to ensure that the building is cleaned properly and the team is functioning efficiently. In hotels, one member of the team is responsible for reporting electronically to the supervisor when rooms are cleaned.

Work environment. Because office buildings generally are cleaned while they are empty, many cleaning workers work evening hours. Some, however, such as school and hospital custodians, work in the daytime. When there is a need for 24-hour maintenance, janitors may be assigned to shifts. Many full-time building cleaners worked about 40 hours a week in 2008, but a substantial number worked part time. Part-time cleaners usually work in the evenings and on weekends.

Most building cleaning workers work indoors, but some work outdoors part of the time, sweeping walkways, mowing lawns, or shoveling snow. Working with machines can be noisy, and some tasks, such as cleaning bathrooms and trash rooms, can be dirty and unpleasant. Building cleaning workers experience injuries more frequently than workers in most other occupations. They may suffer cuts, bruises, and burns from machines, handtools, and chemicals. They spend most of their time on their feet, sometimes lifting or pushing heavy furniture or equipment. Many tasks, such as dusting or sweeping, require constant bending, stooping, and stretching. Lifting the increasingly heavier mattresses at nicer hotels in order to change the linens can cause back injuries and sprains.

EDUCATION AND TRAINING

No special education is required for most entry-level janitorial or cleaning jobs, but workers should be able to perform simple arithmetic and follow instructions. High school shop courses are helpful for jobs involving repair work. Most building cleaners learn their skills on the job. Beginners usually work with an experienced cleaner, doing routine cleaning. As they gain more experience, they are assigned more complicated tasks. In some cities, programs run by unions, government agencies, or employers teach janitorial skills. Students learn how to clean buildings thoroughly and efficiently; how to select and safely use various cleansing agents; and how to operate and maintain machines, such as wet-and-dry vacuums, buffers, and polishers. Students learn to plan their work, to follow safety and health regulations, to interact positively with people in the buildings they clean, and to work without supervision. Instruction in minor electrical, plumbing, and other repairs also may be given.

Supervisors of building cleaning workers usually need at least a high school diploma, but many have completed some college or earned a degree, especially those who work at places where clean rooms and well-functioning buildings are a necessity, such as in hospitals and hotels. In many establishments, they are required to take some in-service training to improve their housekeeping techniques and procedures and to enhance their supervisory skills.

Other Qualifications

Employers usually look for dependable, hard-working individuals who are in good health, follow directions well, and get along with other people.

Certification and Advancement

A small number of cleaning supervisors and managers are members of the International Executive Housekeepers Association, which offers two kinds of certification programs for cleaning supervisors and managers: Certified Executive Housekeeper (CEH) and Registered Executive Housekeeper (REH). The CEH designation is offered to those with a high school education, while the REH designation is offered to those who have a 4-year college degree. Both designations are earned by attending courses and passing exams and both must be renewed every 3 years to ensure that workers keep abreast of new cleaning methods. Those with the REH designation usually oversee the cleaning services of hotels, hospitals, casinos, and other large institutions that rely on well-trained experts for their cleaning needs.

Advancement opportunities for workers usually are limited in organizations where they are the only maintenance worker. Where there is a large maintenance staff, however, cleaning workers can be promoted to supervisor or to area supervisor or manager. Some janitors open their own maintenance or cleaning businesses.

Employment Change

The number of building cleaning workers is expected to grow by 5 percent from 2008 and 2018, more slowly than the average for all occupations. Unlike some occupations, increased productivity is not expected to impact the employment of building cleaning workers. Despite small improvements in cleaning supplies, tools, and processes, roughly the same number of workers will be needed for any given building.

Employment of janitors and cleaners is projected to increase by 4 percent, more slowly than the average for all occupations. As the pace of construction contracts and fewer buildings are built, growth in this occupation should be relatively slow. Many new jobs are expected in healthcare, however, as this industry is expected to grow rapidly, and in administrative support firms as more claiming work is contracted out. Employment of maids and housekeeping cleaners is also expected to increase more slowly than the average, growing by 6 percent from 2008 to 2018. Many new jobs are expected in hotels as demand for accommodations increases, in private households as more people purchase residential cleaning services, and companies that supply maid services on a contract basis, as more of this work is contracted out. Employment of supervisors and managers of these workers, in addition, is projected to grow more slowly than the average, increasing by 5 percent. An increasing number of supervisors will be needed to manage the growing number of janitors, maids, and other cleaning workers.

Job Prospects

Job prospects are expected to be good. Most job openings should result from the need to replace the many workers who leave this very large occupation.

Working Conditions

Modern hotels and motels have the best cleaning equipment for housekeepers to use; however, the work is demanding. Housekeepers must bend, stoop, climb, and reach to clean in corners and inside closets. Moving heavy equipment and furniture can be exhausting.

Housekeepers typically work forty to forty-eight hours each week. They may rotate from a morning to an evening or night shift and are expected to take their share of weekends and holidays. Most housekeepers wear uniforms. Some employers provide them with uniforms or a uniform allowance; others require housekeepers to purchase their own uniforms.

Chapter- 12

Guest Information

The information section keeps track of guests resident in the hotel by keeping an updated "guest alphabetical index rack" also sometime referred to simply as the "information rack". This system consists of a frame which holds 35 to 40 movable carriers into which the copy of the arrival slip bearing the name of the guest is inserted. These names are alphabetically sequenced with the aid of a carrier.

At the beginning of each shift, the information assistants tally the information rack with the room rack located at the reception. The information rack is one in which the arrival slips of guests are stacked alphabetically so that when someone wants the room number of a guest it is easy to located the details provided the name given is correct. The reception section maintains the racks room-wise as they find it easier to allot rooms at the time of registration. During each shift any arrivals and departures are undated by cross-checking with the arrival and departure register. Latest arrival slips are inserted into the information rack while slips of guests who have checked out are removed after drawing a red line over the name in the slips. For missing arrival slips it is the responsibility of the information assistant to have them typed out from the slips in the room rack and inserted into the information rack.

Movable carriers permit insertion or removal of carriers with ease and thus render the easy updating of information rack. This system is called the Whitney rack system.

RECEPTION

Most governments and states insist that a guest registers himself in writing. This is a rule to protect both the hotel owner and the guest. It is also a source of information on the movement of foreigners in the country for the local Foreigners Registration Office. This act of registration may be done by two methods: by the use of registration cards as adopted by large hotels; and through a Registration Register used by small hotels, motels and inns. The basic information required in either case is name, address, nationality, purpose of visit, duration of stay and passport details (in the case of foreigners). The information solicited may be more depending upon the local laws. Sometimes, hotels use registration cards or registers for their own market research activity in which further details are asked for, such as mode of travel, arrived from, next destination, reservation made through, name of company and type of business, etc.

The use of a Registration Card is preferred to a register because of several advantages it offers:

1. More than one guest can register at a time.
2. It can be handed to the typist immediately.
3. It eliminates the cumbersomeness of duplication of information to hand over to the typist to type.
4. A card is more private.
5. A card may be filed conveniently for easy retrievability.
6. A card could have a multiplicity of use-as a folio, as a market research document, as a reservation confirmation, etc.

The registration card is a very important document which is kept under strict control. Normally, each registration card is numbered and this number is referred to in all future documentation. The registration cards are sent daily to the income auditor who checks the new arrivals and departures and sends it back to the front office for permanent filing. Filing may be done in numerical sequence, alphabetically, city or country wise depending upon the further use it Has for the management.

A preamble of activity at the beginning of the day enables the reception to operate smoothly and with minimal guest complaints. While taking over from the night shift it is important to note instructions left by the night shift either verbally or through the log book. These are instructions that are to be followed up during the day.

The next activity is to prepare the control sheet so as to ascertain the expected guest departure for the day. These statistics would be useful to later calculate the room position for the day.

A review of reservation racks is the next activity wherein VIPs expected during the day are allotted rooms in advance and these rooms are blocked against their names. Special guest choice of rooms is also considered, and if available, the room is blocked. Rooms are also blocked that have been taken under repair by housekeeping and these' rooms are not to be sold to a guest. Rooms are also blocked for expected groups and airline crew arrivals. As these involve volume rooms, it is prudent to block the rooms accordingly. The blocking is done at the room rack in the Reception Counter.

Night Duty

The activity at night at the front office is quite different from the day shift. This is the time for recapitulation of the day's performance and for preparation of reports for the management to be submitted next morning. The night staff also bring all records and information up-to-date.

There are a few essential tasks that the night front office assistant must complete: -

1. Take over charge from the day shift by checking the telegrams and telex register for any outstanding telegrams and telexes that have to be sent to guests or kept pending for a guest arriving in the night shift. They must also check the mail and registered parcels. The most important task would be to refer to the log book and understand the instructions before the day shift leaves.

2. Collect registration cards and guest folios of all guests who have checked out and prepare room night sales and analysis.
3. Tally the information rack with the reception rack, telephone rack, and room service rack.

Apart from the above, the night information assistant would execute all the normal functions of the day information assistant, i.e. handle messages, keys, mail and arrange permanent arrival slips.

The night receptionist would, perhaps, be the most critical person as the main -Night recapitulation is done by him. He is also responsible for updating all records and information of the front office. The principal tasks for him to complete are:

1. To check all reservation correspondence for the night shift and see whether reservation slips have been made; and follow up on any special instructions for any of the expected guests.
2. Bring out the correspondence of guests arriving the next day. Attend to any follow up required in connection with the guest's stay.
3. Bring out the reservation rack for the next day commencing at 12 midnight of the night shift. Tally correspondence with the reservation slips and type out reservation slips, if missing.
4. Collect and file expired reservation correspondence of the previous day.
5. Collect and hand to the despatch section any forms required to be sent to the Foreigners Registration Office.
6. Check the mail for existing guests, groups and airlines and send them to their respective rooms. Also check mail for guests expected in the night shift so that they may be kept aside and handed over at the time of their arrival.
7. Check mail for guests who have checked out the previous day and redirect same after ascertaining a forwarding address specifically left by the guest on the registration card.

8. Carry over information and records through the telex and telegram, register,mail packets, register and log book at the end of the shift.
9. Make out a Crew Sheet of airline crews staying in the hotel after referring to the room rack.
10. Prepare list of VIPs staying in the hotel by referring to the room rack, and also a list of VIPs expected by referring to the reservation rack.

The crew and VIP lists are made in several copies which are usually distributed to the General Manager, Lobby Manager, Housekeeping, Room Service, Telephones and Sales Manager. Copies may be sent to others such as Laundry Manager, Chief Engineer, etc. as per the management policy.

RECEIVE MESSAGES

When a person wants to leave a message for a guest staying in the hotel who is not available at a particular point of time, the information assistant hands over a message slip or assists the guest in recording details such as the name of the guest addressed his/her room number, time that message was recorded, the message, the visitor's name and the information assistant's signature. The message is taken down in duplicate. While the original is placed in the appropriate key rack the duplicate is sent to the room itself and slipped under the door. Modern hotels have a message light system. At the information is a panel with all room numbers listed each with a message button. Once each message botton is depressed a message light flashes in the room as well as on the panel. The message light is located at the room console or at the foyer light switches. This light that flashes in the room informs the guest that a message is awaiting at the information counter. The light that flashes on the panel behind the information section enables a guest to collect the message when he collects the key from the information rack. Once the information is conveyed to the guest the message button may be released. Sometimes a guest staying in the hotel may want to leave a message for a visitor who may come in person or may call. This message is recorded on a message slip of a different colour. This slip is inserted into the room slot in the key rack. The colour of the slip is a code to the information assistant to refer to the slip should someone wish to contact the guest. The message should also be

Message Slip

HOTEL XYZ

Date .... Time..................................

To ....

Room No. ....

While you were out

Mr/Mrs./Miss ....

of ....

Telephoned   Please call back

Called in Person   Will call again

Waiting to see you

....

....

....

....

....

....

Accomodation Assistant

informed to the telephone operator and the operators number and the time is recorded. The telephone operator informs the message over the phone to the expected visitor of the guest when he chooses to solicit the same over phone.

Control Guest Room Keys

Absolute responsibility of guest room keys rests with the information assistants. It is vitally important that a strict control is maintained. Keys must be inserted into the correct room slot of the key rack. If this is not followed accurately, an unnecessary chaos could result. Guests would get wrong keys and discover this on reaching their rooms; keys would be declared inadvertantly as lost; keys could get into wrong hands. It is important for the information assistant to try to remember faces of guests staying in the hotel. Thus, anyone asking for a room key is immediately identified. Some hotels have introduced key control cards. To ensure security for guests, issues of keys are made against these cards.

Handle Guest Mail. Cables. Telexes, etc.

Mail is often handled by the information assistant. If the hotel has a large number of rooms, the volume of mail received everyday may be appreciable enough to make the handling of it one of the major and critical tasks of the front office. Mail may vary from letters, business and promotional material, cables and telexes, to large parcels. The timely delivery of the same to guests is important as it might influence his certain plans. Especially an executive could receive some critical or urgent information from his office that would bear on his decisions in connection with his work. To safeguard the hotel from guest complaints regarding mail, most hotels insist on the following:

1. Timing-stamp of all mail at the time of receipt.
2. If the registered insured envelope or parcel is received in an opened state, to record this in the mail log book and have it counter signed by the postman.
3. All registered mail, insured mail, etc. should have the signature of the guest when delivered.

Handle Guest Packages/Registered/Insured Mail

Paging : Paging is the process of locating a guest in a given area within the hotel. when a party calls a guest on the phone and the party specifically knows that the guest he a is contacting is in a specific area, then the information assistant writes the guest's name and room number on the paging board and deploys a bell boy to do the paging with this board. The bell boy then holds the board (which has bells with rings which draw the attentaion of the guest when shaken) a above his head so that guests in an area can see. The bell boy walks through that specified area. The guest, if in that area, immediately contacts the bell boy who esscorts the guest to the phone.

Sometimes a guest expecting a visitor or phone call may have left his where abouts in the hotel on a coloured message slip which is inserted in his room slot on the key rack and with this information the guest is paged as detailed above.

Chapter- 13

Advertising Network Management

Travel Spike has worked with hundreds of hotels and resorts to help them improve their online hospitality advertising and hotel marketing. Our team has many years of hospitality experience working with hoteliers, Internet hotel marketing programs, and online advertising for resorts. We built the leading dynamic package booking engine in the hotel industry which allows your property to bundle rooms with local attractions, events, and package elements. Contact us for more info on our hotel booking engine and our online vacation package reservation system which can be integrated with GDS and other 3rd party reservations systems.

We have worked with small hotels, chains, individual properties, bed and breakfasts (B & Bs), boutique hotels, vacation homes, timeshares, condos, property management companies, vacation home rentals, and large independent hotels. Travel Spike provides digital strategy, email marketing, hotel advertising, and Internet hospitality marketing to increase your occupancy and ADR.

We have revenue management experts, web 2.0 and travel 2.0 expertise, as well as travel experience. We offer a range of web marketing and Internet advertising for the hospitality industry. If you want to reach more travelers, we have travel email databases and email advertising solutions to fit any budget. Your hotel or resort can advertise in our hotel e-mail newsletter where we feature hotel deals, travel packages, travel deals, and special discounts on hotel rooms. We offer a leisure travel email and a luxury travel email where we can feature your property and help you sell more rooms online.

Travel Spike believes firmly in direct booking models to help you lower your distribution costs while selling more online hotel rooms on your own hotel website. We can help you fix up and improve your hotel website and we can drive more qualified bookers to your site. We can send you more travel clicks to your site as we feature your hotel or resort on our travel network and in our hotel deals email specials.

ADVERTISING NETWORK

An online advertising network or ad network is a company that connects advertisers to web sites that want to host advertisements. The key function of an ad network is aggregation of ad space supply from publishers and matching it with advertiser demand. The words "ad network" by itself is media neutral in the sense that there can be a "Television Ad Network" or a "Print Ad Network", but is increasingly used to mean "online ad network" as the effect of aggregation of publisher ad space and sale to advertisers is most commonly seen in the online space.

The advertising network market is a large and growing market, with the top 20 companies earning about $2 billion in revenues during 2007. This represents around 13% of the total display advertising market, forecasted to grow to 18% by 2010. This growth has resulted in many new players in the market, and has encouraged acquisitions of ad networks by large companies entering the market.

Ad networks are primarily involved in selling space for online ads to appear. This online advertising inventory comes in many different forms, including space on websites, in RSS feeds, on blogs, in instant messaging applications, in adware, in e-mails, and on other sources. The dominant form of inventory remains to be third-party websites, who work with advertising networks for either a fee or a share of the ad revenues.

An advertiser can buy a run of network package, or a run of category package within the network. The advertising network serves advertisements from its ad server, which responds to a site once a page is called. A snippet of code is called from the ad server, that represents the advertising banner.

Large publishers often sell only their remnant inventory through ad networks. Typical numbers range from 10% to 60% of total inventory being remnant and sold through advertising networks.

Smaller publishers often sell all of their inventory through ad networks. One type of ad network, known as a blind network, is such that advertisers place ads, but do not know the exact places where their ads are being placed.

In most cases, ad networks deliver their content through the use of a central ad server.

Large ad networks include a mixture of search engines, media companies, and technology vendors.

Types of AD Networks

There are 3 main types of online advertising networks:

1. Vertical Networks: They represent the publications in their portfolio, with full transparency for the advertiser about where their ads will run. They typically promote high quality traffic at market prices and are heavily used by brand marketers. The economic model is generally revenue share. Vertical Networks offer ROS (Run-Of-Site) advertising across specific Channels (example: Auto or Travel) or they offer site-wise advertising options, in which case they operate in a similar fashion to Publisher Representation firms.
2. Blind Networks: These companies offer good pricing to direct marketers in exchange for those marketers

relinquishing control over where their ads will run, though some networks offer a "site opt out" method. The network usually runs campaigns as RON or Run-Of-Network. Blind networks achieve their low pricing through large bulk buys of typically remnant inventory combined with conversion optimization and ad targeting technology.

3. Targeted Networks: Sometimes called "next generation" or "2.0" ad networks, these focus on specific targeting technologies such as behavioral or contextual. Targeted networks specialize in using consumer clickstream data to enhance the value of the inventory they purchase. further specialized targeted networks include social graph technologies which attempt to enhance the value of inventory using connections in social networks.

There are two types of advertising networks: first-tier and second-tier networks. First-tier advertising networks have a large number of their own advertisers and publishers, they have high quality traffic, and they serve ads and traffic to second-tier networks. Examples of first-tier networks include the major search engines. Second-tier advertising networks may have some of their own advertisers and publishers, but their main source of revenue comes from syndicating ads from other advertising networks.

While it is common for websites to be categorized into tiers, these can be misleading. While Google is in the clear majority of advertisement impression served, other networks that could be labeled as tier 2 actually dominate over these tier 1 ad networks as far as the number of customers reached.

Information

Advertising networks provide a way for media buyers to coordinate ad campaigns across dozens, hundreds, or even thousands of sites in an efficient manner. The campaigns often involve running ads over a category (run-of-category) or an entire network (run-of-network). Site-specific buys are not a major emphasis when dealing with advertising networks. In fact, site-specific buys are not even available at some networks, so as not to conflict with in-house sales reps.

Ad networks vary in size and focus. Large ad networks may require premium brands and millions of impressions per month. Small ad networks may accept unbranded sites with thousands of impressions per month.

One of the key issues for publishers is exclusive vs. non-exclusive representation. Exclusive representation generally brings a higher percentage of revenue sharing, but sometimes results in a smaller percentage of ad inventory being sold. In non-exclusive arrangements, publishers may use secondary advertising options to fill the space left unsold by the primary ad network.

Advertising and Hotel Industry

Advertising is defined as a paid public message. In tourism advertising, it is designed to describe an area or a plan. It can be in newspapers, magazines or on radio, television, hoardings, posters, etc. Advertising is the commonest form of promotion reaching the potential travellers..

But advertising cannot be done haphazardly. If your budget is large, you can have the services of an advertising agency which will do the research for you and advise you regarding the selection of media for your message to reach the right kind of people. Advertising agencies have creative writers who write an interesting text for your message and develop headlines for your advertisement. Such people are called copy writers. An advertising agency also has design artists to prepare the design and layout of your advertising message. These are all known as creative people. The services of an advertising agency do not cost much because they get a commission from the media for placing advertisements. This commission is normally fifteen to seventeen per cent, but advertising agencies charge from their clients for preparing designs and layouts.

A good advertising agency can create memorable advertisements for its clients. In 1970, the British Airways (then called BOAC) came up with an advertisement in the USA which offended the members of the British Parliament, but attracted a lot of American visitors to Great Britain. The Advertisement read:

London Bridge is in Arizona,

Queen Mary is in California,

Come to Britain

While it lasts!

Similarly, the USA celebrated the bi-centennial year of American Independence (from Great Britain) in 1976. The British Airways (then BOAC) came up with an advertisement with an amusing title:

Do come Home All is Forgiven.

In the late sixties, there were anti-American feelings among the Frenchmen and students were shouting anti-American slogans asking the 'Yankees' to go home. The Trans World Airlines, an American carrier, came up with an apt advertising. The title read:

Yankee go Home

with TWA!

It was an instant success!

The tourist product is varied. Advertising, therefore, has to highlight the quality of the product to be marketed, It may be an airline, travel agency services or a hotel. The interests of all these segments of travel services overlap and are often complementary. Therefore, sometimes they join hands to launch joint advertising programmes. For instance, the interests of a national carrier and the NTO are similar. The national carrier needs more passengers, preferably to its home destination which is also the primary function of the NTO. By pooling their resources, they can have more impact.

The Singapore Tourist Promotion Board, the NTO of Singapore and Singapore Airlines often advertise jointly in overseas markets. An example:

BIBLIOGRAPHY

- Adcock, Dennis; Al Halborg, Caroline Ross (2001). "Introduction". Marketing: principles and practice (4th ed.). p. 15.
- Administration industrielle et générale - prévoyance organization - commandment, coordination – contrôle, Paris : Dunod, 1966
- Badiru, A. (Ed.) (2005). Handbook of industrial and systems engineering. CRC Press. ISBN 0849327199
- Caperna A., Integrating ICT into Sustainable Local Policies. ISBN13:9781615209
- Dev, Chekitan S.; Don E. Schultz (January/February 2005). "In the Mix: A Customer-Focused Approach Can Bring the Current Marketing Mix into the 21st Century". Marketing Management 14 (1).
- finance. (2009). In Encyclopædia Britannica. Retrieved June 23, 2009, from Encyclopædia Britannica Online: Finance
- Gomez-Mejia, Luis R.; David B. Balkin and Robert L. Cardy (2008). Management: People, Performance, Change, 3rd edition. New York, New York USA: McGraw-Hill. pp. 19. ISBN 978-0-07-302743-2.
- Gove, P. et al. 1961. Finance. Webster's Third New International Dictionary of the English Language Unabridged. Springfield, Massachusetts: G. & C. Merriam Company.
- Grossman, G. and E. Helpman (2005), "Outsourcing in a global economy", Review of Economic Studies 72: 135-159.

- Joshi, Rakesh Mohan, (2005) International Marketing, Oxford University Press, New Delhi and New York ISBN 0195671236
- Kotler, Philip; Gary Armstrong, Veronica Wong, John Saunders (2008). "Marketing defined". Principles of marketing (5th ed.). p. 7.
- Marketing definition "the action or business of promoting and selling products or services, including market research and advertising".
- Measuring the Information Society: The ICT Development Index. International Telecommunication Union. 2009. pp. 108. ISBN 9261128319.
- Paliwoda, Stanley J.; John K. Ryans. "Back to first principles". International Marketing: Modern and Classic Papers (1st ed.). p. 25.
- Paul H. Selden (1997). Sales Process Engineering: A Personal Workshop. Milwaukee, WI. p. 23.
- Salvendy, G. (Ed.) (2001). Handbook of industrial engineering: Technology and operations management. Wiley-Interscience. ISBN 0471330574
- Turner, W. et al. (1992). Introduction to industrial and systems engineering (Third edition). Prentice Hall. ISBN 0134817893.
- Vocational Business: Training, Developing and Motivating People by Richard Barrett - Business & Economics - 2003. - Page 51.
- Walter Ong, Orality and Literacy: The Technologizing of the Word (London, UK: Routledge, 1988), in particular Chapter 4

Index